Dress, Dreams, and Desire

Dress, Dreams, and Desire

A History of Fashion and Psychoanalysis

By Valerie Steele

BLOOMSBURY VISUAL ARTS
LONDON · NEW YORK · OXFORD · NEW DELHI · SYDNEY

BLOOMSBURY VISUAL ARTS
Bloomsbury Publishing Plc, 50 Bedford Square, London, WC1B 3DP, UK
Bloomsbury Publishing Inc, 1385 Broadway, New York, NY 10018, USA
Bloomsbury Publishing Ireland, 29 Earlsfort Terrace, Dublin 2, Ireland

BLOOMSBURY, BLOOMSBURY VISUAL ARTS and the Diana logo are
trademarks of Bloomsbury Publishing Plc

First published in Great Britain 2025

Copyright © Fashion Institute of Technology - The Museum at FIT, 2025

Valerie Steele has asserted her right under the Copyright, Designs and Patents Act,
1988, to be identified as Author of this work.

For legal purposes the Acknowledgments on pp. viii-ix constitute
an extension of this copyright page.

Design concept by Sarco
Cover design by Adriana Brioso
Cover image: Issey Miyake, Bustier, 1983. Gift of Krizia. Copyright Museum at FIT.
Frontispiece (Figure 0.0): Artist Alisa Gorshenina wearing artificial eyes and a jeweled
mouth. Photo by Elizaveta Porodina (@elizavetaporodina).

All rights reserved. No part of this publication may be: i) reproduced or transmitted in
any form, electronic or mechanical, including photocopying, recording or by means of
any information storage or retrieval system without prior permission in writing from
the publishers; or ii) used or reproduced in any way for the training, development or
operation of artificial intelligence (AI) technologies, including generative AI technologies.
The rights holders expressly reserve this publication from the text and data mining
exception as per Article 4(3) of the Digital Single Market Directive (EU) 2019/790.

Bloomsbury Publishing Plc does not have any control over, or responsibility for,
any third-party websites referred to or in this book. All internet addresses given
in this book were correct at the time of going to press. The author and publisher
regret any inconvenience caused if addresses have changed or sites have ceased
to exist, but can accept no responsibility for any such changes.

A catalogue record for this book is available from the British Library.

A catalog record for this book is available from the Library of Congress.

ISBN: PB: 978-1-3504-2818-8
       ePDF: 978-1-3504-2819-5
       eBook: 978-1-3504-2820-1

Typeset by Integra Software Services Pvt. Ltd.
Printed and bound in Great Britain by Bell and Bain Ltd, Glasgow

For product safety related questions contact
productsafety@bloomsbury.com.

To find out more about our authors and books visit www.bloomsbury.com
and sign up for our newsletters.

In memory of my father

CONTENTS

Acknowledgments viii

    Introduction: Fashion as a Deep Surface 1

1. Freud and Fashion 13
2. The Naked Dreamer 31
3. The Masquerade 61
4. The Mirror and the Fragmented Body 85
5. Bitter Enemies 107
6. Desire and Sexual Difference 135
7. To Touch the Gaze 167
8. Bodies to Wear 197

Notes 210
Bibliography 223
Image Credits 239
Index 245

ACKNOWLEDGMENTS

I am a fashion historian, not a psychoanalyst, so I am deeply indebted to the psychoanalysts who answered my questions, offered advice, and in some cases, even read chapter drafts of my manuscript. Naturally, any mistakes that remain in this book are mine. In 2017, I had the great good fortune to meet Lacanian psychoanalyst Anouchka Grose at a conference on "Fashion and Psychoanalysis" held at the London College of Fashion and organized by Claire Pajaczkowska and Ivan Ward of the Freud Museum. When I began working on this book, David Goldenberg provided detailed reading lists about issues in contemporary psychoanalysis and later shared with me his article "Fashioning Hate: Driving the Runway of Desire." Patricia Gherovici, author of *Please Select Your Gender* and *Transgender Psychoanalysis*, helped me understand how Lacanian psychoanalysis can throw new light on contemporary fashion and gender fluidity. Her lecture at the Fashion Institute of Technology, "Bodies to Wear," was especially meaningful. Susie Orbach's books and her lecture at FIT provided insight into our conflicted relationships with our bodies. It is a pleasure to thank Christine Anzieu-Premmereur, who graciously provided information and a photograph of her father, French psychoanalyst Didier Anzieu, whose concept of the skin ego has informed my interpretation of fashion. I am also deeply grateful to historian Mark Micale, who read and commented on several of my chapter drafts. My thanks also to Adam Phillips, the author of so many insightful books on psychoanalysis.

In the world of fashion, I am pleased to thank supermodel Veronica Webb, and fashion designer Bella Freud, for consenting to be interviewed for this book. My thanks also to actress and trans activist Laverne Cox, who helped us obtain a photograph and shared her knowledge about Thierry Mugler. I am also indebted to many brilliant fashion scholars, including Elizabeth Wilson, Caroline Evans, Reina Lewis, and the late Djurdja Bartlett. Antoine Bucher, Corinne La Balme, Thierry Maxime Loriot, Jody Shields, and many others also provided valuable assistance during the years it took to write this book. Sincere thanks to all of the individuals and institutions who contributed images and permissions to this book. They are acknowledged under each image and in the image credits.

It is a pleasure to thank my colleagues at the Fashion Institute of Technology, especially at The Museum at FIT, where this book accompanies a major exhibition. Special thanks to Gladys Rathod and Melissa Marra-Alvarez, who tracked down elusive publications and illustrations, and tackled all the meticulous work involved in finalizing a book manuscript. Thanks to the staff of the Gladys Marcus Library at FIT, especially Margaret Murphy, for assistance with interlibrary loans.

I am grateful to everyone at Bloomsbury, especially my editor Frances Arnold, and the anonymous peer reviewers.

As always, thanks to my husband John Major.

Introduction: Fashion as a Deep Surface

"We all speak Freud, whether we know it or not," wrote historian Peter Gay.[1] Certainly, fashion people speak Freud: Marc Jacobs designed a "Freudian slip" dress. John Galliano created a couture collection for Christian Dior entitled "Freud or Fetish." And Prada presented a fashion film, in which Helena Bonham Carter plays the patient, who takes off her fur coat, lies down on the couch, and begins to talk about her daddy. Her voice fades, and the psychoanalyst, played by Ben Kingsley, quietly stands up, walks over to the fur coat, and begins stroking it. As he surreptitiously slips the coat onto his body and gazes at his reflection in the mirror, we suddenly hear her ask: "What does it all mean?"

Psychoanalysis is concerned with the search for meaning, but the key word here is "search," since meaning is not self-evident or unchanging. Indeed, meaning is often elusive, just as desire is conflicted and ambivalent. Fashion creators can reference psychoanalysis, because most people have at least a "superficial" knowledge of psychoanalytic concepts, and however flawed that knowledge might be, "its impact is not superficial." Not only has the "diffusion of psychoanalytic culture" influenced the wider culture, I would argue that it has also had an impact on changing trends in fashion, and on the ways in which we interpret fashion.[2]

Figure I.1 John Galliano for Dior Haute Couture Autumn/Winter 2000, two figures.
© Robert Fairer.

Figure I.2 Screen grab from Prada's short film *A Therapy* (2012). Directed by Roman Polanski, starring Helena Bonham Carter and Ben Kingsley. Cinematography by Eduardo Serra. Prada/YouTube.

"In psychoanalysis, we treat the objects of desire as clues," writes the British psychoanalyst Adam Phillips. "Every object of desire is an obscure object of desire; leading us to ask both, why this rather than that, and why anything at all?"[3] I am a fashion historian, not a psychoanalyst, but with this book, I hope to show how psychoanalysis provides important clues about the power and allure of fashion, as well as the ambivalence and hostility that fashion also attracts.

Fashion is often dismissed as "superficial," a matter of surface appearances, shallow, not deep, and by extension not serious, meaningful, or important. It is true that fashion is, literally, superficial, since it exists primarily on the surface of the body or as an extension of the body. Philosophers have often invidiously contrasted the carnal, mortal body—especially the female body—with the rational mind and the immortal soul. Mind–body dualism, misleading in so many ways, has also contributed to negative attitudes toward fashion. But I would argue that fashion is meaningful and important, precisely *because* of its intimate relationship with the fleshly human body, which is the foundation of the individual's sense of self.

When I arrived at Yale University in 1978 to study modern European cultural and intellectual history, the body was an emerging topic of study. Cultural historians were also investigating "attitudes toward gender, private life, sexuality and death, all of them critical components of individual identity."[4] But fashion received very little scholarly attention. Serendipitously, during my first term in graduate school, one of my classmates gave a report about two articles in the feminist journal *Signs*, debating the meaning of the Victorian corset: Was it oppressive to women or sexually liberating? It was as though a light suddenly switched on, and I realized: *Fashion is part of culture! I can specialize in fashion history!*

Not long afterwards, a famous professor asked about the subject of my research. "Fashion," I said. "Fascinating!" he exclaimed, with suspicious enthusiasm. "German or Italian?" I stared at him. What in the world did he mean by German fashion? Finally, the penny dropped. "Fashion, as in Paris. Not … fascism," I replied. "Oh," he said, and walked away. There was nothing to say to someone working on such a frivolous topic. This did not bode well for my future in academia.

Nevertheless, I managed to convince several professors that fashion was an acceptable topic, and I was encouraged to explore various theoretical frameworks. For Jules Prown's course on the interpretation of objects, I did a material culture analysis of several Victorian dresses and corsets. For Robert Herbert's social history of Impressionism, I researched images of the Parisienne, while for John Brewer's course on eighteenth-century urban culture and consumerism, I focused on the sexually ambiguous dress styles of London macaronis. Peter Gay, author of *Freud for Historians*, encouraged me to see whether psychoanalytic concepts helped me interpret the history of nineteenth-century women's fashion.

My experience working on the interpretation of objects was especially important, because it forced me to grapple with the embodied nature of dress. The corset, in particular, was intimately associated with women's bodies, and was variously interpreted as respectable, beautifying, and controversial. Freud was also controversial, and I vividly remember a classmate saying, "I don't believe in penis envy!," to which Professor Gay replied, "You don't have to." That still seems like good advice, since few, if any, theorists are right about everything. Freudian psychoanalysis is full of dead ends and false starts.

Freud remains a polarizing figure, and key psychoanalytic concepts, such as penis envy and the Oedipus complex, are widely rejected as false or anachronistic. Psychoanalysis also has an ugly history of misogyny, homophobia, and transphobia. There were years of vociferous opposition before the exhibition *Sigmund Freud: Conflict and Culture* finally opened at the Library of Congress in 1998. The organizers tacitly admitted that there had been controversy when they displayed a poster at the entrance, asking: *"Was he a genius or a charlatan?"*[5]

Most academic psychologists have long dismissed Freud as an embarrassing footnote in the history of psychology. Dominated for years by behaviorists, who rejected the very idea of the unconscious, psychology departments in the United States later turned toward cognitive psychology, which sees the mind as an information processor, and evolutionary psychology, which interprets human behavior through the lens of evolutionary biology. The British school of object relations achieved some acceptance, but trends in psychology and psychiatry that emphasized brain chemistry and neuroscience made psychoanalytic ideas about childhood psychosexual development seem even less relevant.

Having flirted with psychoanalysis off and on for years, historians increasingly rejected it, preferring what Lynn Hunt called a "common-sense or folk psychology." Not that historians were eagerly embracing other types of psychology: "The rise of social history … went hand in hand with the rejection of psychological forms of analysis." Feminist historians, as well as post-structuralists, like Michel Foucault, downplayed the psychological aspects of individual identity in favor of "social constructivism" and "discourse." It is not surprising, wrote Hunt, that "the psyche or self of the individual remains one of the least examined categories of historical analysis, a kind of black box with nothing visible inside."[6]

By the time my first book, *Fashion and Eroticism*, was published in 1985, I had to admit that most "attempts to use psychoanalysis to interpret the meaning of dress have been unsatisfactory."[7] Alison Lurie's *The Language of Clothes* (1981) was too reductionist, focusing on a few (grossly oversimplified) ideas about unconscious sexuality. James Laver's popular books were even worse, full of unexamined ideas about the differences between men and women. Another problem was the stubborn psychoanalytic insistence that "the unconscious is … located beyond the social, beyond history."[8] How could everything change over time and across cultures, including family structure and concepts of the self, and yet the unconscious remained the same? (Contemporary neuroscience suggests that psychoanalysts were probably wrong about this aspect of the unconscious.)

As a universalizing explanation, psychoanalysis was definitely *not* convincing. And yet scholars such as Elizabeth Wilson had shown that it *was* possible to write culturally embedded and psychoanalytically informed history. In other fields, such as visual, literary, and cultural studies, psychoanalysis continued to be valued as a discourse on sexuality and power and on the unconscious and society. With the spread of "French theory," Lacanian psychoanalysis became increasingly popular in certain academic circles.

Meanwhile, fashion continued to be "The F Word" in much of academia. In 1991, when *Lingua Franca* commissioned me to write an article on the subject, very few professors allowed me to identify them by name, because talking about fashion was still widely regarded as "shameful." John Brewer, my former Yale professor, was one of the few who went on record, saying: "To dress fashionably is to be labeled frivolous, to seem to care about the body and, therefore, by implication, to downplay the life of the mind. Most [academic] colleagues view sartorial interest and especially sartorial 'play' or facetiousness with a mixture of amusement, condescension, and fear. Dowdy is safe and serious." Other professors said, anonymously, that fashion was regarded as bourgeois and sexualizing. "My clothes are an expression of who I am," admitted one professor, "but I can't talk about it."[9] Nevertheless, fashion studies began to take off in the 1990s as an interdisciplinary field, although psychoanalysis played only a modest role in most publications. As the field continued to develop, the tendency to think of fashion in terms of representation gave way to "the bodily turn" in fashion studies.

"Fashion is about bodies," wrote sociologist Joanne Entwistle, and in every known culture, human bodies have almost always been "dressed" or "fashioned" in some way.[10]

Figure I.3 *Machine Worker in Summer (Joan Richards)* by Yevonde, tri-colour separation negative, 1937. Purchased with support from the Portrait Fund, 2021. Photographs Collection. NPG x220579. © National Portrait Gallery, London.

This does not mean that people have always worn *clothes*, since "dress," in the most inclusive, anthropological sense of the word, is not necessarily something *added to* or *covering* the body. The category "dress" includes clothes, of course, but it also encompasses a wide range of practices that *modify, augment or decorate* the body, from tattoos and tooth-filing to high heels and hair styles.[11]

The fact that body and dress exist in dialectical relation, embedded in culture, is central to the psychic significance of the clothes we wear. As Eve Golden writes: "The fundamental psychological fact of clothing … is that clothes and the representation of the self can *never* be definitively separated. Like language, its only rival in this, clothing, is an ever present lens through which we see ourselves."[12]

"Fashion" is usually defined as a subcategory of dress that is associated with "the latest style of clothing, hair, decoration, or behaviour."[13] Contrary to popular belief, fashion is not just a modern, western phenomenon. Nor is it limited to women, although women's fashionable dress has received more attention, often from moralists, who have tended to perceive it as a mask that *disguises* or *conceals* something about the wearer. In world historical terms, however, men have usually fashioned their bodies at least as extravagantly as women, and, significantly, they have almost always fashioned themselves *differently* than

Figure I.4 Mademoiselle de Beaumont or The Chevalier D'Éon, 1777. British Cartoon Prints Collection. Library of Congress Prints and Photographs Division, Washington, D.C. 20540.

women, in line with their differently sexed mammalian bodies and different social gender roles.

The word "transgender" is new, but long "before trans," there were historical figures, who "experienced their gender in complex ways."[14] The Chevalier d'Éon (1728–1810), for example, was famous for living and dressing sometimes as a man and sometimes as a woman. At one point, public curiosity was so great that bets were placed about whether d'Éon was really a man, a woman, or a "hermaphrodite" (the period term for an intersexed person). Caricatures sometimes showed a figure dressed half in women's fashionable dress, and half in men's. Ultimately, the shifting back and forth became socially and politically unacceptable, and d'Éon/Beaumont was pressured to choose to dress and live either as a man or a woman.

However, despite the existence of entrenched gender norms, most societies have permitted some degree of cross-dressing or sartorial androgyny. Indeed, modern fashion often plays with sex and gender conventions. The history of psychoanalysis has also been dominated by normative stereotypes of sex and gender, and by a phallocentric bias. Yet Freud always insisted that everyone is bisexual, meaning not only that we all have the potential to be sexually attracted to both men and women, but also that the human psyche contains both "masculine" and "feminine" attributes, however these might be defined.

We tend to think of psychoanalysis as a theory of the mind, and fashion as an embodied practice. But for human beings, body and mind are inextricably linked, just as nature and culture cannot be separated. For Freud, who trained as a physician, the biological body was real, but he also believed that it was "rapidly overlaid with psychical and social significance."[15] Many disciplines distinguish between the biological and the social body. However, the psychoanalytic body is unique, because it is a "libidinized body," a body of "phantastic anatomy," marked by sensory experiences, the sexual and aggressive drives, unconscious fantasies, memories, and emotions.

"The ego is first and foremost a bodily ego," wrote Freud. The human infant becomes aware of itself through "bodily sensations" on the skin, and the "mental projection of the surface of the body" in the mind's eye.[16] Cared for by its parents, the infant gradually acquires agency, a sense of itself in relation to others, and language. Freud's insight into the development of the self as an *embodied subjectivity* has been confirmed by evidence from many fields, including neuroscience. It has even been suggested that "the self should be viewed more as a process than an entity, and the body is integral to that process."[17] Freud notoriously had problems with women and their bodies. Yet, like Simone de Beauvoir, he recognized that our sense of self is constructed over time and within a particular cultural and familial context.

British fashion journalist Suzy Menkes published an article in 2012 describing me as "The Freud of fashion." As evidence, she cited several of my exhibitions, including *The Corset: Fashioning the Body*, *Gothic: Dark Glamour*, and *Love & War: The Weaponized Woman*.

Figure I.5 Ramon Casas, *Decadent Young Woman. After the Dance*, 1899. Oil on canvas. Museu de Montserrat, Abadia de Montserrat, SpainIndex Fototeca/Bridgeman Images.

Using metaphors of surface and depth, she wrote: "In the great tradition of Freudian psychoanalysts, [Steele] prefers to look into fashion's soul and to analyze its meaning, rather than merely to hold up a mirror to its surface."[18] Freud's first, "topographical" theory of the mind pictured it like an archeological site with the treasures of the unconscious buried deep below the surface. But was Menkes also alluding to Jacques Lacan, "the French Freud," best known for the mirror stage? The idea of the "surface" has often been negatively compared with what "lies beneath or within."[19] Yet the unconscious meaning of things is sometimes right in front of our eyes, like the queen's purloined letter in Edgar Allan Poe's story.[20] Or as dress scholars Dani Cavallaro and Alexandra Warwick explained: "Clothing, then, does not just operate as a disguising or concealing strategy. In fact, it could be regarded as a *deep surface*, a manifestation of the 'unconscious' as a facet of existence which cannot be relegated to the psyche's innermost hidden depths but actually expresses itself through apparently superficial activities."[21]

The idea of clothing as a "deep surface" is compelling, because fashion *does* seem to draw on unconscious emotions and fantasies, which are "metamorphosed into symbolic form" on the surface of the body.[22] However, fashion is not *only* a manifestation of the psychoanalytic unconscious, traditionally pictured as an obscure reservoir of sexual and aggressive drives and repressed fantasies. We are certainly conscious of some aspects of our dressed appearance, such as when we decide to wear a new suit to a job interview. Yet we sometimes also fear that our dress will expose unconscious feelings that we would prefer to keep secret, just as a blush or rash can appear, like a neurotic symptom, on the surface of the body.

In 2015, I was invited to speak at a symposium on "Fashion and Psychoanalysis," organized by the Freud Museum and the London College of Fashion. This gave me the opportunity to meet members of a new generation of psychoanalysts, such as Anouchka Grose, who were interested in fashion and knowledgeable about it. Soon, I was discovering new books and articles by psychoanalysts, often women, sometimes Lacanians, who were applying their clinical experience to fashion. Meanwhile, within fashion studies, there was a growing sentiment that *some* kind of psychological approach was necessary to complement the dominant sociocultural frames of analysis.[23] Pioneered by Carolyn Mair, "the psychology of fashion" emerged as a new subspecialty of psychology. Her book *The Psychology of Fashion* (2018) discussed subjects such as mental health and fashion, consumer behavior, and the influence of fashion on body image. Drawing on cognitive behavioral psychology and social psychology, her approach differed from psychoanalysis, which focuses on the unconscious.

As I struggled with Lacan's convoluted prose, I also discovered the work of Didier Anzieu, as well as new books advocating an "emancipated psychoanalysis" that embraced critical theory—from Judith Butler to Michel Foucault. Over the past five years, new articles have appeared constantly in the press—from a report that neuroscience proved that Freud got some things right to an article about how fashion designer Bella Freud (Sigmund's great-granddaughter) had launched a podcast, "Fashion Neurosis," thirty-minute sessions that mimicked classic psychotherapy.

The book you hold in your hands is a cultural history of fashion and psychoanalysis. Strictly speaking, it is not a psychoanalytic history of fashion, although I describe how different psychoanalysts have interpreted fashion. I believe that fashion virtually *demands* multidisciplinary interpretive approaches, because no garment or style has a single, stable meaning, either in the conscious or the unconscious mind. Meanings are constructed and reconstructed within specific contexts. Amplified by the media, some people's interpretations are more powerful, while others' may be richer and more nuanced. But everyone interprets fashion, and our interpretations are inevitably subjective. Moreover, as Gillian Rose pointed out: "Different psychoanalytic concepts brought to bear on the same image [or object, such as a dress] can produce very different interpretations of that image."[24] In this book, I have tried to be explicit about which psychoanalytic concepts I have brought to bear on my interpretations of specific, culturally embedded fashion objects.

Chapter 1, Freud and Fashion, looks at the young Freud's anxious obsession with shopping for clothes, at a time when dress played a significant role in Jewish modernization in Vienna. With his visit to Paris in 1885, he entered the international center of the "new psychology" and also, of course, the capital of (women's) fashion.

Chapter 2, The Naked Dreamer, explores aspects of Freud's work that are related to clothing and fashion, beginning with dream symbolism. It also focuses on his various, often problematic hypotheses about women's special relationship to fashion. Inclined to see women as sexually repressed but exhibitionistic and/or narcissistic, Freud also proposed that "All Women Are Clothes Fetishists."

Chapter 3, The Masquerade, considers the androgynous styles popularized by Gabrielle "Coco" Chanel in the context of a time when new ideals of personal and sexual freedom were often associated with Freud. Born the same year as Chanel, British psychoanalyst Joan Riviere is famous for her essay on "The Masquerade of Womanliness." Her colleague, psychoanalyst, and male dress reformer, J.C. Flügel, authored the first psychoanalytic study of fashion, in which he argued that men should be *more* narcissistic and exhibitionistic.

Chapter 4, The Mirror and the Fragmented Body, analyzes the 1930s fashions of Elsa Schiaparelli in relation to the theories of French psychoanalyst Jacques Lacan. Influenced by Surrealism, Lacan began to reinvent Freudian psychoanalysis with his theory of the mirror stage. Lacan's personal relationship with fashion was also far more extreme and dandiacal than Freud's rigid adherence to professional attire.

Chapter 5, Bitter Enemies, explores psychoanalysis in the United States during the Cold War, when rabidly homophobic analysts like Dr Edmund Bergler characterized gay male fashion designers as women's "bitterest enemies." Eventually, LGBTQ+ activists, feminists, and leftists contributed to the widespread rejection of conventional Freudian psychoanalysis. In the aftermath of May 1968, Lacan would develop new and influential theories about female sexuality, desire, and the gaze.

Chapter 6, Desire and Sexual Difference, draws on Lacanian ideas about desire and sexual difference to explore developments in men's and women's fashions. Beginning with Gianni Versace's safety pin dress, we interpret the work of designers such as Jean Paul Gaultier, Thierry Mugler, Alexander McQueen, and John Galliano, using concepts such as the object (cause) of desire, the phallic woman, and *jouissance*.

Chapter 7, To Touch the Gaze, introduces the work of Didier Anzieu, whose concept of "the skin ego" has inspired renewed attention to the metaphor of fashion as a second skin. Contemporary psychoanalysts such as Pascale Navarri demonstrate how we use fashion both to call attention to ourselves and protect ourselves. Dress scholars also explore how fashion, this "second skin," serves as an interface between the embodied self and other people in the world. Stella North has even argued that fashion could be said to constitute a *part* of the self—"a replaceable, updateable skin."[25]

Chapter 8, Bodies to Wear, addresses the role played by psychoanalysts in the contemporary discourse on gender-fluid fashion and the transgender phenomenon. Many psychoanalysts continue to argue that trans people need to accept anatomical "reality." However, other psychoanalysts, such as Patricia Gherovici, have challenged the traditional psychoanalytic belief in the body as bedrock, arguing that neither the body nor the self is a given, fixed entity. Rather, each of us becomes who we are, through a complex process of self-fashioning.

1
Freud and Fashion

Sigmund Freud (1856–1939) seldom mentioned clothes in his published work, and he paid even less attention to the vicissitudes of fashion. However, in the letters he wrote to his fiancée Martha Bernays, the young Freud described shopping for new clothes, expressing his desire for fine apparel, as well as the anxiety this aroused. Indeed, throughout his life, he placed considerable importance on appropriate attire. Photographs depict Freud as a typical late Victorian bourgeois man, and in many ways he was. Yet he was also a radical, even revolutionary thinker, whose ideas about sexuality and the unconscious transformed the way we view the world, including the way we view fashion. By placing Freud within his historical context, I hope to throw light on the origins and development of his ideas.

Sigmund Freud was born in the Moravian town of Freiberg to Jakob Freud and his much younger second (or third) wife Amalia Nathansohn. Freud once described himself as "the first-born son of a youthful mother" and he remained Amalia's favorite child. Photographs of Amalia depict an attractive, well-dressed woman, and Freud described her as beautiful and vivacious. But her relatives agree that she was difficult and volatile. Her grandson Martin described her as "a tornado." She dominated the family and was highly ambitious for the son she called her "golden Sigi."[1] Everyone in the extended family seems to have preferred the elderly, Talmud-reading Jakob to the difficult Amalie. However, Jakob, a small-scale wool merchant, was a poor provider for the family. Indeed, after they relocated to Vienna (when Freud was four years old), Jakob apparently never held a job again, depending on handouts from relatives, especially the adult sons from his first marriage.

Figure 1.1 Sigmund Freud, c. 1906.
Photo by Imagno/Getty Images.

Despite their relative poverty, the family employed female servants, including an elderly Christian nursemaid, who cared for Sigmund, until she was fired for theft.

Many years later, Freud would make the love triangle he called the "Oedipus complex" central to the theory of psychoanalysis. He named it after the Greek myth in which Oedipus, who was abandoned as an infant, kills his father King Laius and marries his mother the widowed Queen Jocasta. On October 15, 1897, Freud wrote to his close friend Wilhelm Fliess about an idea that had just "dawned on" him, which explained "the riveting power" of Sophocles' play *Oedipus Rex*: "I have found in my own case too, being in love with my mother and jealous of my father, and I now consider it a universal event in early childhood … Everyone … was once a budding Oedipus in fantasy and each recoils in horror from the dream fulfillment."[2]

The same year Freud also confided a long-forgotten childhood memory to Fliess, describing how when he was a small boy, "my libido was stirred up towards *matrem*, … on the occasion of a journey with her from Leipzig to Vienna, during which I must have had an opportunity of seeing her *nudam*."[3] This may have been a screen memory,

Figure 1.2 Sigmund Freud next to his father Jakob Freud. Austria, 1864. Mondadori Portfolio via Getty Images.

but it interesting that the 41-year-old Freud retreated into the decent obscurity of a dead language when describing how he had seen his mother naked. Freud's portrayal of father–son rivalry was vivid, but he largely ignored the issue of sibling rivalry, which is also embodied in ancient myths. In fact, Jakob and Amalia had a second son, who died when Sigmund was still a toddler. Freud once mentioned that he had been "jealous" of this infant, with whom he had to share his mother, although he may have confused this with later feelings of jealousy when his sisters were born. Some years later, another son was born, but Sigmund was already firmly established by then as the favorite child.

With the rise of industrial capitalism in the later nineteenth century, the family gradually ceased to be the basic unit of production. As society became increasingly urban, new forms of domesticity evolved, and bourgeois mothers spent more time with their children. The urban family of Freud's youth was thus an incubator of personal life in the modern era.

The capital of the Habsburg Empire, Vienna was a modern metropolis that attracted immigrants from the surrounding rural areas. Many Jews, in particular, gravitated to the relatively greater freedom from antisemitism that Vienna offered. Freud remembered that, when he was ten or twelve years old, his father Jakob told him a story about his own youth:

> When I was a young fellow, one Saturday I went for a walk in the street in your birthplace, beautifully decked out, with a new fur cap on my head. Along comes a Christian, knocks off my cap into the muck with one blow, and shouts, 'Jew, off the sidewalk!' … Freud asked his father, 'And what did you do?' The reply: 'I stepped into the road and picked up my cap.' His father's submissive response, Freud recalled … 'did not seem heroic to me.'[4]

Jakob meant to show how life was better now for Jews in Vienna, but this was not how Freud perceived it. His father's story involved a hat violently knocked off his head, which implies a kind of symbolic decapitation. Freud responded by identifying with heroes, especially scientific heroes, such as Copernicus and Charles Darwin.

Photographs of young Sigmund with his father and mother depict not only the impact of gender, class, and age on clothing, but also the influence of parental attitudes toward dress. Vienna was a fashionable metropolis and a center of economic and cultural life, much like Paris, the international capital of women's fashion. Menswear in Vienna was influenced by styles set in London, where the three-piece suit was "the unofficial uniform of English upper- and middle-class masculinity."[5] Amalia's attention to her appearance is evident, and probably influenced young Sigmund, who looks quite dapper in his suit.

Freud came of age in the period right after "the emancipation of Austro-Hungarian Jewry," when tailored suits were "visual markers" of Jewish "assimilation and acculturation." In his article "The Man in the Suit: Jewish Men and Fashion in Fin-de-siècle Vienna," Jonathan Kaplan observed that "Dress played a central role in the process of modernization and self-fashioning among Jews throughout Europe." However, for Jews originating in Eastern Europe, in particular, the tailored suit signaled "their willingness to participate in

Figure 1.3 Sigmund Freud and Mutter Amalie, 1872. Photo by Sigmund Freud.
Copyrights: ullstein bild via Getty Images.

the wider society." Within the Viennese context, the suit also indicated a broader middle-class German emphasis on respectability, morality, and self-cultivation.[6] Kaplan's thesis certainly applied to Freud.

But there are almost certainly other aspects to Freud's self-fashioning. In *Déshabillez-moi: Psychanalyse des comportements vestimentaires* (*Undress me: Psychoanalysis of clothing behavior*), psychiatrists Catherine Joubert and Sarah Stern look at how we use dress, mostly unconsciously, throughout our lives:

> Dress harbors in its fibers the memory of the first maternal care. The child is dressed by its mother, herself involved in a family tradition, inhabiting dreams, desires, frustrations. Through clothes, parents leave their mark on the child's body. … With adolescence, clothing accompanies the experience of puberty and permits [the adolescent] to conceal or reveal the sexualization of the body, [and] multiplies the codes and references to the peer group.[7]

Throughout his life, even when he was struggling financially, Freud always tried to be well dressed, and the British-style tailored suit was central to his self-fashioning. As his son Martin Freud recalled many years later:

> He was not the slightest bit vain in the common meaning of the word. He merely submitted without objection to the deeply entrenched medical tradition that a doctor should be well turned out: and so there was never a hair out of place on his head nor on his chin. His clothing, rigidly conventional, was cut from the best materials and tailored to perfection.[8]

Fine fabric and expert tailoring cost money, but Freud obviously believed that it was important, even if he had to pay his tailors in installments.

Freud's facial hair was as conventional as his clothing. During his adolescence, he experimented with a mustache, a dashing style associated with military men. He then adopted a neatly trimmed beard, which he retained all his life. This was neither Karl Marx's bushy revolutionary beard, nor the long beard associated with traditional Eastern European Jewish men. Rather, it was typical of the later nineteenth-century "patriarchal" beard of the Industrial Age. The beard, of course, is what Darwin called a "secondary sexual characteristic" of the adult male body, and is strongly associated with masculinity. Not only did it signify respectability and maturity, it was the beard associated with "the skilled professional as the ideal of modern manliness." Interestingly, physicians were among the professionals who were "particularly enthusiastic champions of the beard even after facial hair had fallen into disfavor at the end of the century."[9] For much of his life, Freud had his beard professionally trimmed almost every day. He was even late for his father's funeral, because his barber was delayed with another customer—an episode that haunted his dreams.[10]

In 1882, a few weeks before he turned twenty-six, Freud met a reserved young woman, who was a friend of his sisters. The following month, they became secretly engaged. Both Freud and his fiancée, Martha Bernays, were interested in dress and appearance. During

Figure 1.4 Sigmund Freud with his wife Martha (Bernays), 1885. Library of Congress Prints and Photographs Division, Washington, D.C. 20540 USA.

the four long years of their engagement, when they could not afford to marry, Freud's letters to Martha frequently mentioned clothes. In one letter, for example, he envisioned living together with Martha in a cozy home, where her closet was filled with "dresses of the latest fashion."[11]

Like his slightly younger contemporary, Viennese architect Adolf Loos (1870–1933), Freud almost certainly thought that men's attire was more rational and modern than women's conspicuous and capriciously changing fashions. In 1898, in a series of articles on men's fashion, Loos argued that what men wanted was "to be well dressed," that is, "to be dressed correctly." By contrast, women aimed to be "beautiful, elegant, chic."[12] Ever since Beau Brummel set the standard for eighteenth-century Englishmen, for European men to be correctly dressed meant wearing appropriate, English-style clothing. "Germans from the best society side with the English," wrote Loos.

> They are satisfied if they are dressed *well* … We have tried to get at fashion with words like 'beautiful,' 'stylish,' 'elegant,' … But this is not the point. Rather, it is a question of being dressed *in such a way that one stands out the least* … An article of clothing is modern when the wearer stands out as little as possible at the center of culture, on a specific occasion, in the best society.[13]

Figure 1.5 Alfred (seated) and Stefan Zweig, 1898. Photographed by Kunst Salon Pietzner, Vienna. The Stefan Zweig Collection, Daniel A. Reed. Library Archives & Special Collections, State University of New York at Fredonia.

Dress, Dreams, and Desire

By wearing the appropriate type and quality of English-style tailored suits, Freud was always "correctly dressed," thereby identifying himself as a modern man. Even in the nineteenth century, however, there were occasions when men wore colorful or decorative clothes. Military men, for example, wore uniforms. Indeed, Freud once confided that when he saw several generals in a café, they kept "reminding me of parrots … mammals just don't dress in such colors, with the exception of the reddish-blue of mandrils' posteriors."[14] It has often been suggested that women (and gay men) are attracted to men in uniform, because uniforms tend to highlight the body and/or because soldiers are associated with virility.

Masculinity remained the normative gender, while femininity was perceived and constructed both as lesser and as other. Unsurprisingly, Freud shared many of the beliefs and prejudices of his class and culture, although he was also part of a transitional generation, in which arranged marriages began to give way to love marriages. As traditional definitions of masculinity and femininity slowly evolved, tentative steps toward greater freedom for women often resulted in defensive reactions on the part of men. The young Freud certainly made it clear to his fiancée Martha that he could only imagine her as a beloved sweetheart and wife.

However, for a long time, he was too poor to marry. Once when Martha sent him a necktie, he wrote: "The tie produces for me the hitherto unheard-of luxury of a change of ties, for I still possess another decent one."[15] Yet he advocated spending money on clothes: "You must let me know what the jacket is going to cost," he wrote her. "If I cannot afford it now, I want to … [pay for it] later, next month. But don't deny yourself, my precious, any little luxury; I don't."[16] He often confided in Martha about his latest "reckless" purchase, be it a silver watch ("Without a watch, I am really not a civilized person") or "the two suits I need so urgently." He asked "Do you approve?" and claimed that he only patronized a particular tailor because the man was a friend of Martha's family: "I knew you would be pleased about Tischer; I did it only for your sake, for I am rather over-awed by his high prices." Yet when the "second magnificent suit" arrived, Freud wrote: "God only knows what I owe him already! I will pay him in installments."[17]

Less than a month later, Freud announced that he needed new clothes for his oral exams:

> Top hat and gloves to be bought, and then what kind of coat am I to wear? I have to appear in a dress coat – am I to hire it or have it made? I have just been to see Tischer and ordered a frock coat, but … I also need a black coat as well … It is so appalling not to have any money, my darling. I cannot imagine who invented the tale about women's dresses being so expensive that a man simply dare not marry! I shudder at the thought of my tailor's bill.[18]

Clothes were obviously an emotionally loaded subject for Freud, closely tied to his self-image. At one point, for example, he observed that his wardrobe might not be "very grand," but it would at least be "respectable."[19] His English-style suits differentiated him from orthodox Eastern European Jews, but even dressed as a secular, assimilated Jew, he was confronted with antisemitism. In one letter to Martha, for example, after describing how he had bravely stood up to some antisemites on the train, he wrote:

> My self-confidence had been somewhat increased by the battle with the infidels, but sank again when I saw myself in the mirror. No, I don't look at all noble; neither the blackest coat nor the whitest shirt could conceal my obvious plebeianism. But an elegant princess loves me nevertheless, and when I have money, which is as good as certain (my self-assurance tells me so) then I shall dress her in the most beautiful clothes and it will never occur to a soul that she could have married anyone but a prince.[20]

As with everyone who engages with "retail therapy," Freud's real and fantasied purchases of new clothing seemed to temporarily ward off anxieties related both to his status as a Jew in an antisemitic society and his precarious socioeconomic position.

Freud in Paris

In 1885, the young Dr. Freud received a fellowship to study nervous disorders in Paris. It was an exciting opportunity, because the French capital was the international center of the *psychologie nouvelle*.[21] The scientific study of the mind flourished first in French psychiatry, in part because anxiety about "degeneration" was especially acute in nineteenth-century France, due to the country's low birth rate and declining geopolitical status.[22] However, medical and legal experts throughout Europe and the United States were studying "abnormal" minds.

The sexual "perversions," in particular, were a subject of growing interest in the late nineteenth and early twentieth centuries, a period that came to be known as the "golden age of sexology." Medical and legal professionals increasingly focused on specific categories of sexualities, developing new psychiatric classifications, such as "homosexual," "exhibitionist," and "transvestite." Much later, Michel Foucault famously argued that what we now call "homosexuality" was once theorized and experienced as a practice (of sodomy) and only later as an identity.

The idea of gender identity as separate from sexual identity did not yet exist, although sexologists and psychiatrists recognized that a degree of cross-dressing was sometimes associated with homosexuality and lesbianism, although not always. Some men seemed to be sexually aroused by wearing women's clothes, but most women, it was thought, wore men's clothes primarily for functional reasons.

Hysteria and Hypnosis

Freud was especially enthusiastic about studying with the illustrious neurologist Jean-Martin Charcot, who was best known for his research on hysteria and hypnosis. Hysteria was an ancient diagnosis for "female problems," dating from before the fourth century BCE, when Hippocrates coined the term *hysterikos* (of the womb). Even in the late nineteenth century, most doctors still insisted that hysteria was exclusively a female disorder.

Charcot, however, argued that hysteria was a disease of the nervous system, not the uterus, and therefore men, too, could be hysterics. This idea was very slow to be accepted, and many dictionaries continued to define hysteria as "feminine temperament turned into neurosis."[23] It was only during the First World War that the many cases of "shell shock" convinced doctors that men, too, could suffer from traumatic unconscious ideas that caused physical symptoms, such as paralysis.

Charcot was in charge of the Salpêtrière hospital, where several thousand impoverished women were interned, and where his famous lecture demonstrations took place. The "Tout Paris" attended Charcot's public demonstrations, in which he hypnotized female patients, who then enacted the supposed "stages" of a hysterical attack. Charcot also hired photographers to document the "passionate attitudes" taken by his patients, and sometimes acted out neurological symptoms himself. Many years later, in his 1893 obituary essay on Charcot, Freud described him as a *visuel*, someone whose clinical intelligence was essentially visual.

Charcot's demonstrations influenced not only visiting doctors, like Freud, but also creative artists and writers. In 1887, André Brouillet painted *A Clinical Lesson at the Salpêtrière*, which depicted Charcot demonstrating on his famous patient Blanche Wittman. Her dress is pulled down, revealing the top of her corset and exposing her breasts as she collapses dramatically into the arms of Charcot's assistant. Freud would keep a lithograph of this painting in his office throughout his life. When Anna Freud was a young girl, she asked her father what was wrong with the lady in the picture, and Freud told her that the woman's corset was too tight! The print can still be seen in the Freud Museum in London, although, being black and white, it does not show, as the painting does, that Blanche Wittman was apparently wearing red lipstick.

Hippolyte Bernheim, a French professor of medicine in Nancy, would later prove that it was not only Charcot's "hysterics" who were hypnotizable—*anyone* could be susceptible to hypnotic suggestions. But it was also the case that a number of Charcot's patients deliberately performed the stages of hysteria "in order to capture attention and gain stardom"—as a former patient, Jane Avril, recalled in her memoirs, which also described her life as the famous can-can dancer memorialized by Toulouse-Lautrec.[24]

In the absence of modern technology, hysteria became the catch-all diagnosis for any symptoms without a known cause. Today many people are inclined to dismiss both the hysteria diagnosis and Freud's thinking as products of a misogynistic era of neurology. Yet although the term "hysteria" was dropped from the *Diagnostic and Statistical Manual of Mental Disorders* (DSM-1) in 1952, the terms "hysterical" and "histrionic personality type" still remain in the DSM, and refer to excessive emotional display, predominantly in women.

Figure 1.6 André Brouillet, *A Clinical Lesson at the Salpêtrière*, 1887. Image source: Wikimedia Commons (public domain).

Psychiatrists and psychoanalysts are still confronted with patients whose unhappiness and neurotic symptoms seem to be caused or exacerbated by ideas or feelings that operate "beneath the threshold of consciousness." In cases when there is no organic disease, but a person still has a psychological complaint, "you're back in Charcot-land," writes psychoanalyst Anouchka Grose. She also points out that: "If hysteria can be loosely characterized as a neurotic illness with a psychosexual cause, then contemporary people are no nearer to solving it than people at any other time."[25]

Several months after arriving in Paris, Freud was invited to attend one of Charcot's soirées at his opulent Saint-Germain mansion, filled with art and antiques. Freud was so nervous that he spent the entire day getting ready: "I had my hair set and my rather wild beard trimmed in the French style; altogether I spent fourteen francs on the evening. As a result, I looked very fine and made a favorable impression on myself." He also bought "a new shirt and white gloves." Meanwhile, Freud's colleague Ricchetti, "who hitherto had been going about in the most incredibly shabby clothes, had been persuaded by his wife to buy a new pair of trousers and a hat." However, Ricchetti had been misinformed by his tailor that "he could go in a redingote, with the result that he was the only guest not in full evening dress." Fortunately, Freud had the cultural capital to know that he should wear his new tailcoat. He proudly reported: "My appearance was immaculate." He admitted that he almost wore an "unfortunate ready-made white tie," but he replaced it at the last minute with a "beautiful" black tie from Hamburg.[26]

The Parisian Sphinx

Freud's preoccupation with his own self-fashioning was a leitmotif throughout his youthful correspondence. But there seem to have been relatively few references to Parisian women's fashions in his letters to Martha, although he teasingly reported that Mademoiselle Charcot had worn "a Greek costume" at one of her father's soirées, "and since your jealousy probably won't have lasted very long I can tell you that she looked quite attractive." On one occasion, however, in a letter to Martha's sister Minna Bernays, the young Freud made an extraordinary allusion to Parisian fashion and femininity: "I am under the full impact of Paris and, waxing very poetical, could compare it to a vast, overdressed Sphinx who gobbles up every foreigner unable to answer her questions."[27]

For the future inventor of the Oedipus complex to compare Paris to a man-eating, "overdressed" female sphinx is fascinating. But what did it mean—in 1885? Why did Freud perceive the Parisian sphinx as "overdressed"? Did this imply that she was wearing *too many* clothes (perhaps to ensure that her nakedness was well covered), or that her clothed appearance was *too much*? Paris and the Parisians certainly intimidated Freud, who could read French but was unable even to answer the questions of a Parisian waiter. We know that he visited the Louvre, specifically the antiquities section, where he saw

Figure 1.7 Gustave Moreau, *Oedipus and the Sphinx*, 1864. Oil on canvas. The Metropolitan Museum of Art, New York. Bequest of William H. Herriman, 1920.

the Egyptian sphinx. That probably reminded him of the Greek legend recounted by Sophocles, who described how a monstrous sphinx, half lion and half human, was killing the people of Thebes until Oedipus ended the carnage by correctly answering the riddle that the sphinx had posed to all challengers. Freud later identified with Oedipus, and saw himself as having solved the riddle of the human mind.

In fin-de-siècle Europe, it was not uncommon for educated men to characterize women as mysterious and dangerous sphinxes, and many artists depicted them that way. Indeed, Gustave Moreau's famous painting, *Oedipus and the Sphinx*, was exhibited in the Salon during the very year that Freud was in Paris. There is no evidence that Freud saw the painting; indeed, it is unlikely that he did, since he had no interest in modern art. However, the elegant and feminine appearance of Moreau's sphinx is conspicuous. She even wears a diamond tiara. Later, Freud would buy a print of Ingres' painting of *Oedipus and the Sphinx* (1808), in which a petite yet buxom sphinx also wears a tiara.

The stereotype of the Parisienne had long emphasized how her ultra-fashionable dress contributed to making her more feminine and sexually desirable than other women. Freud was almost certainly familiar with the related idea, common in German-speaking countries, and famously expressed in 1878 by F.T. Vischer, that contemporary women's fashion was "*eine Hurenmode*" [whorish fashion] of "fantastic excesses," and the French,

Figure 1.8 Octave Uzanne, *La Femme à Paris*. Cover illustration of La Parisienne as a sphinx by Leon Rudnicki. Photo by: Universal History Archive/Universal Images Group via Getty Images.

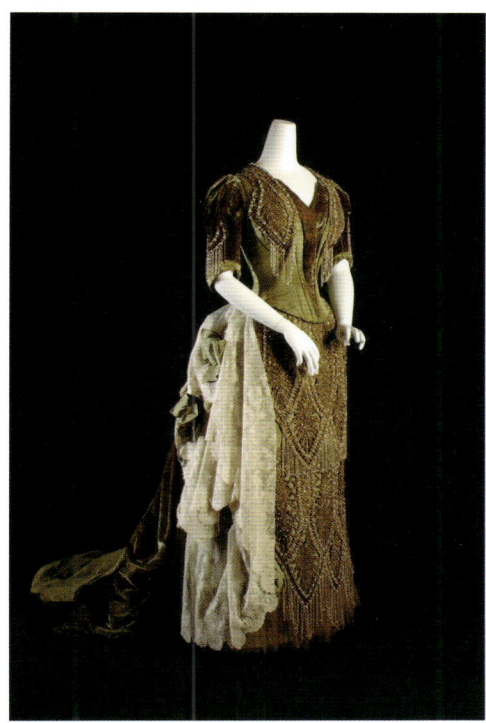

Figure 1.9 Emile Pasquier, ballgown, 1889–1890, France. Photo © The Museum at FIT.

especially "the milliners" and "all of the demimonde" of Paris, were "world rulers in this sphere."[28]

Even in Paris, capital of feminine fashion, a woman could attract disapproval if her love of dress seemed excessive, or if it conflicted with other aspects of the female role of wife and mother. Pundits worried that fashion blurred the lines between *le monde*, the "world" of society, and the *demimonde*, the shadowy "half-world" of commercial sex. Courtesans and actresses were, indeed, fashion trendsetters, although the styles they launched did not so much *expose* the courtesan's body, as elaborately *embellish* her person.

Fetishism

In 1887, a year after Freud returned to Vienna, French psychiatrist Alfred Binet published *Le Fétichisme dans l'amour*, in which he transcribed the term "fetishism" from European ideas about "primitive religion" into the field of sexual psychology. Freud certainly read this text by Binet, who cited Charcot. Because the concept of fetishism has exerted such an influence, it is worth pausing briefly to consider its history. As European traders and explorers traveled in west Africa, they encountered African religious beliefs and practices, which they regarded as irrational, even demonic. They applied the term "fetish" (from the

Portuguese *feitico*, or charm) to the amulets, protective talismans, and "idols" that Africans were thought to "worship."[29] Especially influential was Charles de Brosses' book *Du culte des dieux fétiches* (1760). All the "terrestrial and material objects" that Africans worship are "called Fetishes," wrote de Brosses. For this reason, he declared of the wider phenomenon: "I will call it Fetishism."[30]

Karl Marx read *The Cult of Fetish Gods* as part of his research into religion and superstition. The idea that "primitive" people make fetishes and then, irrationally, worship them led him to develop his own ideas about the fetishism of commodities. Already in the 1840s, he began to apply this idea of irrational belief to economic concepts, such as the Spanish conquistadors' worship of gold. Indeed, he argued that certain European nations were "still dazzled by the sensuous glitter of precious metals, and are, therefore, still fetish-worshippers of metal money."[31]

In *Capital: A Critique of Political Economy* (1867), Marx went on to argue that a commodity is not just an object that human beings make and use, such as a linen coat, since, under capitalism, commodities are produced and exchanged within a context of exploitation and mystification. Commodity fetishism is the mistaken belief that the commodity has a natural, intrinsic value, apart from the labor that went into it. According to Marx, the commodity functions as a sign that is overvalued, even worshipped, while the person who actually made it is alienated and objectified. Thus, a particular "social relation between men … assumes … the fantastic form of a relation between things."[32] It is highly unlikely that Binet read Marx, but he had almost certainly read de Brosses.

In *Le Fétichisme dans l'amour*, Binet described how certain "degenerates" experienced "intense genital excitation" when contemplating "inanimate objects," especially articles of clothing. Citing Charcot and Valentin Magnan on the way these sexual "deviants" felt "adoration" for "bizarre-seeming" objects such as "night caps, the nails in women's shoes, [and] white aprons," Binet concluded that "The term fetishism suits quite well this type of sexual perversion." At the same time, however, he insisted that "Everyone is more or less a fetishist, when in love." It was just a question of "a big and a small fetishism," the former pathological, the latter quite normal.[33] Freud read Binet's analysis of sexual fetishism, and cited it in 1905, but it was only in 1927 that he developed his own ideas on the subject.

In its "pathological" form, sexual fetishism seemed to be a primarily masculine perversion, although researchers also identified some female fetishists. However, according to all accounts, most sexual fetishists were men, and the majority of them focused on stereotypically "feminine" materials, such as silk and fur, or items of dress, such as high-heeled shoes or boots, lingerie, and aprons, as well as female body parts, like long braids of hair, which some fetishists surreptitiously cut off and collected.

Edouard Manet's painting *Nana* (1877) depicts the actress Henriette Hauser dressed only with her lingerie, a blue satin corset, matching stockings, a bracelet, and high-heeled shoes. The trend toward colorful, luxurious lingerie was adopted first by "the aristocracy of vice," but within a few years, it had become more widely fashionable. "Secret" garments,

Figure 1.10 Edouard Manet, *Nana*, 1877. Oil on canvas. Hamburger Kunsthalle, Hamburg, Germany/ Bridgeman Images.

like these, were seen only in the intimacy of the boudoir or bedroom, where Hauser's male companion sits fully dressed. The sexual allure of the body not only seemed to "rub off" on undergarments, but these also acquired an erotic allure of their own. According to Manet, "The satin corset is the nude of our time."[34]

Clothes and Collecting

In 1886, Freud returned from Paris to Vienna, and finally married Martha Bernays. They had six children in fairly quick succession, not unlike Freud's own parents. As a married man, Freud apparently turned the task of shopping for his clothes over to his wife Martha. Their eldest son, Martin (who was named after Charcot), recalled that Martha Freud was always very careful with expenses, except when she "ordered all my father's clothes," when she "tried to reach absolute perfection, always taking the greatest care in ordinary well-cut clothes made from British cloth."[35] (Even the expensive laced shoes he had bought in Paris had "English soles"!)[36]

Martha herself was not very fashionable (unlike Freud's mother), but she enjoyed dressing well, and encouraged her daughters to be well dressed, although the youngest, Anna Freud, was a disappointment in this respect. "Never renowned for her sartorial splendor, Anna Freud looked quite shabby," when she entered the Rosenberg's carpet shop in Vienna before the Second World War. Years later, in London, Olga Rosenberg recalled thinking, "she must be a beggar," when "the poorly clad" young woman identified herself and asked to buy a carpet for her father.[37]

Freud never explicitly analyzed the unconscious role that clothes played in his own life, although his personal style has influenced generations of psychoanalysts, both real and fictional. Psychoanalysts who study shopping have been influenced by the work of Freud's colleague Melanie Klein (1882–1960), who pioneered play therapy with young children and theorized the "pre-Oedipal stage." Kleinian analysts suggest that the "consumption" of goods ultimately refers back to the baby's experience of incorporating the "good breast," that is, the nourishment and pleasurable sensations associated with nursing. If we are stressed or anxious, we may smoke or eat too much, or try to "fill psychic hunger" with "greedy shopping." We project "our idealized selves onto consumer goods" and then "re-introject these idealized objects." Buying consumer goods provides gratification, at least in the short term, because it gives a "feeling of agency," while also acting as a "defense against bad feelings."[38]

Freud's nephew, Edward Bernays, emigrated to the United States where he became a pioneer of US public relations in the 1920s, using psychoanalytic ideas to help clients like the American Tobacco Company sell their products. At a time when men were the vast majority of smokers, Bernays launched a behind-the-scenes campaign directed at young feminists, which identified cigarettes as "torches of freedom." As the 1929 New York Easter Parade began, dozens of women simultaneously lit cigarettes to promote the idea that smoking in public was an act of female emancipation.

Austrian psychologist Ernest Dichter also emigrated to the United States in the 1930s, where he introduced the idea that brands have "personalities," because "people project themselves into" certain brands and form attachments with others who use the same brands. Consumers feel "a sense of kinship" with certain brands, and feel good about themselves whenever they make a new purchase. Adolescents are especially obsessed with brands, because they are experiencing so many identity issues at puberty, and fashion becomes "an important area of cultural production."[39]

In recent years, there has been growing interest in the study of "excessive" or "compulsive" buying. While this is often interpreted in terms of a problem with impulse control or obsessive-compulsive behavior, "buying goods to bolster one's self-image" is apparently typical of "most buying behavior." As one "shopaholic" put it: "I felt really depressed about myself ... I probably wanted to make myself feel that I was something better than what I was." In the book *I Shop, Therefore I Am* (2000), Helga Dittmar writes: "When people engage in impulse buying," they are especially likely to purchase "material symbols ... relevant to those aspects of self that are felt to be lacking."[40] Yet research also indicates that shopping for clothes makes many people anxious, and the feeling is often closely related to "anxiety over potential social embarrassment." Drawing on an ethnography of shopping, dress scholars Alison Clarke and Daniel Miller argue that "it is above all anxiety that determines what people actually wear."[41]

In 1896, after the death of his father, Freud began acquiring the many objects that would comprise his famous antiquities collection. Freud's choice to collect objects from antiquity bears an obvious resemblance to his comparison of psychoanalysis with archeological excavations. Psychoanalysts have described collecting as "an unruly passion." Not unlike the child with a teddy bear or the fetishist with a shoe (or, indeed, the shopper), the collector "assigns power and value to these objects," which give pleasure, calm anxiety, and "enhance or restore a narcissistically injured person's sense of self."[42]

2

The Naked Dreamer

After the death of his father in 1896, Freud began a self-analysis, which included interpreting his dreams. In this way, he developed "the idea of a dynamic or *personal unconscious*."[1] As he observed: "The concept of the unconscious had long been knocking at the gates of psychology and asking to be let in."[2] Philosophers and writers had already intuited that not all mental activity is conscious. But it was difficult to prove that the unconscious even existed, let alone that it influences our behavior. Freud suggested that the existence of the unconscious could only be inferred, through neurotic symptoms, slips of the tongue or pen ("Freudian slips"), or dreams—all occasions when we "say" something we did not consciously intend to say, but which reveals a wish.

In *The Interpretation of Dreams* (1900), probably his most famous book, Freud argued that dreams are about "forbidden wishes," usually sexual wishes, which have been repressed, pushed down into the unconscious, from which they emerge only in disguise. From the beginning, many people deplored Freud's "obsession" with sexuality. Others seemed even more threatened by "the very idea that humans have unconscious motivations."[3] Yet already by the early twentieth century, many artists believed that "human creativity … stems from unconscious access to underlying, unconscious forces."[4] In paintings by artists such as Gustav Klimt, even abstract motifs seemed to allude to

Figure 2.1 *Cupid and Psyche*, 1589, by Jacopo Zucchi (1540–1589-90), oil on canvas. Villa and Galleria Borghese, Rome, Lazio, Italy. © NPL – DeA Picture Library/G. Nimatallah/Bridgeman Images.

sex, with shapes resembling sperm and stylized genitalia. Although Félix Vallotton probably never read Freud, his *Intérieur avec femme en rouge de dos* (1903) depicts a dreamlike scene in which a mysterious woman in red pauses on her way through an enfilade of open doors, past furniture draped with discarded items of clothing, toward a staircase leading to a bedroom. This painting, which seems to be about sexual desire and anxiety, practically cries out for a psychoanalytical interpretation. Freud's sex and dream theories would ultimately also have an impact on how we interpret dress.

Figure 2.2 Portrait of Adele Bloch-Bauer I, 1907, by Gustav Klimt, oil, silver, and gold on canvas. Photo by Imagno/Getty Images.

Figure 2.3 Félix Vallotton, *Intérieur avec femme en rouge de dos*, 1903, Kunsthaus, Zurich. Photo: Peter Barritt/Alamy Stock Photo.

Sexual Symbolism

Everyone who reads *The Interpretation of Dreams* becomes familiar with the idea of sexual symbolism. According to Freud, umbrellas and neckties, as well as other long and/or hard objects such as knives and guns, often symbolize the penis or phallus. Receptacles, such as purses and pockets, as well as rooms and boxes, often symbolize the vagina or sometimes the uterus. Shoes can potentially symbolize the genitals of either sex. High-heeled shoes and boots, for example, are usually interpreted as phallic symbols, but a shoe can also symbolize the vagina into which the phallic foot is slipped.

One of Freud's patients, a married woman, dreamed that she was wearing a hat with a crown that stuck up and two side pieces that hung down, one lower than the other. When she could not think of any associations to this image, he suggested that the hat symbolized the male genitals. At first she flatly rejected this interpretation, but after a pause, she asked whether all men had one testicle that hung lower than the other, like her husband. On the other hand, when he told his famous patient "Dora" that her dream about a jewel box referred to the female genitals, she told him, "I knew *you*'d say that." When she played with her reticule, a type of small purse, he interpreted this gesture as symbolizing masturbation.[5]

Figure 2.4 Jack Jacobus, Ltd. side-button boots of leather and silk. 1895–1900, England. Gift of Victoria and Albert Museum. Photo © The Museum at FIT.

"The necktie which hangs down and is not worn by a woman is clearly a masculine symbol," declared Freud later in his *Introductory Lectures on Psychoanalysis* (1915–1916). The symbolism of an object does not necessarily correlate just to its shape, however. If an item of clothing is typically worn by men, or has a name that is gendered masculine, Freud tended to perceive it as a phallic symbol. For example, when a young male patient dreamed of an ill-fitting overcoat (*Mantel* in German), Freud interpreted this as a condom. But there were still other reasons why the necktie was coded as a phallic symbol. In a talk at the Vienna Psychoanalytic Society, Freud said that: "The strongest reason in the unconscious is that the necktie is something that one can choose, that one can have as pretty as one wants it—which is, unhappily, not the case for the penis."[6]

Freud did not invent the idea of sexual symbolism. Humans have utilized symbols since the prehistoric period. The body, in particular, seems to lend itself to symbol and metaphor. Phallic amulets, for example, have existed in many cultures, where they function magically to ward off the "evil eye" and promote fertility. Small children also sometimes innocently utilize sexual symbolism, like a little boy in Washington D.C., who ran naked into the living room with an erection, saying, "Look, Mommy, look! I'm the Washington Monument!" He had certainly not read Freud, but he spontaneously associated his little penis with a massive stone erection.

Figure 2.5 Bag, c. 1907. Photo © The Museum at FIT.

Figure 2.6 Karl Lagerfeld for Chanel, shoes, cruise 2009. Photo © The Museum at FIT.

Yet the idea of sexual symbolism often arouses resistance. I once lectured about sexual symbolism in fashion to an audience of engineers and cellphone designers. Afterwards, a man approached and said, suspiciously: "We have one kind of cellphone that we call a candy bar and another that we call a clamshell. You seem to be implying that there is something sexual about that." Candy bar? Clamshell? I was surprised at his naivety, especially since contemporary designers often deliberately play with sexual symbolism. However, it is also true that the universalizing use of sexual symbols can be absurdly reductive. Freud himself allegedly said, "Sometimes a cigar is just a cigar."

To Be Naked

Among the "typical" dreams that Freud described were "embarrassing dreams of being naked." But what does it mean for a human being to be naked? As an educated European Jew, Freud knew that in ancient Israel, nakedness was regarded as degraded and shameful, while clothing was associated with the "glorious garment" of divinity. Indeed, throughout much of the ancient world, in Egypt and Babylon, as well as Israel, nakedness was associated with shame and lack. By contrast, in ancient Greece, idealized nakedness (nudity), especially athletic male nudity, was celebrated, and associated with ideal beauty and "clarity of vision." The good, the true, and the beautiful were closely related, and with Plato, the metaphor of "the naked truth" became linked to the idea of knowledge as the "unveiling" of a mystery.[7]

Figure 2.7 Masaccio, *The Expulsion from the Garden of Eden*, 1426–27. Wilkipedia Commons.

Freud apparently never referred to the fateful curiosity of what a later psychoanalyst called "the first couple."[8] But he knew the story of Adam and Eve, who were innocently naked until after they ate the forbidden fruit, when "the eyes of both of them were opened and they knew that they were naked; and they sewed fig leaves together and made themselves aprons." As the Ur-garment, the fig leaf was portrayed in innumerable Christian paintings as a sign of humanity's fallenness and mortality.

Many paintings feature strategically placed leaves even when depicting scenes that occurred prior to the fall. But in Masaccio's *The Expulsion from the Garden of Eden* (1426–7), the couple are pictured completely naked—in contrast to the angel, who is robed and armed. They also embody their shame differently: "He hides his eyes and she hides her breasts and pubic hair." In their book *Shame and Sexuality: Psychoanalysis and Visual Culture*, Claire Pajaczkowski and Ivan Ward propose that "Man's averted gaze and woman's covered body" indicate that "man is the bearer of the gaze and woman is its object."[9] The gendered politics of looking would play a central part in Freud's ideas about the eroticism of dress.

Protection from the elements is another reason for *covering* much of the body with clothes. Freud often quoted from Shakespeare, and *King Lear* (3.4.28–32) features a powerful passage on "Poor naked wretches, … / That bide the pelting of this pitiless storm / How shall your houseless heads … and window'd raggedness, defend you / From seasons such as these?" Notice how Shakespeare described a body that was only *partly* covered as "naked."

Victorians, like Freud, had "ambivalent … attitudes towards the unclothed body." Brought up to regard the heroic male nude of antiquity as "the pinnacle of a civilized aesthetic," they were conditioned to interpret "the unclothed African, Australian, Aboriginal, or Pacific Islander" in terms of "primitiveness and savagery." European missionaries and colonial administrators constantly complained about the insufficient attire and lack of shame exhibited by colonized peoples.[10] However, as Ruth Barcan observed in her history of nudity: "There is no simple opposition between being clothed and being naked," because different cultures and eras have had different ideas about what constitutes nakedness and "what counts as clothes."[11]

Darwin and the Power of Sexuality

Most animals wear a coat of fur, feathers, or scales. Among existing primate species, only *Homo sapiens* lost their fur.[12] Charles Darwin's theory of evolution by natural selection does not necessarily explain this loss. However, in *The Descent of Man, and Selection in Relation to Sex* (1871), Darwin suggested that humans' relatively "naked" skin might have evolved as a means of *sexual* selection, becoming "the prime bodily ornament of the human species," comparable to the peacock's tail, while the hairless "hot-spots" of apes evolved into hairy and sexual areas on human bodies. Further developing Darwin's hypothesis, others have argued that "precisely because naked skin is the only ornament …

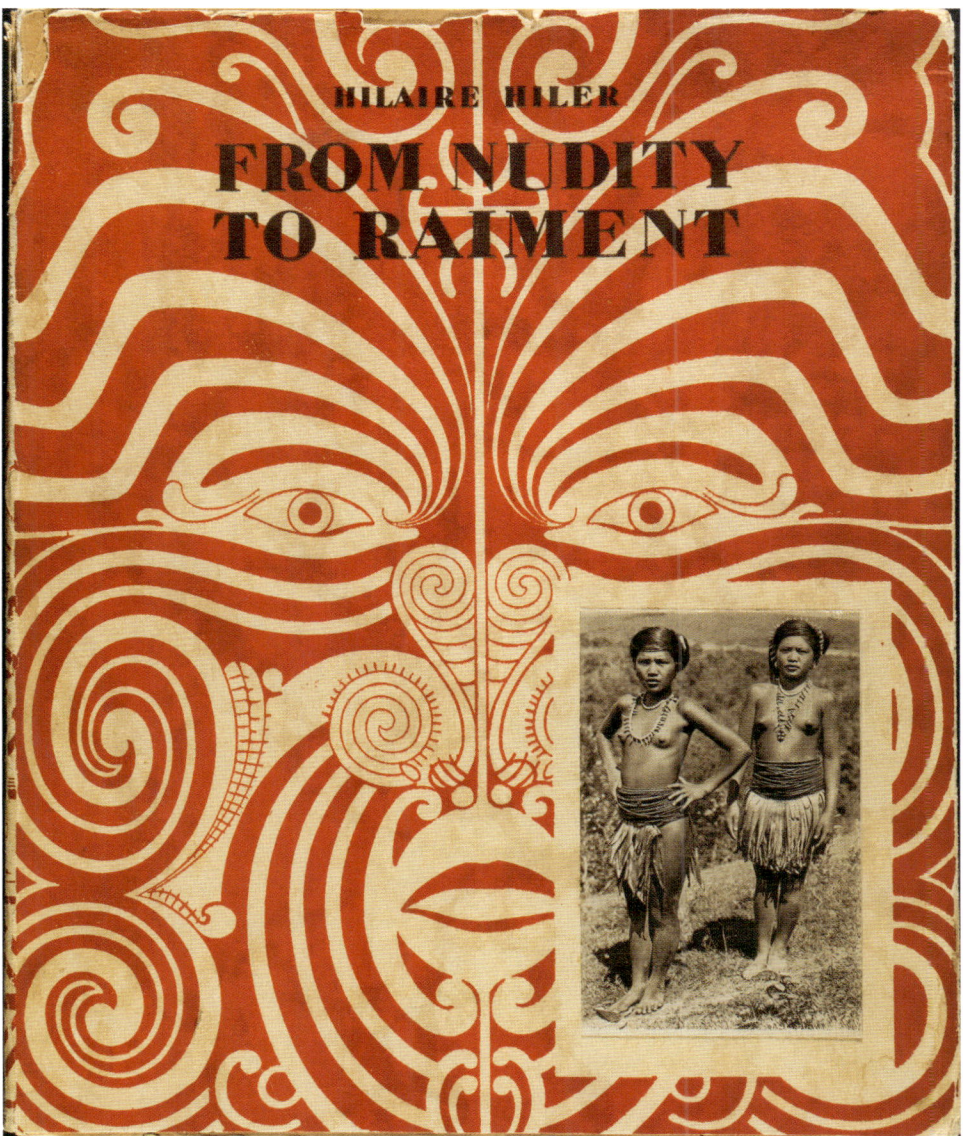

Figure 2.8 Cover of *From Nudity to Raiment*, by Hilaire Hiler, featuring a photograph by Charles Martin of Bontoc Igorot women wearing skirts of leaves. Courtesy of the author.

[it] is itself able to function as the setting for further additions and ornamental markings of every kind. In this sense, naked skin is a superb feat of sexual selection."[13]

Darwin's emphasis on the power of sexuality encouraged the idea that perhaps sexual *display*, rather than sexual modesty, was the original message of dress and bodily adornment. Ethnologists of Freud's era mentioned the penis sheaths and *cache-sexes* of "primitive" cultures, which could be interpreted as calling attention to the genitals. The body decorations of nonwestern people were also sometimes compared with "irrational" and "immodest" European fashions, such as the Renaissance codpiece or the Victorian corset and bustle. Cartoonists even implicitly suggested that the Biblical fig leaf was an ambivalent symbol of modesty, since it called attention to what it supposedly attempted to hide. Freud concluded: "At the root of every taboo, there must be a desire."[14]

Embarrassing Dreams of Being Naked

There are few universals in world history, and we don't know why the naked, *unmodified* body has been so widely rejected. Nakedness "has been remarkably under-theorized."[15] But in order to understand the significance of dress, we need to recognize that it only exists in relation to the idea of nakedness. Freud's innovation was to explore the unconscious significance of nakedness and dress. "It is only in our childhood … that we feel no shame at our nakedness," argued Freud. Many people today would argue that *they* feel no shame about being naked. However, Freud is really emphasizing how children feel pleasure displaying their naked bodies (evidence of infantile sexuality), and have to *learn* to feel ashamed. As Freud put it: "One can scarcely pass through a country village in our part of the world without meeting some child of two or three who lifts up his little shirt in front of one." Older, urban children also find pleasure in being naked in front of other people, as Freud observed: "Undressing has an almost intoxicating effect on many children even in their later years, instead of making them feel ashamed. They laugh and jump about … while their mother or whoever else may be there, reproves them and says: 'Ugh! Shocking! You mustn't ever do that!'"[16] Notice how Freud calls attention to certain aspects of nakedness in relation to dress, such as how the child "lifts up his little shirt," or how nakedness is identified with "undressing," which has an "intoxicating effect" on some people, but which others regard as "shocking."

Freud admitted that some people have dreams of nakedness without feeling embarrassed, but he believed this to be rare. The dream "censor" is so vigilant, he argued, that the dreamer does not even need to be completely naked, but only insufficiently or inappropriately dressed, in order to feel ashamed. Freud himself had once dreamed that he was "very incompletely dressed" while rapidly going up a flight of stairs when he met a maid on the stairs. "I felt ashamed and tried to hurry," he wrote, but suddenly, "I was glued to the steps and unable to budge." Meanwhile, the maid was oblivious to his state of partial undress. Drawing on his memory of the previous day, Freud recalled that he had "taken off [his] collar and tie and cuffs" before walking upstairs from his office to his apartment.[17] This remnant of the day was incorporated into the manifest content of the dream.

Elana Shapiro has suggested that, as an assimilated Jew living in an antisemitic environment, Freud may have felt anxious about a Gentile maid seeing him improperly dressed.[18] This is plausible, but almost certainly not the entire story. Indeed, Freud gave a slightly different description of this dream to his friend Fliess. In that version, he had been climbing the stairs rapidly, when the woman suddenly came up behind him, and although feeling ashamed, Freud also experienced erotic excitement. Freud never publicly shared a complete self-analysis of any of his dreams, but when Didier Anzeiu interpreted this particular dream, he found erotic "sensations of flying (going up nimbly) and rigidity (glued to the spot)," as well as wishes for health (Freud climbed the stairs rapidly despite being a heavy smoker).[19]

In her book *La robe: Essai psychanalytique sur le vêtement* (1983), Lacanian analyst Eugénie Lemoine-Luccioni described an exhibitionistic dream that one of her female patients recounted: "I am nude. Freud is there. We speak. He gives the impression that this is of no importance. He is dressed, but we can continue like that … ." At which the analyst thinks: "Curious! *She* is nude, *he* is dressed, as in so many paintings … It is rare in any case that *he* would be nude and *she* would be dressed."[20] I love this example, because it shows the influence of history and society on the personal unconscious.

The Pleasure Principle

In Freudian psychoanalysis, the pleasure principle is the human tendency to seek pleasure and avoid pain. Contemporary fashion often plays with images of the naked body. The dream of nakedness is a good example of the unconscious pursuit of pleasure, which often comes up against both external and internalized resistance. Consider the Lanvin dress printed with the image of a classical sculpture of a naked female torso. If a woman dreamed that she wore this dress, it might mean that she unconsciously wanted to be naked and experience pleasure in showing off her body. If she actually wore the dress, she might well be conscious of that wish. However, the wish to be naked might also be affected by other considerations, beyond the sexual repression that Freud observed. The fact that the dress references classical sculpture brings to mind Kenneth Clark's theory about the distinction between the "naked" and the "nude" in art.[21] Feminist art historians have questioned Clark's queasiness with the fleshy nakedness of actual women, and his praise for the idealized nudity of artistic female bodies, which they regard as sanitized and controlled. Yet as beauty standards have become ever more exigent, women today (and men also) are increasingly conscious of the wish or injunction to "Look better naked!"

And what about the Jean Paul Gaultier trouser suit, whose jacket is printed with the trompe l'oeil image of a muscular male torso? This was produced as part of Gaultier's womenswear collection, and was worn on the runway by a woman. If a woman dreamed that she wore this suit, should we interpret it as a wish to be transformed into a man? But the wish to be a man can mean different things to different people. A woman told me that when she was an adolescent, she took mescaline and hallucinated that she had a penis. "This is great!" she thought. "No wonder men are so full of themselves." Yet she also recalled thinking that the best part was how it made her feel "impenetrable." Of course,

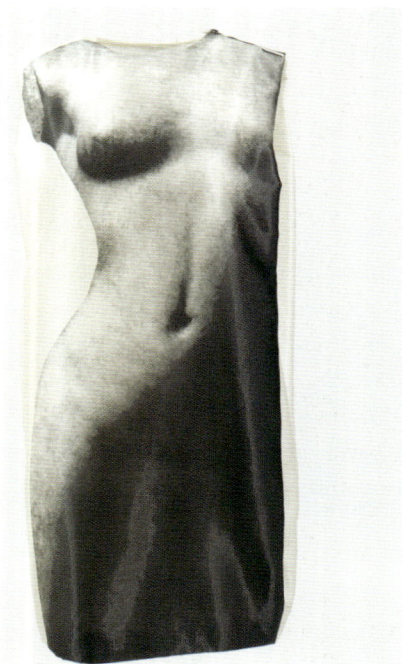

Figure 2.9 Lanvin, "naked torso" dress, Summer 2013. Photo © The Museum at FIT.

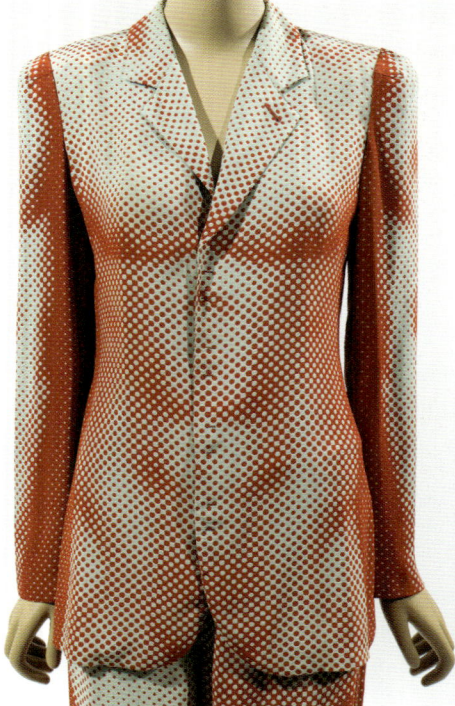

Figure 2.10 Jean Paul Gaultier, Femme trompe l'oeil cyber muscle suit, Spring 1996. Photo © The Museum at FIT.

Figure 2.11 Jeremy Scott for Moschino, Chocolate bar dress, Fall 2014. Photo by Jacopo Raule/Getty Images.

having a penis does not protect an individual from being penetrated, although the fantasy of an all-powerful *phallus* might.

According to Freud, the sex drive goes far beyond genital pleasure, per se, to encompass a range of other pleasures, including oral pleasures. The chocolate bar dress designed by Jeremy Scott for Moschino evokes familiar oral pleasures, like consuming sweet candy, while also hinting at other desires by transforming the female body into something "good enough to eat." The pleasure we find in clothes, especially new clothes, is one of the reasons why fashion plays such an important role in "the dream world of capitalism," as well as in our own private daydreams about how fashion can transform us.[22]

The Role of Trauma

Is the dream of nakedness only the expression of an infantile exhibitionistic wish? Freud implied as much in *The Interpretation of Dreams*. But in *Beyond the Pleasure Principle* (1920), he suggested that dreams could also function as attempts to master trauma. The recurrent nightmares suffered by the First World War veterans supported his revised theory, which placed much greater emphasis on human aggression and destructiveness. Recent research in post-traumatic stress disorder also confirms that traumatic elements often play a role in dreams of feeling embarrassed at being naked. The female patient of a male analyst, for example, recalled several such dreams, including the following:

> I was in a classroom at college. The professor asked a question of the group, and I stood up to answer it, only to discover to my embarrassment that I was naked from the waist up. Neither the professor nor the rest of the class seemed to notice, however, as someone else had gotten up to answer the question at the same time.[23]

After identifying the professor with both her analyst and her current indifferent lover, she wept when she recalled how, as a teenager, she had paraded around the house in a brassiere, trying to attract her father's attention. "He was completely blind to my existence." In other case studies, male patients also reported desperately trying to attract the attention of their parents, who remained indifferent or rejecting.

To remain unseen or unacknowledged by our significant others is painful. As Pajazkowski and Ward point out: "We can be overwhelmed with shame and self-consciousness if we are scrutinized too closely, or if we are ignored."[24] Exhibitionism, in the sense of "showing off," has its roots in children's legitimate desires to see and be seen. Children not only show off their naked bodies, they also call attention to their physical accomplishments: "Look at me! I can ride a bike!" Or they reference their dressed appearance and pretend identity: "Look at me! I'm a princess!" "Look! I'm Spiderman!"

Like dreams, fantasies may express unconscious wishes, attempt to master trauma, or seek to resolve psychic conflicts. In his paper on "Hysterical Phantasies and their Relation to Bisexuality" (1908), Freud described the case of a patient "who pressed her dress up

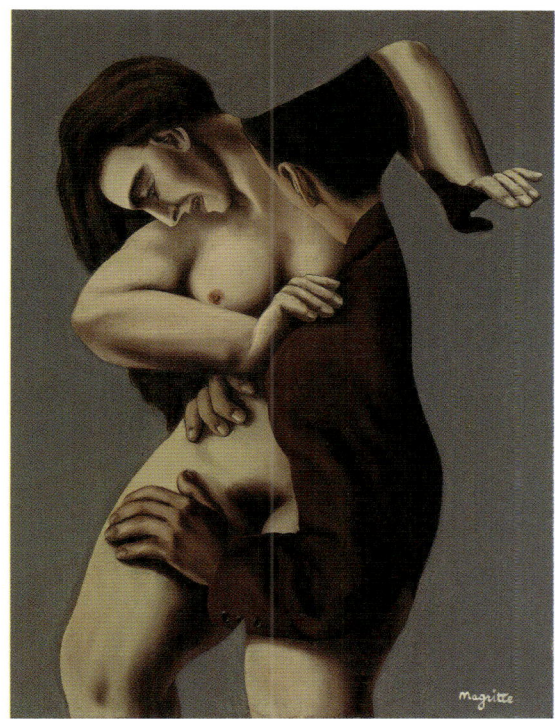

Figure 2.12 René Magritte, *Les Jours gigantesques (The Titanic Days)*, Paris, 1928. Private Collection. Photo © Christie's Images/Bridgeman Images. © 2024 C. Herscovici/Artists Rights Society (ARS), New York.

against her body with one hand (as the woman), while she tried to tear it off with the other (as the man)."[25] René Magritte's disturbing painting *The Titanic Days* (1928) recalls this fantasy, which Freud associated with the psychoanalytic idea of bisexuality as the individual's identification with both the male and female aspects of the self.

Freudian versus Jungian Dream Analysis

Like Freud, Swiss psychiatrist Carl Jung (1875–1961) believed that dreams were significant. Indeed, he claimed to have analyzed more than 80,000 dreams over the course of his career. Jung was initially enthusiastic about Freud's theory of psychoanalysis, and the two men traveled together to the United States in 1909. But Jung objected to Freud's emphasis on sexuality, while Freud was disturbed by Jung's "unscientific" interest in religion and alchemy. In 1913, Freud broke off relations with Jung, who left the psychoanalytic movement to form his own school of analytic psychology.

In 1916, during the First World War, when Freud returned to the subject of "symbolism in dreams," he still argued that the "great majority of symbols in dreams are sexual symbols." However, perhaps in response to Jung's criticism, he did concede that "the human body as a whole, parents, children, brothers and sisters, birth, death, [and] nakedness" are also given

Chapter 2 The Naked Dreamer

symbolic representation in dreams. Parents may appear in the guise of king and queen, for example, while the body may be disguised as a house, "nakedness by clothes or uniforms."[26]

Psychoanalysts today do not automatically interpret dream images in terms of universalizing sexual symbolism, instead emphasizing that the individual's *own* associations with the dream will provide more accurate clues to its latent meaning. That does not mean that sexual symbolism has disappeared from psychoanalysis, but it has evolved. As one psychoanalyst put it: "Nowadays a certain type of phallic potency would often be represented by a motorcycle."[27] Dreams can also be interpreted, not in terms of individual symbols, but as an entire *mise-en-scène*, encompassing characters, costumes, settings, and events. As the artist Marisol once said: "A work of art is like a dream, where all the characters, no matter in what disguise, are part of the dreamer."[28] The traditional Freudian distinction between the manifest and the latent dream is thus blurred.

Jung desexualized sex to a kind of vital energy, and focused on the "collective unconscious" as a reservoir of universal symbols. He thus interpreted dream imagery in terms of eternal "archetypes" (figures such as the hero, the shadow, and the mother). Artists and creative writers have been receptive to both Freud's and Jung's ideas about dream symbolism and the unconscious, because they see dreams and daydreams as important sources of inspiration for their own imaginative creations. Jungian archetypes, especially feminine archetypes (such as the lover, the queen, and the priestess), have exerted considerable influence on art and fashion.[29] I have met several people in the fashion world who were interested in Jung, and it is certainly often fascinating to read his books. Yet his work is undeniably mystical, as when he writes: "In dreams we put on the likeness of that more universal, truer, more eternal man dwelling in the darkness of eternal night."[30]

Catherine Bronniman's *La robe de psyche: Essai de lien entre psychanalyse et vêtement* (*Psyche's Dress: Essay on the Connection between Psychoanalysis and Clothing*) (2015) is one of the few books on fashion that takes a Jungian approach, exploring subjects such as the process of individuation, the persona, the shadow, the archetype, as well as the "collective unconscience, which contains the complete spiritual heritage and the evolution of humanity." In Jungian psychology, dress often represents the *persona*, a mask that the individual presents to the world, which contrasts with the hidden part of the self, the *shadow*.[31] Then there is the *anima*, "the personification of all the feminine psychological tendencies in the psyche of a man," while the *animus* is the "the interior man" in the woman's psyche. All this is richly evocative, but also polarizing, with femininity associated with love, nature, and intuition, while the masculine is associated with initiative, audacity, and intellect. For Jung, it was feminine Eros versus masculine Logos.[32]

There seems to be a correlation between Jungian archetypes and various fashion looks, although it is unclear to what extent fashion designers have actually read Jung or had Jungian analysis. Fashion designer Rick Owens, for example, sometimes seems to have drawn on archetypes, as in his Spring 2009 collection, entitled "Priestesses of Longing." For Jungians, the archetype of the priestess represents the water element, and is intuitive, sensual,

Figure 2.13 Rick Owens, ensemble, Spring 2009. Gift of Rick Owens. Photo © The Museum at FIT.

and restorative. This seems congruent with the dark romanticism of Owen's avant-garde designs, although I am not suggesting that he was directly inspired by Jungian archetypes.

The doppelganger motif, the theme of the uncanny double, which was of interest to Freud, was also important for Jung, who associated it with the shadow. Here, too, fashion designers have found rich sources of inspiration. Jun Takahashi of Undercover has more than once featured twins in his fashion shows, and while at Gucci, Alessandro Michele also drew on the theme of doubles. The exhibition *A Queen Within: Adorned Archetypes*, organized in 2017, featured more than 100 looks by designers such as Alexander McQueen, which the curator interpreted in terms of seven different archetypes of the queen, or, metaphorically, of woman, from mother earth to enchantress.[33] Yet for all its visual and emotional appeal, Jung's archetype psychology has not had the impact on cultural criticism that Freudian and Lacanian psychoanalysis have had.

Three Essays on the Theory of Sexuality

Three Essays on the Theory of Sexuality (1905) was Freud's most radical book, in which he revised and expanded the very notion of sexuality. Almost everyone at that time believed that, except for a few "degenerates," everyone had a biological instinct to heterosexual genital intercourse. (Many people still believe this.) But Freud argued that so-called "normal" sexuality (penis in vagina) does *not* simply arise naturally from biological instincts, because human sexuality is not just about reproduction, it is about *pleasure*.

Freud famously used the Latin word *libido* (lust or desire) to describe the hypothetical energy behind the transformations of the sexual drive. In the first of the three essays, on the sexual aberrations, he explained that the object of the sexual drive (the person to whom one is attracted) could be male or female … or both. Thus, homosexuality "cannot be regarded as degenerate." Indeed, he implied that there was no polarity between heterosexual–homosexual, normal–perverse, or even masculine–feminine. Everyone has masculine and feminine aspects, he argued, and the "disposition to perversions of every kind is a general and fundamental human characteristic." He described how common, even ubiquitous, were sexual styles from fetishism to cross-dressing. The aim of the sex drive could be many types of pleasure-seeking, involving the mouth, anus, genitals, and/or the skin, which Freud described as "the erotogenic zone par excellence." But no matter the specific sexual aims, "touching and looking" were always part of sex.[34]

The Libido for Looking

In 1905, Freud stressed that the "libido for looking" was one of the components of the sexual drive, which could assume an active form (scopophilia or voyeurism) or a passive form (exhibitionism). The term "exhibitionist" was first used in 1877 by French physician and psychiatrist Charles Lasègue to refer to men who deliberately exposed their genitals to strangers. The medico-legal definition of exhibitionism remains essentially the same today: the act of genital exposure to unsuspecting strangers, which is usually regarded as both a crime and a paraphilia (perversion). Then, as now, the vast majority of such exhibitionists are men, although there do exist women who are exhibitionists, such as one who "compulsively exposed her genitals to certain women, literally flashing and stalking them."[35] This certainly sounds active, even aggressive, but according to Freud, exhibitionism, "the act of displaying oneself … has the passive sexual aim of being looked at."[36]

Figure 2.14 Grandville (Jean-Ignace-Isidore Gerard), *Venus at the Opera*, 1844. INTERFOTO/Alamy Stock Photo.

Ultimately, Freud would suggest that both "shameless" children and fashionable women were, if not exactly exhibitionists, at least *exhibitionistic*, while men were the ones primarily engaged in sexual looking. European society certainly positioned women as dressed-to-be-looked-at, while men were apparently all eyes, as we can see in Grandville's eerie and extraordinary lithograph *Venus at the Opera* (1844). But the reality was more complex.

Élisabeth de Caraman-Chimay, the Countess Greffulhe (1860–1952), one of the most beautiful and fashionable women of *la belle Époque*, once confessed to Robert de Montesquiou: "I don't think there is any pleasure in the world comparable to that of a woman who feels that she is being looked at by everybody, and has joy and energy transmitted to her." In *La Divine Comtesse*, under the heading "Before the Mirror," Montesquiou again quoted her: "I returned from the opera and was astonished with the transfiguration that the crowd made me undergo … How can one live when one can no longer provoke this great anonymous caress, after having known and tasted it?"[37] She also loved to look at herself, and in 1896, she collaborated with the photographer Paul Nadar on at least two images, which show her in front of a full-length mirror, wearing a dress that she almost certainly created in collaboration with the couturier Charles Frederick Worth.

Chapter 2 The Naked Dreamer

Figure 2.15 Countess Greffulhe, 1896. Photograph by Paul Nadar. Palais Galleria, Musée de la Mode de la Ville de Paris. © Eric Emo/Galliera/Roger-Viollet.

When the Countess Greffulhe referred to the gaze of the crowd as "this great anonymous caress," she directly links what Freud called the "libido for looking" and the "libido for touching." In infancy, touching, grasping the breast with the hands, precedes looking. But when an adult gazes at another person, this may stimulate a fantasy about touching that person, and/or being touched, for touch always goes both ways. Because we touch especially with our hands, gloves have long carried erotic connotations, and paintings have often contrasted a naked hand with another that wears a glove. Barbara Kruger's artwork *Untitled (You are seduced by the sex appeal of the inorganic)* references touch but also the allure of fashion as artifice and commodity.

The libido for looking would play a crucial role in Freud's understanding of the significance of nakedness and dress: "Visual impressions remain the most frequent pathway along which libidinal excitation is aroused, indeed, natural selection counts upon the accessibility of this pathway when it encourages the development of sexual beauty in the sexual object." In one of the few specific references to dress in *Three Essays on the Theory of Sexuality*, he wrote:

> The progressive concealment of the body which goes along with civilization keeps sexual curiosity awake. This curiosity seeks to complete the sexual object by revealing its hidden parts. It can, however, be diverted ('sublimated') in the

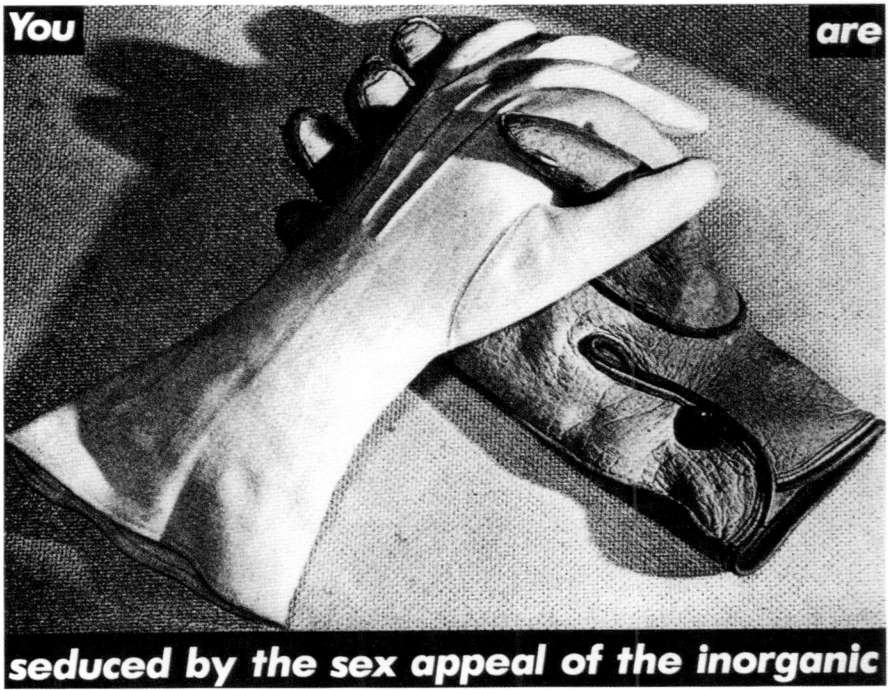

Figure 2.16 Barbara Kruger, *Untitled* (*You are seduced by the sex appeal of the inorganic*), 1981. Gelatin silver print, 96.2 × 127.6 cm, 37 7/8 × 50 1/4 inches. Courtesy of the artist and Sprüth Magers.

direction of art, if its interest can be shifted away from the genitals on to the shape of the body as a whole.[38]

Did the concealment characteristic of women's dress in late Victorian Europe and North America reflect a culture of extreme sexual repression? Many people today unthinkingly accept this cliché. Indeed, Freud contributed to popularizing the idea by emphasizing "civilized" sexual morality as a source of modern nervous illness.[39] Yet his description of the attraction of concealment indicates that people's experience of fashion was more complicated. In his novel *The Man Without Qualities*, Austrian writer Robert Musil eloquently denied that the body-concealing character of prewar dress could be reduced to feelings of shame:

> In those days women wore clothes that encased them from throat to ankles … The water-clear candour of exhibiting oneself naked would then have been regarded, even by a person … not hampered by any feelings of shame … as a relapse into the animal state, not because of the nakedness but because of the renunciation of the civilized sexual stimulus afforded by clothes … Human beings at that time still had many skins … dress … forming a many-petaled, almost

impenetrable chalice loaded with an erotic charge and concealing at its core the slim white animal that made itself fearfully desirable, letting itself be searched for.[40]

A Loophole for Women's Exhibitionism

"The libido for looking and touching is present in everyone in two forms, active and passive," wrote Freud in *Jokes and Their Relation to the Unconscious* (1905). However, for Freud, activity was almost always associated with masculinity and passivity with femininity—and it is here that he makes his clearest statement yet on women, dress, and bodily exposure: "In women, the inclination to passive exhibitionism is almost invariably buried under the imposing reactive function of sexual modesty, but not without a loophole being left for it in relation to clothes."[41] In other words, women repress much of their exhibitionism, but dress allows them to exhibit at least some parts of their body—more, in fact, than men were permitted on formal occasions, such as an evening at the theater.

Indicating an awareness that fashions in dress are situated in time and space, Freud added: "I need only hint at the elasticity and variability in the amount of exhibitionism

Figure 2.17 Eva Gonzàles, *A Box at the Théâtre des Italiens*, 1874, oil on canvas. Musée d'Orsay, Paris, France/Bridgeman Images.

that women are permitted to retain in accordance with differing conventions and circumstances."[42] In Freud's day, for example, an evening dress might have a low décolletage and bare arms, whereas a day dress had a high collar and long sleeves.

Already by 1906, long before Freud became internationally famous, Viennese journalist Karl Kraus published an essay on "The Eroticism of Clothes," in which he drew on Freud's work to argue that:

> We hardly know to what degree our entire eroticism is an eroticism of clothing. Even our idea of nakedness is still indissolubly bound to the idea of clothing … The clothing of the opposite sex is a sexual symbol. An item of female clothing becomes an erotic fetish for the man and cross-dressing … entices the homosexual drives dormant everywhere.[43]

The references to nakedness, sexual symbolism, fetishism, cross-dressing, and homosexuality almost certainly alluded to Freud's recent publications, as well as the work of sexologists such as Richard von Krafft-Ebing. Kraus seems to have been the first to realize that Freud had, without intending it, outlined the beginning of the first psychoanalytic study of dress.

All Women are Clothes Fetishists

Freud never developed an organized theory about the eroticism of clothes, but he did draft various brief hypotheses about why *women* seemed to be so interested in fashion. On the evening of February 24, 1909, Freud presented a paper at a meeting of the Vienna Psychoanalytic Association, in which he tried to explain women's relationship to fashion: "In the world of everyday experience, we can observe that half of humanity must be classed among the clothes fetishists. All women, that is, are clothes fetishists … Only now we understand why even the most intelligent women behave defenselessly against the demands of fashion." Alluding to his exploration of the libido for looking, Freud wrote: "Dress plays a puzzling role in them [women]. It is a question again of the same drive [that is, to look], this time, however, in the passive form of allowing oneself to be seen, which is represented by clothes, and on account of which, clothes are raised to a fetish."[44]

Women's desire to exhibit their naked bodies is repressed, but also partially gratified through the exposure of their *fashioned bodies*. Women often derive *pleasure* from fashion, since, like the naked body, the adorned body may be experienced as something to be proudly displayed to others, and to oneself. Then Freud took a different turn:

> For [women], clothes take the place of parts of the body, and to wear the same clothes means only to be able to show what the others can show … Otherwise it would be incomprehensible why many women, following the demands of fashion, also want to wear, and do wear, pieces of clothing which do not show them to their best advantage, which do not suit them.[45]

Freud was *not* describing fashion here as an aesthetic phenomenon, since it often demanded that women wear unflattering clothes. Nor was this the status-oriented competition often associated with fashion. If clothes take the place of "parts of the body," what parts are these? The missing penis? If women all "wear the same clothes … in order to show what the others can show," what did he think they were all showing? Freud was still thinking through his ideas, but he was beginning to link women's interest in fashion with passivity and castration.

At some point, the minutes of the 1909 meeting were lost, only to be discovered in 1988, when Freud's paper was finally published. However, the newly discovered text had little impact on psychoanalytic thought, having been superseded by Freud's famous essay "Fetishism" (1927), in which he notoriously argued that "the fetish is a substitute for the woman's (the mother's) penis that the little boy once believed in and … does not want to give up." As an adult, the male fetishist knows that women do not have a penis, writes

Figure 2.18 Pair of fetish buttoned boots, European, c. 1895. Francesca Galloway, London. Image © Francesca Galloway (Photograph Katrina Lawson Johnston).

Dress, Dreams, and Desire

Freud, and yet, such is his "aversion ... to the real female genitals" that he needs to "endow" them with a fetish that serves as "a token of triumph over the threat of castration and a protection against it."[46] He had already observed in 1905 that the fetish object tended to be "some part of the body (such as the foot or hair) ... or some inanimate object," usually one relating to a "person's sexuality (such as a piece of clothing or underlinen)."[47]

Freud was not the only doctor exploring sexuality and the unconscious, nor the only one investigating the role of dress. According to historian Jann Matlock, "Clothing obsessionals played a central role in the gender of perversion in turn-of-the-century France, and a pivotal role in our understanding of sexual difference."[48] Medical and legal authorities were fascinated by sexual fetishism and cross-dressing, which they regarded as particularly intriguing perversions. In 1908, for example, French neuropsychiatrist Gaëtan Gatian de Clérambault (1872–1934) reported on the cases of several women who were apprehended stealing pieces of silk and masturbating with them. This was *precisely* the kind of behavior

Figure 2.19 G. de Clérambault, *Femme Marocaine Voilée*, 1917–1920. © Musée du quai Branly – Jacques Chirac, Dist. RMN-Grand Palais/Art Resource, NY.

that led men to be labeled fetishists. Yet in "*Passion érotique des étoffes chez la femme*" (1908), Clérambault insisted that, at most, the women could be classified under the term "pseudo-fetishism." After all, he argued, male fetishists engaged in "veritable debauches of the imagination" celebrating their fetishes in "an homage to the opposite sex," while these "sick women ... masturbate with the silk without any more reverie than a solitary gourmet savoring a fine wine."[49]

By flatly denying that women were capable of being fetishists, Clérambault was taking an extreme position for the time. But he was a strange person, deeply misogynistic, and obsessed with fabric and drapery. While serving in the French Army in North Africa, he took some 40,000 photographs of women (and some men) dressed in traditionally enveloping outer garments. Clérambault did not create titillating photographs of veiled women, only to pull the veil away to reveal their nakedness. More interested in the cloth than the naked body beneath, he also gave lectures on drapery at the École des Beaux-Arts. In her famous essay "The Sartorial Superego," Lacanian theorist Joan Copjec observed that both "exotic" Middle Eastern veils and European women's silky, ornamental fashions were often negatively compared with modern western men's "functional" clothes. Like developments in modernist architecture, this discourse on dress formed part of a "utilitarian rejection of useless enjoyment," as well as a fantasy of women's "surplus pleasure."[50]

Freud would later reject his hypothesis that "all women are clothes fetishists." Long dismissed by psychoanalysts as a dead end, it might yet throw light on some of women's unconscious fantasies about fashion and its relationship with the naked body. Indeed, the concept of "female fetishism" has seen something of a revival in recent years, as writers like Lorraine Gamman look at woman's attraction to "sexy girl shoes" and wonder "What's At Stake – Female Fetishism or Narcissism?"[51]

Female Narcissism

The ancient Greek myth of Narcissus told of a handsome youth, who fell in love with his reflection in a pool of water. Freud drew on this myth to describe a type of self-love that he called "narcissism." He posited the existence of a "primary and normal narcissism" in children of both sexes. But he argued that young women experience "an intensification of the original narcissism" at puberty, "especially if they grow up with good looks."[52] Freud *could* have observed a similar phenomenon among male adolescents, who also become extremely interested in their bodies. But he did not, presumably because he was already convinced that women were more narcissistic than men, with the significant exception of homosexual men, who "take *themselves* as their sexual object ... and look for a young man who resembles themselves and whom *they* may love as their mother loved *them*."[53]

Figure 2.20 Hans Memling, *Vanity*, central panel from the *Triptych of Earthly Vanity and Divine Salvation*. c. 1485. Musee des Beaux-Arts, Strasbourg, France. Art Heritage/Alamy Stock Photo.

"Women, especially if they grow up with good looks, develop a certain self-contentment," wrote Freud, whose portrayal of the female narcissist may have been modeled partly on his good friend, the glamorous Lou Andreas-Salomé:

> Strictly speaking, it is only themselves which such women love with an intensity comparable to that of the man's love for them ... Such women have the greatest fascination for men, not only ... [because] they are the most beautiful, but also because ... another person's narcissism has a great attraction for those who have renounced part of their own narcissism and are in search of object love ... It is as if we envied them for maintaining a blissful state of mind.[54]

On first reading, there does not seem to be anything *lacking* in Freud's portrayal of the narcissistic woman, since a degree of self-love is both necessary and desirable. The idea of female narcissism also implies that women are not, after all, so passive and sexually repressed. Their exhibitionism and narcissism are active and at least partly conscious. Yet it did not bode well, when Freud mentioned in passing that most men had "renounced part of their own narcissism," seeking instead to love a woman. Why were women apparently incapable of loving another person? Freud admitted that women loved their children, but, he added, only as a part of themselves.

The image of a woman gazing into a mirror has long been a symbol of vanity, and Freud's concept of female narcissism bears a strong resemblance to the traditional idea of female vanity. Although vanity had been described for centuries as a sin, Freud notoriously dismissed religion as an "illusion." In any case, religious asceticism had clearly not eradicated the human desire to see images of beautiful women, such as Hans Memling's *Vanity* (c. 1500). Naked except for her shoes and jeweled headband, she gazes at herself in a mirror. *Vanity* is the central painting in a triptych, which is flanked by the figures of Death and the Devil. Nudes also posed as Venus, goddess of love and beauty, who is sometimes depicted with her illegitimate son Cupid, holding the mirror in which she admires herself.

Ultimately, Freud would conclude that women's narcissism was caused by envy. He had already mentioned penis envy in 1905, arguing that when little girls "see that boys' genitals are formed differently from their own," they "immediately ... are over-come by envy for the penis—an envy culminating in the wish ... to be boys themselves."[55] In adolescence, young women's penis envy was triggered again by the onset of menstruation. As Freud put it later: "the physical vanity of women" was a defensive "compensation for their original sexual inferiority."[56]

That women's narcissism was among "the psychic consequences of the anatomical differences of the sexes" was widely accepted after 1925.[57] However, not all psychologists or psychoanalysts agreed, either that narcissism was bad, or that it was primarily female and resulted from penis envy. Indeed, the early twentieth century witnessed "a wide-ranging discussion that was—notably—as much concerned with the pleasures as with the pathologies of narcissism."[58]

Sylvia Bliss, author of "The Significance of Clothes" (1916), interpreted adornment as compensatory but also pleasurable for *both* men and women. An American psychologist, Bliss believed that the human inclination to decorate the body stemmed from a "fundamental feeling of incompleteness" that analysts had misinterpreted as female.[59] Yet this promising idea gained no traction. Instead, Freud's obsession with penis envy united his ideas about female exhibitionism, female fetishism, and female narcissism—and ultimately resulted in the long-held psychoanalytic belief that women's love of fashion was a compensation for their "lack."

3

The Masquerade

After the First World War, when women adopted more boyish and body-revealing fashions, many men complained bitterly that postwar society had become a "civilization without sexes," where "the modern woman" was reduced to this being "without breasts or hips," who "dances without a corset," and cuts her hair short. Contemporaries saw her as "a creation of the war."[1] However, in prewar avant-garde and bohemian circles, the image of the modern woman had *already* begun to shift from a voluptuous, corseted Venus to a slim, athletic Diana.[2] The catastrophe of the First World War accelerated prewar developments by giving young middle-class women greater personal and financial independence, including the freedom to style themselves in new ways. Soldiers on leave from the trenches were often shocked and anxious to see how women had changed.[3]

Known in English-speaking countries as "the flapper" and in France as *la garçonne*, the boyish girl or bachelor girl became a recognized social type and an icon of the Roaring Twenties. As Freud's early work on sexuality finally began to be widely translated in the 1920s, psychoanalysis became popularly associated with the sexual liberation of women and members of sexual minorities, especially gays, lesbians, and "transvestites." The heroine of Victor Margueritte's novel *La Garçonne* (1922) abandoned her unfaithful fiancé for an independent life involving both male and female lovers. Margueritte regarded his novel

Figure 3.1 *Les Garçonnes*, 1928.
Photograph by Jacques Henri Lartigue.
© Ministère de la Culture (France),
MPP-AAJHL.

as a feminist critique of society, but many readers, including most older feminists, were horrified by the young heroine's lack of "morality." Whereas first-generation feminists had advocated for women's civil rights, members of the younger generation were more concerned with personal and sexual freedom.

The scandalous Hollywood film *Flaming Youth* (1923) starred actress Colleen Moore as a young flapper, who wore short dresses and silk stockings, went to petting parties, and dated an older man who had been her mother's lover. When Moore was shown reading a book by Freud, her publicity agents immediately announced that she had actually *read* Freud. Clearly, she was a new woman, attracted to "the new ideals of personal life and sexual freedom."[4] Moore played similar roles in other films, such as *Why Be Good?*

In *Les Garçonnes: Modes et fantasmes des Années folles*, Christine Bard suggests that women's self-fashioning in the 1920s existed "under the sign of ambivalence." Since fashions in dress and hair typically function to maintain sex and gender distinctions, the *garçonne*'s adoption of masculine styles in the early twentieth century "transgressed a double taboo." Not only did she violate traditional sex and gender distinctions in dress and behavior, the *garçonne*

Figure 3.2 American actress Colleen Moore with Neil Hamilton in the 1929 film *Why Be Good?* Photo by First National Pictures/Michael Ochs Archives/Getty Images.

also evoked the emerging image of the lesbian. This image had begun to be disseminated as early as 1889, when Berlin psychiatrist Richard von Krafft-Ebing argued that: "One can almost always suspect uranism [homosexuality] in women who wear short hair or dress like men or practice sports."[5]

The nineteenth-century medicalization of "sexual perversions" was problematic, but it also had unexpected consequences, leading "both 'perverts' and their scientists" to construct the modern concept of "sexual identity." As a result, queer and trans people increasingly pioneered styles that signaled their sexual and gender identities to others of their "kind."[6] Certainly, a Sapphic subculture with its own dress codes and meeting places was visible in Paris by the 1890s, although, as with most sexual subcultures, its most visible members tended to be either socially elite individuals or socially marginal ones.[7]

"The novelty of the 1920s resides perhaps in the idea that 'vice' was no longer confined to the margins (a decadent aristocracy and the lower depths), but infected the heart of bourgeois society," writes Bard. "Another conviction of the epoch: vice, formerly hypocritically hidden," was now "exhibitionistic" due to "Freudian justifications."[8] Notice how Bard utilizes the language of the period to expose how one way of thinking about sexuality (vice, decadence, infection) meets another, where people give "Freudian justifications" for flaunting their sexuality.

Inverts are Alluring

Robert McAlmon, American expatriate publisher, was thrilled by what he perceived as a new vision of sexual and sartorial freedom in the bars of 1920s Paris, writing: "Paris is changing itself into a laboratory where a freer and more tolerant world is being invented: 'inverts' are alluring, lesbians are imposing boy-style, and transvestites have the rights of citizens. People fantasize about androgyny, debates about the third sex are launched, bisexuality is in fashion, and an uncomplicated libertinism is imagined."[9]

As he got in touch with his own queer sexuality, McAlmon optimistically declared that both fashion and fantasy embraced androgyny, bisexuality, and the third sex. Lesbians may not have "imposed" boy-style, but they pioneered it and took advantage of its popularity. By 1930, lesbian bars and nightclubs, like Le Monocle, helped establish a long-lasting "sexual schema—now called 'butch/femme'." As *La Vie Parisienne* reported in 1932, Le Monocle was "a cabaret of a very special kind, in which the clientele is composed exclusively of priestesses from Lesbos." Like many such cabarets, it hired staff members who "dressed like men."[10]

There was no "girlish boy" style comparable to the *garçonne* look pioneered by lesbians, although, as McAlmon pointed out, "inverts" and "transvestites" presented themselves in various "alluring" styles—from elegant silk dressing gowns to full drag. Some men adopted feminine touches, such as wearing bracelets or cosmetics. There was also a small men's dress reform movement in England that promoted casual sportswear, such as shorts

Figure 3.3 Two women smoking. Photo by Henry Guttmann Collection/Hulton Archive/Getty Images.

and sweaters, which many young men adopted for non-ideological reasons. McAlmon's enthusiasm for "androgyny" and "bisexuality" were very much of the period.

One of the stars of 1920s Paris was the Texas-born aerialist and drag artist known as Barbette (1899–1973). Jean Cocteau wrote how Barbette pleased those who saw him as a woman, those who saw him reveal himself to be a man, and those "others whose souls are moved by the supernatural sex of beauty."[11] Cocteau commissioned a series of photographs by Man Ray documenting his transformations between man and woman.

Berlin in the 1920s and 1930s was another center of queer and trans life, although laws against homosexuality and cross-dressing remained in force. Magnus Hirschfeld (1868–1935), a gay sex researcher based in Berlin, coined the term "transvestite" in 1910; its primary meaning was a person who cross-dressed, but he seems to have intended the word to cover a range of what we would now call "transgender" identities.[12] Hirschfeld was a pioneering advocate for homosexual and transgender rights, who co-authored and acted in the 1919 film *Anders als die Andern* (*Different from the Others*), in which Conrad Veidt starred as a gay man who is blackmailed and commits suicide. Hirschfeld had seen this happen to some of his patients. In the film, he played himself, saying: "The persecution of homosexuals belongs to the same sad chapter of history in which the persecutions of

Figure 3.4 Man Ray, *Barbette Dressing*, c. 1926. Gelatin silver print. Ford Motor Company Collection, Gift of Ford Motor Company and John C. Waddell, 1987. Image copyright © The Metropolitan Museum of Art. Image source: Art Resource, NY. © Man Ray 2015 Trust/Artists Rights Society (ARS), NY/ADAGP, Paris 2024.

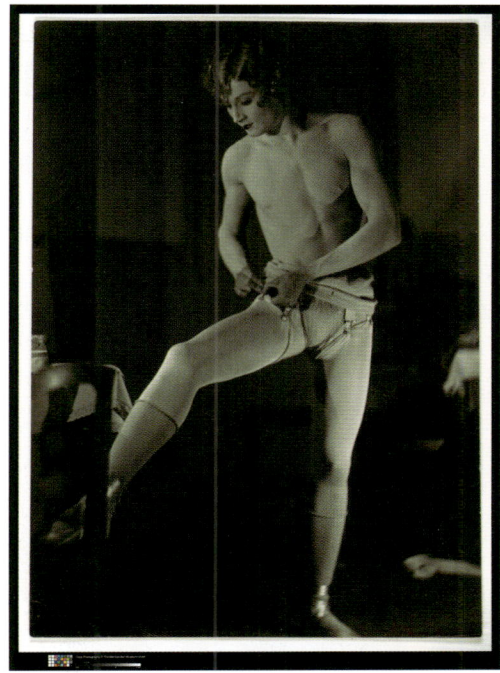

Figure 3.5 Jeanne Mammen, *She Represents*. Illustration from the *Führer durch das 'lasterhafte' Berlin* (*Guide to Immoral Berlin*). Author: Konrad Haemmling, Leipzig, 1931. Inv. Tc 10226/9. Historical Prints Division. Location: Staatsbibliothek zu Berlin/Stiftung Preussischer Kulturbesitz/Berlin/Germany. Credit: bpk Bildagentur/Staatsbibliothek zu Berlin/Stiftung Preussischer Kulturbesitz/Berlin/Germany/Art Resource, NY. © 2024 Artists Rights Society (ARS), New York/VG Bild-Kunst, Bonn.

witches and heretics is inscribed … May justice soon prevail … love achieve victory over hatred!"[13]

Freud also supported the movement to end the laws against homosexuality and cross-dressing, although he and Hirschfeld had different views on the etiology of sexual attraction. Whereas Hirschfeld believed people are "born this way," Freud argued that all humans are essentially bisexual, and described homosexuality as merely "a variation of the sexual function."[14] Freud even argued that heterosexual attraction also "needs elucidating and is not a self-evident fact."[15]

In his wonderful book *Freud's Mexico*, Rubén Gallo describes how poet Salvador Novo (1904–74) "came out of the closet with a vengeance" in the 1920s, defying machismo and conservative Catholicism to affirm his identity as a gay man. "In his youth, Novo started with a 'wild' understanding of psychoanalysis as a theory of sex." He acquired all sixteen volumes of Freud's work then in Spanish translation, heavily annotating passages devoted to sexuality. In *Three Essays on the Theory of Sexuality*, for example, he marked the places where Freud rejected the idea that homosexuality was a type of "degeneracy," arguing that it was "found in people … distinguished by especially high intellectual development and ethical culture." When a mistranslation described homosexuality as a "sad anomaly,"

Figure 3.6 Photograph of a costume party held at the Institute for Sexual Research (Institut für Sexualwissenschaft) in Berlin, c. 1920s. Magnus-Hirschfeld-Gesellschaft e.V., Berlin.

Dress, Dreams, and Desire

Figure 3.7 Manuel Rodríguez Lozano, *Retrato de Salvador Novo*, 1924. Oil on cardboard. Courtesy of Museo Nacional de Arte INBAL.

Novo wrote (in German), "*Es ist nicht traurig*! (There is nothing sad about it!)." And when Freud referred in passing to the "scientific spokesmen" of homosexuals, Novo inquired: "Edward Carpenter? Havelock Ellis?"[16]

"[Novo] used psychoanalysis to think through sexual identity," writes Gallo, "to act out his own fetish for chauffeurs, to develop a theory of the wireless unconscious, and ultimately to engage in a self-analysis that culminated with … his version of *The Interpretation of Dreams*." His attraction to drivers was immortalized in the painting *El Taxi* (1924) by Manuel Rodríguez Lozano, which depicts Novo with plucked eyebrows and red lips in a taxi at night; he wears a dressing gown, rather than a tuxedo or smoking jacket, perhaps implying that the taxi was "a bedroom of sorts." Not only was he one of Mexico's leading writers on psychoanalysis, "Novo became the only poet to brandish psychoanalysis as a weapon" in the fight against prejudice and in support of same-sex desire.[17]

Gabrielle Chanel and the Modern Woman

Gabrielle "Coco" Chanel (1883–1971), the most famous fashion designer of the 1920s, was known for her chic and androgynous dandyism. "Chanel expresses the heart and soul

Figure 3.8 Gabrielle "Coco" Chanel, c. 1929–30. Courtesy of the author.

of the modern woman," declared *Vogue* in 1923. Even before the war, back when she was still only a kept woman, Chanel had rejected the feminine dress codes of her day, creating a personal style based on elegant simplicity and elite masculine distinction. When she opened her first boutiques in 1913 and 1916, and then established her couture house in Paris in 1919, she transformed her personal style into her brand identity. Although almost every couture house in 1920s Paris created clothing in the *garçonne* style, only Chanel became identified with the style.

Simultaneously designer and trendsetter, Chanel constructed and modeled the dominant image of the modern woman. But what did "this new identity for women" mean for Chanel? And for her legions of followers?[18] Social psychologists write about identity as "a self-in-context: a self that is embedded in social relations and situations," including "how an individual perceives, interprets, and presents his or herself."[19] However, most psychoanalysts emphasize the lifelong process of *identification*, which begins in childhood and is largely unconscious. Significantly, both concepts are inextricably linked to the idea of *differentiation*; Chanel wanted, very much, to differentiate herself from most images of womanliness.

Can psychoanalysis tell us anything about the sources of Chanel's creativity? Her biographers have often observed that Chanel was irremediably wounded by her illegitimate birth and her chaotic, impoverished childhood. For the rest of her life, she lied compulsively about her childhood and, in particular, about what happened when her long-suffering mother died and her father abandoned her in an orphanage. She seldom mentioned her mother, but often emphasized her father's financial success (which was nonexistent), as well as his affection for her, suggesting both that she identified with him, and that he was also the object of her love. As a young woman, Chanel worked as a seamstress; then tried and failed to make it as a café-concert singer. Although she claimed that Coco had been her father's pet name for her, it was more likely to have been taken from one of the songs she performed, such as "Ko Ko Ri Ko" or "Qui a vu Coco?" Already possibly a part-time prostitute, she became the *irregulière* of a wealthy man. This part of her life Chanel also veiled in lies. She seized her chance for financial independence, when two of her lovers set her up as a milliner. She then began designing and selling clothes.

I believe that Chanel expressed her rage, hatred, and destructiveness in her revolutionary fashions. Sociologist Georg Simmel wrote:

> The fact that the demimonde is so frequently a pioneer in matters of fashion is due to its peculiarly uprooted form of life. The pariah existence to which society condemns the demi-monde produces an open or latent hatred against everything that has the sanction of law, of every permanent institution, a hatred that finds its ... most innocent and aesthetic manifestation in striving for ever new forms of appearance. In this continual striving ... there lurks an aesthetic expression of the desire for destruction.[20]

Her friend Paul Morand saw in Chanel an example of "that advanced guard of country girls … who go out, confront the dangers of the city, and triumph, doing so with that solid appetite for vengeance that revolutions are made of."[21]

Significantly, Chanel rejected the overtly erotic fashions promoted by the era's *demimondaines* and copied by society women. Indeed, she frequently expressed disdain and disgust for other women, her anger almost radiating off the page. It is likely that one function of her "look" was to differentiate herself from other women, poor women, like her mother, but also sex workers and respectable women. Chanel destroyed the fashions of the early twentieth century by creating her own personal style, derived from that of her upper-class male protectors, which she then sold to women around the world. Speaking of herself in the third person, Chanel once told Salvador Dalí: "She took the English masculine and made it feminine. All her life, all she did was change men's clothing into women's: jackets, hair, neckties, wrists. Coco Chanel always dressed like the strong independent male she had dreamed of being."[22]

Chanel's admirers would later argue that she had "liberated" women from restrictive feminine fashions, but she was neither a dress reformer nor a feminist. However, if we look at Chanel as a modern female dandy, in love with distinction, we see that her clothes, like her famous little black dress, have a deceptively simple, less-is-more aesthetic. According to psychoanalyst Christopher Bolas: "Artists are gifted only in their exceptional use of otherwise ordinary human capacities, usually because they know more about the intelligence of form." If an artist or, in this case, a fashion designer creates new forms, other people (usually of the same generation) may feel a collective identification with these evocative forms.[23] Certainly, many women in the interwar period seem to have identified both with Chanel's glamorous persona and her fashions, which included dandyish suits, as well as some of the shortest dresses of the 1920s.

The success of the *garçonne* style has often been interpreted as the expression of a widespread female desire for "emancipation," but this could mean different things for different women in the 1920s. French doctor, feminist, and psychiatrist Madeleine Pelletier (1874–1939) declared: "My costume says to the male: I am your equal … If those who wear short hair and starched shirt collars have all the freedom, all the power, well then! I too will wear short hair and a starched shirt collar."[24] Pelletier, however, wore full male attire, which was far from the stylized androgyny that Chanel personified.

Indeed, the very ambiguity of the *garçonne* style was probably one reason for its success. Not every woman wore a masculine Eton crop or a man-tailored suit accessorized with a monocle. Short hairstyles could be marcelled, bleached platinum, artfully shaped, and accessorized with Art Deco earrings. For many women, the style symbolized fashionable modern femininity: active, alluring, slim, and young. After all, young girls often had short hair, just as they traditionally wore short skirts. The modern woman had short hair and smoked, but she also exposed her legs in "nude" stockings and wore lipstick.

Figure 3.9 Irving Penn, *Chanel Sequined Suit* (1926), New York, 1974. Photograph by Irving Penn. © The Irving Penn Foundation.

The *garçonne* style was not the only fashionable look of the 1920s, of course. Other couturières, like Madeleine Vionnet, created sensuous bias-cut gowns, while Jeanne Lanvin emphasized charming femininity with her *robes de style* and matching dresses for mothers and daughters. In the long term, Chanel's combination of the masculine and the feminine would remain highly influential. But by the late 1920s, fashion was moving toward greater femininity, as the straight up-and-down silhouette of 1925 gave way to longer dresses that clung to the body's curves. Chanel also began designing more conventionally "feminine" dresses at this time, although her personal style in the 1930s cleaved more than ever toward a dandyish androgyny.

Joan Riviere and the Masquerade of Womanliness

English psychoanalyst Joan Riviere (1883–1962) is best known for her 1929 article "Womanliness as a Masquerade," which described how successful professional women felt the need to put on femininity like a mask. Born the same year as Chanel, and christened Joan Hodgson Verrall, her life and career also throw light on women's relationship to the concepts of "femininity" and "masculinity," as these have been applied to fashion. In contrast to the many biographies devoted to Chanel, Riviere's life has received relatively little attention. But, as with everyone, her early experiences influenced her later life.

The eldest surviving child of a solicitor and a former governess, Joan might easily have attended university. (Her uncle taught classics at Cambridge, where she mixed with intellectual and artistic circles.) But she was unhappy in boarding school and rather than matriculating, she left to spend a year studying art and music in Germany, where she also learned the language. Returning to London, she apprenticed herself to a court dressmaker. This was an odd choice for a woman of her milieu, and psychoanalyst Athol Hughes later wondered "whether dressmaking was a form of masquerade … in which she took on a womanly role to disguise masculine strivings and competitiveness."[25] This seems to me highly unlikely, since Riviere had long been personally interested in fashion, as well as involved with the women's suffrage movement. At age twenty-three, she married the barrister Evelyn Riviere, and two years later had a daughter Diana.

Joan Riviere continued to design and create her own dresses throughout her life, and by all accounts she was an elegant woman. One contemporary described her as "tall, strikingly handsome, distinguished-looking, and somehow impressive." Katherine West, whose mother was a friend of Riviere's, remembered her as a "tall, Edwardian beauty with a picture hat and a scarlet parasol—walking up and down … in lively conversation with a gentleman. Perhaps they were discussing … the Post-Impressionists. Or perhaps they were talking about Freud—since this chic and decorative creature Joan Riviere was, of all things, Freud's first translator and a pioneer lay analyst."[26]

Riviere was one of a growing number of women who became involved in the relatively new field of psychoanalysis, initially as a patient. She was very close to her father and when he died in 1909, she had a nervous breakdown. At some point, she entered analysis with Ernst Jones. It was not a satisfactory analysis; after assuring Freud (falsely) that he had never had a sexual relationship with her, Jones complained that she suffered from "typical hysteria," "sexual anaesthesia," "colossal narcissism," and "masculine identification." However, he also recommended her to Freud as a translator. Eventually, she had a second brief analysis with Freud, and became a valued member of the British Psychoanalytic Society, where she was especially close to Melanie Klein.[27]

In his book *Secrets of the Soul*, Eli Zaretsky argues that many women were drawn to psychoanalysis after the First World War "for the same reason they were attracted to short hair … [because] it promised release from the material weight of family life [and] spoke to a specific problem that post-war women faced, the problem of 'women's difference,' which in the 1920s came down to the question of women's sexuality." Or, as he also wrote: "Psychoanalysis … stood for the emancipation of sexuality from reproduction."[28] This was almost certainly part of the appeal of psychoanalysis for a woman such as Riviere, but her involvement with psychoanalysis and her impact on the field went further than this.

Figure 3.10 Joan Riviere, c. 1931. Joan Riviere collection, the British Psychoanalytical Society Archive, P02-D-12. Reproduced by kind permission.

Riviere's "Womanliness as a Masquerade" was published in the *International Journal of Psychoanalysis* in 1929—a year after Englishwomen over twenty-one received the vote, and ten years after the professions in England opened to women. As she wrote:

> Not long ago intellectual pursuits for women were associated almost exclusively with an overtly masculine type of woman. This has now changed … In university life, in scientific professions and in business, one constantly meets women who seem to fulfill every criterion of complete feminine development. They are excellent wives and mothers … they have no lack of feminine interests, e.g., in their personal appearance … At the same time they fulfill the duties of their profession at least as well as the average man. It is really a puzzle to know how to classify this type psychologically.[29]

It was "a puzzle," as she put it, because most people, including most psychoanalysts, still assumed that "normal" women were "feminine" and therefore did not pursue careers.

Yet the party line on female psychology was increasingly challenged by women psychoanalysts. Riviere, for example, worked closely with Melanie Klein, the pioneering child psychologist, whose discovery of the pre-Oedipal phase of children's development transformed psychoanalysis. Whereas Freud emphasized female penis envy, Klein pointed out that both girls and boys envy the mother's ability to produce babies, while the mother's breasts play at least as significant a role in children's psyches as her imaginary penis. Neither Klein or Riviere rejected the idea that penis envy existed, but they thought it played a much less important role in the female psyche than Freud believed. Riviere also flouted Freudian dogma by insisting on the coexistence of clitoral and vaginal orgasms.

In her now-famous article, Riviere argued that "women who wish for masculinity may put on a mask of womanliness to avert anxiety and the retribution feared from men." She gave as an example one of her patients, a successful American professional, who suffered from severe anxiety after public speaking, unless she immediately afterward began "flirting and coquetting" with male colleagues, "father figures," who might otherwise have been threatened by her intellectual performance. Another of Riviere's patients, "a clever woman, wife and mother, a university lecturer," wore "particularly feminine clothes" whenever she lectured to colleagues (not students), and spoke in a "flippant and joking way, thus displaying her masculinity to men as a 'game'."[30]

Since the very idea of women speaking in public and presenting themselves as figures of authority went against centuries of misogyny, it is not surprising that such a woman's male colleagues might feel threatened by her intellectual performance, or that she would feel the need to assuage them by performing femininity. If a woman succeeded in a traditionally male role, and then felt anxious, Riviere believed that she had unconsciously experienced her success as though she had "stolen" her father's penis (power), thereby "castrating" him. Riviere was not unlike the accomplished professional women she described.[31] Indeed, the women she described in "Womanliness as a Masquerade" may have been, in part, a disguised self-portrait.[32]

In a famous passage, Riviere explained how successful professional women would put on "womanliness" like a mask:

> both to hide the possession of masculinity and to avert the reprisals expected if she was found to possess it – much as a thief will turn out his pockets and ask to be searched to prove that he has not the stolen goods. The reader may now ask how I define womanliness or where I draw the line between genuine womanliness and the "masquerade." My suggestion is not, however, that there is any such difference, whether radical or superficial, they are the same thing.[33]

In other words, genuine womanliness (or authentic femininity) *does not exist*, there is only the masquerade. The idea of femininity as a masquerade, *of women dressing up as women*, has obvious relevance to fashion, which constructs various representations of femininity, some so exaggerated as to verge on parody, while others appropriate multiple codes of masculinity to the point where they approach cross-dressing. Although Riviere's concept of the masquerade was largely ignored at the time, it later gained attention with the renewed debate about women's sexuality within psychoanalysis, especially the work of Jacques Lacan and in feminist critiques of psychoanalysis, especially that of Judith Butler.

J.C. Flügel and the Psychology of Clothes

Freud had suggested that fashion provided a "loophole" for women's exhibitionism. A quarter of a century later, Riviere's colleague the British psychologist and psychoanalyst John Carl Flügel (1884–1955) argued that *both* men and women experienced "clothes ambivalence," because the unconscious conflict between exhibitionism and modesty is "displaced" from the naked body onto clothing, which then functions as a "compromise," since it both covers the body and attracts attention to it. Thus, our entire attitude toward dress is "ambivalent." Furthermore, Flügel argued, "clothes ambivalence" involves not only the *exposure* of parts of the body, but also the *emphasis* on particular body parts, and the use of "clothes symbolism," especially phallic symbolism.[34]

Freud had mentioned "variability" in the exhibitionism permitted to women. But Flügel was acutely aware of the radical changes that had recently occurred in women's fashion, and in his book *The Psychology of Clothes* (1930) he zeroed in on *specific* variations: "Perhaps the most obvious and important of all the variations of fashion is that which concerns the part of the body which is most accentuated." Victorian fashion covered women's legs and emphasized the *curves* of the female torso, through low-cut bodices and padded bustles. But a dramatic change occurred in the 1920s, when "legs have emerged after centuries of shrouding." Flügel related the modern "accentuation of the body" to a cultural idealization of "youth."[35]

In 1937, prolific fashion writer James Laver credited Flügel with the idea that "the erogenous zone is always shifting, and it is the business of fashion to pursue it."[36] Later, Laver attributed his theory to anonymous "psychologists," writing:

> If the psychologists' theory of the Shifting Erogenous Zone can be accepted, once a focus of interest loses its appeal another one has to be found. In the early 1930s the emphasis shifted from the legs to the back. Backs were bared to the waist and, indeed, many of the dresses of the period look as if they had been designed to be seen from the rear.[37]

Flügel correctly observed that women's fashion has emphasized or exposed different parts of the body at different times. However, Laver was mistaken in believing that these changes were caused by heterosexual men losing "interest" in the outmoded body part. Skirts did become longer in the 1930s and evening dresses did often expose the back, but not because men's sexual attention had shifted to a new erogenous zone. The real causes were more complicated, involving factors such as the Hays Code, which restricted Holly-

Figure 3.11 Maison Roger, dress, c. 1877. Photo © The Museum at FIT.

Figure 3.12 Callot Soeurs, evening dress, c. 1924. Photo © The Museum at FIT.

Figure 3.13 Augusta Bernard, evening dress, 1933. Photo © The Museum at FIT.

wood films from exposing "too much" of the breasts: the exposure of the naked female back was less problematic, because less obviously erotic, although its exposure may have enhanced its erotic appeal.

Flügel also noticed that while women's fashion had changed dramatically in the early twentieth century, men wore almost exactly the same clothes they had fifty years earlier. This led him to wonder: Why do modern women show off so much more of their bodies than men do? Why were women's clothes so much more colorful than men's clothes? Because Flügel knew so much about fashion history, he was reluctant to accept the dominant psychoanalytic belief that women's fashions reflected their inherently greater "narcissism" and "exhibitionism." He knew that men in the western world had not always concealed their bodies in sober, uniform attire. Indeed, for centuries, they had worn colorful, decorative, eye-catching fashions that emphasized various parts of their bodies—legs, shoulders, chest, even the penis itself.

Flügel openly envied the modern woman's freedom to "indulge" in bodily display, and he bitterly complained that men had long been subject to "greater repression of Narcissism" and "male exhibitionism." Indeed, he looked forward to a time when modern men could relax their "severer clothes-morality." He even predicted a "nude future."[38] In his obituary of Flügel, Ernest Jones wrote that *The Psychology of Clothes* seemed "to have been inspired by a personal foible, a dislike of conventional starched clothing and a keen interest in Dress Reform."[39] The dress reform movement had traditionally focused on women's corsets and long skirts, which were decried as both unhealthy and unaesthetic. A few reformers, such as Oscar Wilde, had also targeted men's suits, long trousers, and top hats. By the 1920s, when women had ceased wearing corsets and long skirts, attention turned to men's clothes.

Founded in 1929, the Men's Dress Reform Party (MDRP) advocated lighter, looser, and more colorful men's clothes. Often associated with the simple life movement, the New Health Society, and the British eugenics movement, men's dress reformers in England believed that healthier and more beautiful clothes for men would produce "a healthier and more beautiful race." Flügel was a founding member of the MDRP and spoke at their first rally in August 1929, saying: "Psychology has taught us to have faith in consciousness, in reason. We have rationalisation in industry. It is time there was rationalisation in clothes. Our motto should be 'Better and Brighter Clothes'."[40] On this occasion, Flügel wore a striped blue flannel suit with shorts, knee socks, and an open-collar shirt. Other members of the MDRP also favored soft, open-collar shirts (no starch, studs, or neckties) in materials such as rayon, and jackets or knitted sweaters worn with shorts, breeches or kilts, rather than trousers. Men were already beginning to wear comfortable, casual clothes like these on holiday, but they risked ridicule if they wore them in the city. Shorts were especially problematic, because they were associated with young boys. Colorful, soft clothes that exposed the lower legs and were open at the throat also resembled the styles worn by modern women.

Flügel's famous theory of the "Great Masculine Renunciation" was intended to explain how and why men had abandoned colorful, revealing, fashionable dress for drab uniformity. Flügel's theory has subsequently been modified by dress scholars, such as Christopher Breward, but its general outlines remain widely accepted. The French Revolution (along with the Industrial Revolution and the spread of capitalism) contributed to a profound change in the fashion system. Until the late eighteenth century, both men and women of the elite wore decorative and fashionable dress, which distinguished them from the masses of ordinary people. With the new vestimentary regime, the great visible division was between decorative women, who consumed fashion on behalf of their fathers and husbands, and men, who adopted a uniform associated with shared political and economic power.

Yet dress scholars have tended to reject Flügel's belief that men "suffered a great defeat in the sudden reduction of male sartorial decorativeness at the end of the eighteenth century."[41] In her article "Masculine Renunciation or Rejection of the Feminine?," dress historian Chloe Chapin pointed out that Flügel was so concerned with men's historic "loss" that he failed to see how the concept of "fashion" had become negatively reimagined as a "feminine" and irrational realm, which the majority of men duly rejected.[42] As a result of his obsession with men's "defeat," Flügel could only see modern women's fashion as a sign of their greater freedom and power. Whereas Riviere interpreted the masquerade of womanliness as a form of "defensive femininity"[43] in the face of male power, Flügel

Figure 3.14 J.C. Flügel wearing hat and shorts with other members at the first Men's Dress Reform Party rally, 1929. British Library/Granger. © The Granger Collection Ltd d/b/a GRANGER Historical Picture Archive.

insisted that: "The defiant use of powder puff and lipstick is a token at once of triumph and of independence, signalling a victory in the spheres of both sex and of society – a victory over old habits of sexual repression and social subordination."[44] The language of a war between the sexes was not uncommon during the 1920s, and fashion was often used as evidence of this. But Flügel was atypical, in as much as he hoped that modern men would become *more* narcissistic and exhibitionistic in their dress, although he anticipated that such developments would be widely interpreted as revealing "homosexual tendencies," loss of "manliness," or even a type of "castration."[45]

Nakedness versus Phallic Dress

Nudism or *Nachtkultur* was popular in the 1920s, especially in England and Germany, so Flügel was not alone in arguing that "the future of dress" might be "the ultimate disappearance of clothes, except for occasional protective purposes." John Langdon-Davies' *Lady Godiva: The Future of Nakedness* (1928) and Gerald Heard's *Narcissus: An Anatomy of Clothes* (1924) also predicted that clothes were destined to disappear. As a eugenicist, Flügel argued that if we improved our bodies, then "clothes would no longer be felt as necessary or desirable." A century later, however, this has still not occurred. His related prediction, that people would become "reconciled" to their bodies, certainly has not come to pass, although we have become increasingly (often destructively) employed "in the cause of bodily perfection."[46]

While advocating nudity, Flügel also pioneered the concept of "phallic" clothing, writing that: "The object most frequently symbolized by clothes is the phallus." He argued that phallic symbolism in dress is usually a "proud display of potency," although he agreed with Freud that an overabundance of phallic symbols could indicate "castration fears." He identified the codpiece as the most extreme example of "phallic symbolism" in European fashion history.[47]

Worn by European men from the late fifteenth to the early seventeenth century, the codpiece was a type of penis sheath, "a special bulging portion of the hose," often vividly colored, and "embellished by padding in such a way as to simulate a perpetual erection."[48] "Cod" was the sixteenth-century English term for the testicles, and the codpiece originated as a modest bagged appendage, intended to interject greater *modesty* into male fashion by covering the gap between the very short doublet and the thigh-high hose. Surprisingly little was written about the codpiece during its existence, as it gradually swelled and then faded away, although François Rabelais featured enormous codpieces in his satiric books, and Michel de Montaigne described the codpiece a "laughter-moving and maids look-drawing piece." Like Flügel, dress historians have usually simply assumed that the codpiece served as an "aggressive virility display."[49]

Modern literary scholar Will Fisher presents a more convincing interpretation of the codpiece: as a "prosthetic" device to materialize ideas about masculinity.[50] It was not just "a sign of masculinity, but … quite literally helped to mold the body and make the man." However, the "bagged appendage" type of codpiece "equated masculinity with reproduction," while the padded sheath style "linked [masculinity] with sexual conquest, and specifically with phallic penetration." Fisher speculates that even though the codpiece disappeared, "the emergent ideology of masculinity did not." Indeed, the new "performative masculinity" implied that the codpiece was only a supplement to the penis, and he was not a man "if he has only a codpiece without a 'pin' to put in it." Fisher concludes: "We might therefore say that the cultural investment in the penis arises out of, and in conjunction with, the decline of the codpiece. It may, moreover, also have been at least partially an attempt to disavow transferability and detachability of masculinity and masculine/patriarchal power."[51] Although "the cultural investment in the penis" may not be quite as restricted in time and space as Fisher suggests, there are, indeed, different styles of masculinity, which are undoubtedly related to different styles of dress.

Although he only partially understood the significance of the codpiece, Flügel seems to have been the first to describe "sartorial phallicism" and "the phallic significance of clothes." Some people, he wrote, are like children who have not yet learned how "to sublimate their exhibitionistic interests on to clothes." With others, however, the chief conflict may be between the satisfactions of nakedness on the one hand and sartorial phallicism on the other. "The full gratification to be obtained from the phallic significance of

Figure 3.15 Agnolo Bronzino, *Portrait of Guidobaldo II della Rovere, Duke of Urbino*, 1531–32. Galleria Palatina, Palazzo Pitti, Florence, Italy. Luisa Ricciarini/Bridgeman Images.

clothes can often only be obtained when the pressure of clothes is distinctly felt ... even to the extent of creating ... discomfort." But in the words of a man who through analysis obtained insight into his own condition, "these tightness and stiffnesses are all discomforts gladly suffered for the sake of an idea"—the idea, that is, of "having a continuous erection." According to Flügel, the same man who liked tight, stiff clothes also liked "to be in a loose, soft silk garment," and "considers that he grows better-looking with every garment he takes off."[52]

By the late twentieth century, phallic symbolism would be conspicuous in both fashion and the interpretation of fashion. Whereas Freud had recognized that a top hat might be a phallic symbol, he was oblivious to the phallic symbolism of the man's tailored suit Flügel anticipated the emerging awareness of the suit as a type of "armor safeguarding certain men's bodies from the position of vulnerability and penetrability that has, in turn, been stigmatized as the domain of feminine and racialized bodies." Flügel also foresaw how "muscle" can also "give rise to a new mode of phallic engineering."[53] By the late twentieth century, women not only wore tailored suits, they had joined men in the quest for hard, mesomorphic bodies. Students today find Flügel's work very dated, but it also contains fascinating insights into our relationship with clothes. When *The Psychology of Dress* was eventually translated into French, it bore the title *Le Rêveur Nu* (*The Naked Dreamer*). In the long run, Flügel may have been correct in anticipating that young people would increasingly regard ideas about modesty and "sex differences in dress" as social conventions subject to modification.

4

The Mirror and the Fragmented Body

Chanel dismissed Elsa Schiaparelli (1890–1973) as "that Italian artist who makes clothes."[1] She meant it as an insult, but Schiaparelli regarded dress designing as "an art," and some of her most iconic looks were created in collaboration with artists, such as Salvador Dalí. From the beginning of her career, in 1927, she was creating illusionistic designs, such as a sweater "tattooed like a sailor's chest with pierced hearts and snakes" and "a skeleton sweater that shocked the bourgeoisie." Initially sporty, her clothes became increasingly "architectural" with a "wooden soldier" silhouette. The result was a hard chic with padded shoulders and a fitted waist, juxtaposed with a decorative, feminine surface. She proudly claimed to be known for her "apparent craziness and love of fun and gags."[2]

Schiaparelli's autobiography, *Shocking Life* (1954), began with the words: "I merely know Schiap by hearsay. I have only seen her in the mirror." Shifting from the first to the third person, the author presented herself as a split personality: lazy and hard-working, generous and mean, charming and hateful. By breaking her surname into a single syllable, "Schiap," she contributed to this sense of fragmentation. Looking could be hostile: "Those whom she dislikes find themselves looked right through as if they were transparent," or reassuring, as when she repeated the words: "I have seen her in the mirror." But looking in the mirror

Figure 4.1 Portrait of Elsa Schiaparelli, September 1, 1937. Horst P. Horst, *Vogue*, © Condé Nast.

could also be deceptive or confusing, as when Schiaparelli recalled visiting a nightclub in 1930s Berlin, where she caught a glimpse of herself on a mirrored staircase: "There!" I said to Jerome, "at last there is a smart woman." "Heavens!" exclaimed Jerome, "but don't you recognize yourself?"[3]

What is our self? And what is the role of the mirror in creating our self-image? Consider Horst's photograph of Schiaparelli, produced for *Vogue* in 1937. She wears a jacket with a strict military cut, lavishly embroidered with feminine plant motifs, together with an asymmetrical turban-like hat. We see her image within an oval frame, which resembles the gilt frame of a mirror. But if we look more closely, we realize that what appeared to be a mirror is actually a hole in the wall. In her brilliant article "Masks, Mirrors, and Mannequins: Elsa Schiaparelli and the Decentered Subject," Caroline Evans writes that it is the "illusory nature of the mirror—and of representation itself—lies at the heart of Schiaparelli's work."[4] She alludes, of course, to Jacques Lacan's theory of the mirror stage. But before exploring that important concept, let's stay with the familiar story of Schiaparelli's engagement with Surrealism.

Spanish-born Surrealist artist Salvador Dalí (1904–89) described *The Interpretation of Dreams* as "one of the capital discoveries" of his life.[5] At the International Surrealist Exhibition of 1936, he appeared wearing a diving suit to symbolize his immersion in the unconscious. Unfortunately, the helmet became stuck and Dalí nearly suffocated, until someone managed to remove it with a screwdriver. Dalí was crazy about Freud, who had deconstructed the traditional view of the unified, conscious self, replacing it with an image of the psyche that was riven with unconscious conflicts. However, whereas Freud wanted to use reason to *interpret* the unconscious, the Surrealists plunged into dreams and the unconscious, embracing the idea of a self that was haunted by otherness.[6]

Dalí and Schiaparelli began collaborating in 1936. Among their creations were iconic looks, such as the notorious shoe hat. "All my life I have been preoccupied with shoes … to the point of making a kind of divinity of them," wrote Dalí, alluding to the supposed religious origins of sexual fetishism. "In 1936 I went so far as to put shoes on heads; and Elsa Schiaparelli created a hat after my idea."[7] The shoe hat deliberately evoked Freudian sexual symbolism, as well as Freud's idea that dreams often involved displacement. In this case, the shoe was transposed from foot to head, and one version had a bright pink heel, reinforcing its phallic associations. Schiaparelli recalled that "The Hon. Mrs. Reginald Fellowes, 'Daisy' to her friends, the most-talked-about well-dressed woman, the supreme word in elegance, had the courage to wear it."[8] Gala Dalí, the artist's wife, also wore the shoe hat—and she certainly understood its symbolism. Whether Schiap's other clients did is unclear.

The shoe hat was designed to be worn with a black tailored suit, the jacket, with lip-shaped buttons and embroidered and appliqued pink lips at the pockets, suggesting a connection between the pocket, the mouth, and the vagina. The lips and vagina, like

Figure 4.2 Model wearing suit and shoe hat by Elsa Schiaparelli, 1937. Photo by ullstein bild/ullstein bild/Getty Images.

the tongue, the nipples, and the penis, are colloquially known as the "pink parts" of the body—and Schiaparelli famously named a bright shade "Shocking Pink." Whether separately or together, Schiaparelli and Dalí emphasized that the relationship between body and dress was fraught with eroticism—both perverse and playful. Like all of Schiaparelli's suits, this one is characterized by a hard chic, featuring broad, padded shoulders that tapered to a narrow waist. In psychoanalytic terms, her suits are phallic garments, although on top of the masculine silhouette, she lavished a wealth of brilliant color and "feminine" trimmings. This is a perfect example of the Surrealist assimilation of Freudian ideas, such as dream interpretation and sexual symbolism. But there is nothing yet about mirrors.

Jacques Lacan and Freud's French Revolution

Jacques Lacan (1901–81), the charismatic and controversial French psychoanalyst, has often been described as "the French Freud," because he reinvented Freudian psychoanalysis, interpreting it through the lens of Parisian intellectual thought, as this evolved from Surrealism through Hegel's master–slave dialectic, linguistics, and structuralism. Over the course of his life, Lacan not only transformed psychoanalytic theory and practice, he also created a unique "psychoanalytic culture" in France.[9] Through Lacan's friendship with Dalí, and Dalí's collaborations with Schiaparelli, Lacanian psychoanalysis influenced fashion—and its interpretation.

Lacan is important for the study of fashion, because he moved the relationship between fashion, Surrealism, and psychoanalysis beyond Freudian dream work, sexual symbolism, and exhibitionism to new ideas about the alienated self, body image, fragmentation, and aggression. His work on the mirror, the eye, and the gaze, like his later ideas about the phallus, the masquerade, and *objet petit a* have all been used productively to interpret fashion. Lacan's personal style is also relevant. Indeed, he invites us to explore it when he begins the Overture to *Écrits* by quoting Buffon's epigram: "The style is the man himself."[10]

Born in 1901 to a prosperous Roman Catholic family of vinegar merchants, Jacques Lacan was the first child and eldest son of Alfred Lacan and Emilie Baudry. Although outwardly conventional, the family was riven by jealousy and discord. As a young man, Lacan "violently rejected" his family and religion, and later almost "never spoke of his parents or family." Too young to be called up during the First World War, he was nevertheless exposed to the sight of wounded soldiers who were cared for in a wing of his school. In 1920 he entered medical school, where he decided to specialize in psychiatry.[11]

"In about 1923 [Lacan] heard about Freud's theories for the first time."[12] It was probably André Breton, the "Pope of Surrealism," who introduced him to Freud's work. Breton had also attended medical school, where he studied with Freud's early mentor, Charcot. Breton initially preferred Charcot's spectacular accounts of hysteria and hypnosis, but he eventually also became attracted to Freud's ideas about sexuality and the unconscious—or what he *thought* were Freud's ideas. Freud himself believed that the Surrealists completely misunderstood his work, because they rejected his rational, therapeutic model in favor of an irrational, poetic version of psychoanalysis.

Significantly, Lacan came to psychoanalysis via the Surrealist movement. He was close to a number of Surrealist artists and writers, including Georges Bataille (author of *The Story of the Eye*, whose wife, the actress Sylvia Bataille, later became Lacan's second wife), Hans Bellmer (creator of a series of sculptures and photographs of fragmented female "dolls," which inspired one of Alexander McQueen's most controversial collections), and Salvador Dalí. Lacan had long been interested in the visual aspects of paranoia. He knew Dalí and was familiar with his 1930 article "The Rotten Donkey," in which the artist argued that "paranoia functioned in the same way as an hallucination, that is, as a delusional interpretation of reality."[13] By 1931, Lacan had begun to synthesize psychiatry, psychoanalysis, philosophy, and Surrealism.

Among his professors was Gaëtan Gatian Clérambault, an authority on erotomania, fabric fetishism, and paranoia, whom Lacan later rhetorically described as his "only master in psychiatry."[14] (We met Clérambault before, in 1909, when he denied that women could be fetishists, and produced thousands of photographs of North Africans in drapery and veils.) Clérambault's obsession with the gaze culminated in his spectacular suicide in 1934, when, blinded by cataracts, he seated himself in front of a mirror and shot himself in the mouth, leaving a document inviting any interested colleagues to examine his eyes.

Lacan's 1932 medical dissertation on "paranoid psychosis and its relation to personality" was largely devoted to a case study of one of his psychiatric patients, whom he called "Aimée," who had attacked the actress Huguette Duflos with a knife. Diagnosed as suffering from persecution mania, she was confined in the Sainte-Anne asylum. She was also a frustrated, self-taught writer, and Lacan appropriated her manuscripts, parts of which he incorporated into his dissertation. He never returned them.[15] Years later, Lacan's biographer reported that "Aimée" said that she "found Lacan too attractive and too much of a clown to be trusted."[16] (We will hear more about her later.)

In 1933, Lacan and the Surrealists became fascinated by the much more famous crime of the Papin sisters, two servants who savagely murdered their employers, gouging out their eyes. As scholar Martin Jay later observed: "Just as Freud had found clues to the workings of the 'normal' psyche in his studies of hysteria, so Lacan's analysis of paranoid psychosis led him to posit a universal stage through which all humans pass, a stage displaying marked similarities to the pathological crimes of spectacular violence committed by the Papin sisters and Aimée."[17] (Although Aimée wounded Huguette Duflos in the hand, this was hardly a crime of "spectacular violence.")

The Mirror Stage

Lacan is famous for theorizing the "mirror stage," which emphasized the role of vision in the construction of the self. Neither the first nor the last to observe how very young children come to recognize their own image in the mirror, Lacan drew on Henri Wallon's mirror test.[18] But he made a very different argument. According to Lacan, "the little man," physically weak and uncoordinated, had hitherto perceived himself as a "fragmented body." In the mirror, however, the child sees a total and unified *image* of his body. This "identification" with the ego ideal is a crucial step in the formation of the ego. However, the visual construction of subjectivity is also profoundly "alienating," because the reflection in the mirror is not really the child himself. What he sees is an *other*, just an *image*, like "the imago of one's own body" that we sometimes see "in hallucinations and dreams."

The transition from a sense of fragmentation to one of wholeness is, therefore, a "misrecognition." At most, the sense of wholeness is "orthopedic."[19]

Critics who take literally the idea of the mirror miss the point: Lacan realized that what he called the mirror stage involved "the exchange of gazes" between the child and its mother.[20] He just did not prioritize that particular bond. The idea that *the mother's gaze is the child's first mirror* was first emphasized by British pediatrician and child psychoanalyst Donald Winnicott. Focusing not on the infant alone, but on the relationship between the infant and its caregiver, Winnicott developed the idea of the "good-enough mother," who will hold and look at her child with love, "warts and all." Ideally, the mother and child will mutually recognize and affirm each other. However, Winnicott argued that if the mother is severely depressed, psychotic or otherwise absent, the child will have difficulties learning to see itself with loving eyes.[21]

Lacan, like Winnicott, was familiar with Melanie Klein's work, which emphasized the existence in very young children of powerful feelings of rage and fear, which (she believed) would have been experienced, preverbally, as terrifying images of bodily fragmentation. While we cannot know what preverbal children experience, many people do have nightmares about losing body parts, such as teeth, and when we are upset, we talk about feeling as though we are "falling apart."

Contemporary psychoanalyst Alessandra Lemma argues that Lacan is too quick to insist that "the mirror lies" when it tells you that "your body is not fragmented." Although the unified image of the self may be misleading, it is not entirely false. Furthermore, everyone needs a degree of "defensive narcissism," she writes, adding:

> The good-enough mother's loving gaze needs to hold up a benignly distorting mirror … [because] when the mother cannot help the child to install internally a pair of "rose tinted glasses," a more persecutory gaze may dominate the inner world. When that happens, the self may become overly reliant on image and mirrors in order to feel whole and may also feel compelled to modify the body in order to achieve an idealized form.[22]

Lemma's clinical work on body dysmorphia throws light not only on Schiaparelli's references to mirrors, but also to another episode in her autobiography, when her mother began "making disparaging remarks about her looks. She was always being told that she was as ugly as her sister was beautiful. So Schiap, believing that this was really so, thought up ways of beautifying herself." One attempt involved planting seeds "in her throat, ears, mouth," so she would "have a face covered with flowers."[23] Dalí would later incorporate this image into his work, some of which appeared in fashion magazines. Did fashion represent for Schiaparelli another attempt to beautify herself? This is probably partly true, not only for her but for many fashion designers. Yet Schiaparelli's work was not seamlessly idealizing. Indeed, it was often quite disturbing, not unlike the all-too-common sight of wounded veterans.

The Fragmented Body

After the First World War, there were around one million amputees in France alone. Working with former combatants, Paul Ferdinand Schilder observed that sometimes, after a leg was amputated, the patient would retain a vivid impression that his leg was still there; he might even try to walk and fall down. In his book *The Image and Appearance of the Human Body* (1935), Schilder introduced the term "body image," which he defined as "the picture of our own body which we form in our mind."[24] This idea of "body image" would go on to play an important role in psychology. If a person with a damaged body could still feel whole by mentally replacing a missing leg with a phantom limb, then so might a person with an intact body unconsciously perceive it as fragmented. Or the experience of bodily fragmentation might re-emerge in dreams or under conditions of stress.[25]

In her book *Surrealist Masculinities*, Amy Lyford suggests that the violence, terror, and physical mutilations that men experienced during the First World War resulted in an ugly mixture of war trauma and gender anxiety.[26] Men's anxieties about damaged male bodies were sometimes repressed and then projected in imagination onto the bodies of

Figure 4.3 André Kertész, *Muguet Seller on the Champs-Élysées*, 1928. © The Estate of André Kertész/courtesy Stephen Bulger Gallery.

Figure 4.4 March 4, 1938 cover of *Harper's Bazaar*. Courtesy of *Harper's Bazaar*, Hearst Magazine Media, Inc. © 2024 – Approval A.M. Cassandre/Artists Rights Society (ARS), New York.

women. Certainly, many artists associated with Surrealism were fascinated by the idea of the fragmented female body.

Violence and fragmentation were also visible in the fashion world of the interwar period, as Lucy Moyse Ferreira observed in *Danger in the Path of Chic: Violence and Fashion Between the Wars*. Although fashion is often perceived as escapist fantasy, magazines like *Vogue* and *Harper's Bazaar* frequently featured surreal images of fragmentation, such as disembodied eyes and severed heads, as well as the artificial simulacra of body parts, like the dress forms that resembled limbless female torsos.[27]

Fashionable garments could also evoke bodily fragmentation, physical violence, and even death. The Tears dress (1938) was a collaboration between Dalí and Schiaparelli that drew on imagery from three of Dalí's paintings: *Necrophiliac Springtime* (owned by Schiaparelli), *The Dream Places its Hand on a Man's Shoulder*, and *Three Young Surrealist Women*

Figure 4.5 Elsa Schiaparelli, Tears dress from the "Circus Collection," fabric designed by Salvador Dalí. Paris, France, 1938. © Victoria and Albert Museum, London.

Holding in their Arms the Skins of an Orchestra. This silk evening gown and matching head scarf, both of which featured a printed trompe l'oeil design by Dalí of ripped fabric or skin, convey a visceral sense of violence. They evoke the anatomical illustrations or statues known as *écorches*, which show the muscles that are visible when the skin is removed—but here displaced from a woman's body onto her dress. "The Tear-Illusion dress serves as a commentary on femininity and beauty, as a fragile costume that only appears to be seamless and intact," writes Rachel Alpha Johnson Hearst. "The woman's body is a decorated surface that masks interiority, which … provokes an aggressive and violent response."[28]

There was something genuinely shocking about the fashions that Schiaparelli created with Dalí—something violent and eccentric that was very different from the work of most other fashion designers of the period, who tended to create smooth, apparently intact representations of the clothed female body. Schiaparelli has inspired designers of subsequent generations, some of whom may also have sensed that identity may be illusory or fragmented. The Tears dress, for example, anticipates punk styles by Vivienne Westwood, as well as the deconstructionist 1980s styles by Rei Kawakubo of Comme des Garçons, which journalists described as "destroy" fashion.

The Procrustean Arbitrariness of Fashion

Is fashion unnatural? There is a scene in William Klein's satirical film *Qui Êtes-vous, Polly Magoo?* (1966) in which a pompous professor argues that the hidden meaning of the Cinderella story is "the value of tiny feet and beautiful clothes." He triumphantly concludes: "fetishism, mutilation, pain. Fashion in a nutshell." Feminists have often perceived fashion similarly, as the violent and arbitrary *mutilation* of the "natural" human body.

Lacan was no feminist, but in his essay "Aggressiveness in Psychoanalysis" (1948), he wrote:

> There is a specific relationship between man and his own body that is also more generally manifested in a series of social practices: from tattooing, incision, and circumcision rituals in primitive societies to what might be called the procrustean arbitrariness of fashion, in that it contradicts, in advanced societies, respect for the natural forms of the human body, the idea of which is a latecomer to culture.[29]

In Greek mythology, Procrustes was a robber who offered travelers a bed, and then stretched their bodies or cut off their legs to make them fit the bed—just as Cinderella's stepsisters cut off their toes and heels to try to fit into the glass slipper.

Although Lacan referred in passing to the recent development of "respect for the natural forms of the human body," he knew quite well that body modifications have existed in all known cultures. For Lacan, "the procrustean arbitrariness of fashion" evoked "all the aggressive images that torment mankind," Freudian images of castration, of course, but also Kleinian pre-Oedipal images of "mutilation, dismemberment, dislocation, evisceration, devouring, and bursting open of the body," which Lacan called "imagos of the fragmented body."[30] Certainly, his portrayal of the "relationship between man and his own body" is compelling on the level of archaic fears and desires triggered by the mirror stage, and constantly retriggered. Both the fear of a fragmented body and the desire for wholeness are closely associated with fantasized images of the body.

Women, Fashion, and Mirrors

Mirrors were long believed to hold magical powers. One of the most famous images of a magic mirror comes to us from Walt Disney's film *Snow White and the Seven Dwarfs* (1937). When Snow White's wicked stepmother, the evil queen, conjures her mirror to identify "the fairest of them all," she is motivated not only by vanity, but also by murderous envy of the younger and more beautiful Snow White. "Women are supposed to depend on their mirrors to know who they are," writes Diana Tietjens Meyers, in her book *Gender in the Mirror*. "For women, to know oneself is to know one's appearance and the worth of that appearance in the parallel economy of heterosexual partnership … How apt that the French call a woman's boudoir mirror her *psyche*."[31]

Figure 4.6 The wicked stepmother in the Disney film *Snow White and the Seven Dwarfs,* 1937. Directed by William Cottrell, David Hand, Wilfred Jackson, Larry Morey, Perce Pearce, Ben Sharpsteen. Produced by Walt Disney Productions. Disney Enterprises, Inc.. Screen grab.

Figure 4.7 Dress by Madeleine Vionnet, 1931. Paris, Musée des Arts Décoratifs. © Les Arts Décoratifs.

Throughout history, women have often used fashionable dress and cosmetics in an attempt to look younger and more beautiful, to look "as pretty as a picture." According to Simone de Beauvoir, woman's beauty "is made to arrest man's gaze," leaving her an object, "caught in the immobile trap of the mirror's silvering."[32] Feminist studies have long called attention to the reifying aspects of the "male gaze," but the internalized, "persecutory" gaze of the (m)other may be even worse, because it is more difficult to defend against, negatively affecting women's relationship to their bodies, clothes, and identities. Our "body image" is the product of others' gazes, and the gazes of the Other.

Lacan's mirror stage is part of the register that he called "the Imaginary"—the order of images and illusions. Or rather, it marked the watershed between the Imaginary and the Symbolic—the order of language and law. But the "mirror stage" is not just a stage in the child's development. It is also, metaphorically, a dramatic stage on which everyone, at all ages, performs before an invisible audience. "The notion that the image of the self always comes from outside is especially helpful," writes Lemma, because the self "internalizes otherness—the other's desire—as the condition of his own desirability."[33] Or, as Anouchka Grose puts it: "The beginning of the mirror stage is marked by an identification with one's own reflection. At the end of the mirror stage one identifies with the imago of one's peers."[34]

Lacan's ideas have become increasingly important in recent theorizing about body image and its disturbances. As Lemma writes:

> Our experience of the world is inevitably mediated from the unique perspective of our body. But how we put [the pieces of our body] together in our minds to form a representation of our body only partly depends on actual anatomy. …
> It also depends on how the body is seen by others, on how it is experienced in relationship with others.[35]

In other words, the picture of our body that we have in our minds depends in large part on how that body is seen by others.

We don't know whether Schiaparelli knew Lacan personally, but Dalí knew both of them, and it is likely that she knew at least something about the man and his ideas. She was definitely familiar with the outlines of psychoanalysis, referring in her autobiography to concepts such as the "subconscious," as well as [women's] "unconscious jealousy" and "inferiority complexes."[36] It does not really matter, though, how much she consciously knew, because her designs told their own story.

"Psychoanalysis suggests that picturing the body is fundamental to the construction of a gendered identity, while fashion allows the displacement of feelings about the body on to dress," wrote Caroline Evans in the entry on "Fashion" in *Feminism and Psychoanalysis*. "Once women's fashion is identified as a field of representations of the female body it then becomes a significant text of how the dominant culture constructs femininity."[37] The fashion designer plays a special role in the creation of representations of the female body. Many designers try to use fabric and corsetry to create the illusion of an ideal body.

Figure 4.8 Elsa Schiaparelli, evening jacket, Spring 1939. Francesca Galloway, London. Image © Francesca Galloway (Photograph Katrina Lawson Johnston).

Madeleine Vionnet famously rejected corsets, but she also rejected customers whom she regarded as too fat. When a woman wore one of Vionnet's bias-cut gowns, the masquerade of femininity was seamless, but the gown required that the wearer already have a beautiful body, by the standards of the time.

How did Schiaparelli construct femininity? She obviously made different looks, but probably the most representative was the tailored and decorative dinner suit, which was an popular throughout the fashion world in the later 1930s, being both practical and photogenic. Schiaparelli's last few collections before the Second World War were also among her most famous. Her famous "Zodiac" collection (Winter 1938–39) alluded to popular ideas about the stars and astrology, as well as the historic Palace of Versailles, built by the Sun King, Louis XIV. Emotionally, the collection seems to have paid loving tribute to her uncle, a famous astronomer, who had once kindly told her that the "beauty marks" on her face were in the shape of the constellation Ursa Major, the Big Dipper. Unlike her mother who repeatedly told her that she was ugly, her uncle implied that she was beautiful and special.

There were many ornate and beautiful designs in this collection, but, as curator Dilys Blum writes: "One of the most stunning ensembles of the Zodiac collection was Schiaparelli's mirror-studded dinner suit."[38] The jacket of this dinner suit, made of black silk velvet, was embroidered by Lesage with two gilt strip cartouches in the shape of gold rococo hand mirrors with "fractured" faces. To be more precise, each cartouche was filled with twenty-seven small rectangular mirrors. The jacket buttons, on which Schiaparelli lavished attention, were in the form of classical female heads.

The jacket is sometimes known as the "Hall of Mirrors" evening jacket, alluding to the mirror-paneled doors and decorations of the Galerie des Glaces at the Palace of Versailles. For centuries, most mirrors consisted of multiple smaller pieces of mirrored glass, rather than one large plate of glass. But for a modern viewer, the effect is of fractured glass. It was not just that Schiaparelli revealed her own identity to be fragmented; when the Nazi *Blitzkrieg* began, Schiaparelli's mirrors seemed to predict that Europe was about to be violently shattered again. Yet because the upside-down hand mirrors on her evening jacket were positioned over the wearer's breasts, some dress scholars have argued that these "symbols of female vanity become a warrior's breastplate."[39]

Beyond the historical significance of Schiaparelli's designs, there is also the question of our relationship to the mirror and to fashion: Does fashion armor us to face the world? Or does our effort to create an ideal image shatter us into a thousand pieces? Elizabeth Wilson has suggested that modern fashion is "one means whereby an always fragmentary self is glued together into the semblance of a unified identity."[40] Although Lacan emphasized divided subjectivity and the aggressive, fragmenting aspects of fashion, fashion encompasses both aspects, the unifying and the fragmenting.

The Style is the Man

What is the significance of Lacan's style? In contrast to Sigmund Freud, who adhered to conventional, respectable male attire, Jacques Lacan was notorious throughout his life for his "sartorial eccentricity."[41] Some of his clinical performances were also "very much in the line of Dada or Situationism. He talked gibberish to his patients, threw plant pots out of the window at them as they left, and apparently once dropped his trousers in a session."[42] Lacan never followed the rules and clearly believed that they did not apply to him. He never completed his training analysis with Rudolph Loewenstein, who later declared him "unanalyzable." When Lacan was eventually expelled from the International Psychoanalytic Association, he launched his own organization(s).

After his first marriage to the elegant Marie-Louise Blondin in 1934, Lacan became a fashionable dandy. This evolved into an extremely mannered, obsessive way of dressing: On one occasion in 1946, he spent hours looking for "a special kind of black doeskin to have made into a pair of evening shoes to go with a particularly sumptuous suit."[43] He could also speak brilliantly for hours without notes, although his language tended to be opaque and convoluted, and often featured wordplay. When he left his first wife and family to live with Sylvia Bataille, his style became even more eccentric. Their daughter Judith was for years his only publicly recognized child, even though, due to French law, she could not bear his name.

Beginning in the 1950s, Lacan became increasingly famous. His lecture on "The Signification of the Phallus" in 1958 helped revive interest in Riviere's idea of the masquerade. As Lacan put it: "Paradoxical as this formulation might seem, it is in order to be the phallus, that is, the signifier of the Other's desire, that a woman rejects an essential part of femininity, namely, all its attributes, in the masquerade." A page later, Lacan added: "The fact that femininity finds refuge in this mask, by virtue of the *Verdrangung* [repression] inherent in desire's phallic mark, has the curious consequence of making virile display in human beings seem feminine."[44] Did Lacan regard his own sartorial display as feminine?

By the 1960s, Lacan was attracting celebrities to his public lectures, acquiring many followers, and many detractors. In the fall of 1968, for example, Jean-Michel Rabaté was a new student at the École normale supérieure, where his initial impression of Lacan's lecture was that it sounded "deep, Dadaist, and hilarious, and yet no one laughed." He wrote:

> Here I was, facing an aging performance artist (Lacan was sixty-seven then) whose very garb had something of the cabaret comedian's outfit, with a dandiacal Mao costume, a strange shirt, and the most tortured elocution one could imagine, broken by sighs, wheezes, and sniggers, at times slowing down to a meditative halt, at times speeding up to culminate in a punning one-liner.

Figure 4.9 Portrait of Jacques Lacan, October 1967. Photo by Giancarlo BOTTI/Gamma-Rapho via Getty Images.

Figure 4.10 Larry Shox, "Celestial Eye" suit, 1985. © The Museum at FIT.

Figure 4.11 Daniel Roseberry for Schiaparelli, Autumn/Winter 2023/2024 haute couture collection. Photo by Peter White/Getty Images.

Curiously, he was being listened to in utmost silence by an audience intent on not missing one word.[45]

Despite (or because of) Lacan's bizarre appearance and behavior, Rabaté was intrigued and returned.

His biographer Elisabeth Roudinesco recalled how "Lacan, looking very majestic with his mane of white hair, would often arrive in a checked purple suit and a gray astrakhan overcoat; he always wore a light-colored shirt with a mandarin collar." She quoted a colleague who noted that "the numerous small pleats in his shirts were ironed almost religiously."[46] Lacan's friend and colleague Françoise Dolto once asked Roudinesco, "why he was so awkward in everyday life, so anxious about his image, and so obsessed with his outward appearance. Why did he feel such a need to disguise himself, to go to masked balls and wear such extravagant clothes?"[47]

When she attended his seminars in the early 1970s, Sherry Turkle noticed that: "Lacan wore a long jacket, longer than a standard jacket. He wore a bow tie ... Sometimes his jacket was velvet, embroidered with a kind of soutache." Significantly, Turkle also observed that "the first two rows were taken up by young men who were dressed more or less in his style—in 1973-4 this meant, at the very least, a bow tie. A hand-tied bow tie ... thin and black. *Les noeuds papillons*."[48] Imitation is central to the phenomenon of fashion, of course, as Georg Simmel observed more than a century ago. Differentiation is the other side of the picture. We imitate those whom we admire and want to be like, while we differentiate ourselves from others whom we value less. But ego ideals vary in different contexts. If many Lacanian psychoanalysts imitated the eccentricity and exhibitionism that characterized their leader, other psychoanalysts have tended to imitate a more casual version of the conservative propriety of Freud.

In her fascinating article "Shrinking Clothes," Anouchka Grose described how British analysts are still often advised to wear conservative, "almost theatrically boring" clothes, because in "the Anglo-Saxon tradition," the patient has a transference to "the person of the analyst." According to Nina Coltart's widely read book *How to Survive as a Psychotherapist* (1993): "A therapist who is obviously self-conscious, in either an anxious or a narcissistic way, about her clothes, would be quite off-putting to a patient." Coltart even advised women analysts against wearing trousers! By contrast, Lacanians have greater sartorial freedom, because "in the French tradition, the patient's transference is not so much to the analyst as to their knowledge." As Lacan said, "Psychoanalysis can make you less ignorant, but it can't stop you being an idiot."[49] Grose herself says that she ultimately gravitated toward the Lacanian school of psychoanalysis, in part because of her love of fashion.

Salvador Dalí, Elsa Schiaparelli, and Jacques Lacan continue to influence high fashion and popular culture. Larry Shox's Celestial Eye Suit (1985), for example, was featured in Richard Martin's book and exhibition *Fashion and Surrealism*. Daniel Roseberry, artistic director of Schiaparelli, often draws on his predecessor's imagery, as with his eye jewelry, or haute couture mirrored suit. Another interesting contemporary example comes from Mexico, which the Surrealists regarded as a special country.

"I was thinking about Surrealism's idea of the fragmented body," says Mexican designer Montserrat Albores Gleason of PTRA. Her "Walking lip" dress was inspired by Man Ray's painting of Lee Miller's lips, as well as by Dalí's lips sofa. She also sought to address the "problem" of the "split between the real body and the body in the mind," and the anxieties this caused. With her dress, she hoped to create "an external skin which expands and shrinks along with the imaginary perception of the body." Not only would such a dress adapt to "this mutable body," it would also "represent the source of the mutability: the mouth." However, the "mouth" is created by "a central cut-out" that could "easily be read as a rip in the fabric," especially as its shape and size would vary as the wearer moved. Also relevant, she adds, would be the "desire associations" of the viewer and the wearer.[50]

Lacan's influential work on desire and sexual difference will be the focus of Chapter 6.

Figure 4.12 PTRA, "Walking lip" dress, 004 Collection, 2019. Photograph Victor Trani, courtesy PTRA.

5
Bitter Enemies

No sooner had the Second World War ended than the Cold War began. From the 1940s to the 1980s, especially in the United States, the profession of psychoanalysis turned away from radical ideas about sexual freedom toward an "investment in orthodoxies of desire and identity."[1] Homosexuality, in particular, was demonized as innately "pathological," and was often associated with gender nonconformity, which was also denounced. Ego psychology became part of a medical system emphasizing normalization and adjustment to reality, which influenced "virtually all other thought-systems."[2] Cold War Freudianism even influenced the way people thought about fashion.

In *Fashion and the Unconscious* (1953), Austrian-born American psychoanalyst Edmund Bergler (1899–1962) claimed to have analyzed more than 100 homosexual fashion designers. Intrigued by the "paradoxical fact that women are dressed by their bitterest enemies," Bergler concluded that a repressed masochistic fear and hatred of the female body lay behind the "dress absurdities" designed by "the homosexual czars of fashion creation."[3] It was not, of course, a *fact* that homosexuals were women's "enemies," although many of the most famous and successful fashion designers, in Paris and New York, were gay men. However, Bergler and his colleagues provided ample evidence that psychoanalysts were bitter enemies to their queer and female patients.[4]

Figure 5.1 Christian Dior, 1955. Photo by Willy Maywald. © 2024 Association Willy Maywald/Artists Rights Society (ARS), New York/ADAGP, Paris, 2024.

When one of his patients wondered out loud why he had "always wanted to design women's dresses," Bergler smugly replied: "I've told you repeatedly, that a homosexual is only a fugitive from women … one always returns to one's first love." According to Bergler, the man suddenly shouted: "I HATE WOMEN, I HATE WOMEN, I HATE THEM!" Bergler thought to himself, "If he hates women, his fashion creations must reflect this." Then he said: "Well, if you hate women as passionately as you claim, isn't it possible that you are using your profession to revenge yourself on them—that you're not dressing women, but caricaturing them?" According to Bergler, the patient was amused, but the next day he asked anxiously: "If you change my homosexuality, will my designing talent collapse too?" Bergler replied: "Your talent represents a sublimation, hence … an inner conflict *productively* solved." He went on to boast: "As was to be expected, the patient's fears were unfounded. Today, many years after the change to heterosexuality (he is married and has children), he is still in the same field of endeavor, and is one of the important men in it."[5]

Spectacular Femininity and Invisible Gay Men

Among "the homosexual czars of fashion creation," Christian Dior (1905–57) was the single greatest influence on women's fashion from 1947, when his ultra-feminine "New Look" transformed the fashionable silhouette, until his untimely death in 1957. Dior's "spectacular femininity" made him a polarizing figure, lavishly praised and harshly criticized for his highly stylized silhouettes, which often featured cinched waists and an extravagant use of fabric. Many women adored Dior's luxurious, highly stylized fashions, although other people, then and later, believed that his influence marked a step backward for women.[6]

Bergler never mentioned Dior or any other designer by name, but he regarded most contemporary women's fashions as "so silly and even preposterous, so nearly a caricature of clothing, so awkward or uncomfortable to wear, that they invite speculation." He argued that all such "punitive fashions" were based on "the homosexual's hidden enmity" against women, which originated in his "terror" of the "cruel pre-Oedipal mother." Yet he also observed that "many of these homosexuals excel in fantasy and in sartorial ingenuity."[7]

The postwar era has often been described as the "golden age" of couture, when predominantly male couturiers, such as Christian Dior, Hardie Amies, Pierre Balmain, Cristobal Balenciaga, Jacques Fath, Hubert de Givenchy, and Norman Hartnell, created women's fashions characterized by glamorous femininity. After the modern styles of the interwar period and the practical clothes of the war years, the shift toward feminine, almost Belle Epoque silhouettes created a sensation. There was even a return to corsetry, as women increasingly adopted structured foundation garments or wore dresses with their own built-in foundations.

Figure 5.2 Marlene Dietrich in Dior by Horst P. Horst, 1947. Horst P. Horst, *Vogue*, © Condé Nast.

The sexually dimorphic curves of the feminine body were exaggerated, while long skirts featured yards of luxury fabric. The erotic—even sexually fetishistic—aspects of the style were seldom openly discussed at the time, but seem evident in retrospect. Actress Marlene Dietrich not only wore Dior in her personal life, she had it written into her film contracts that she had to be dressed in Dior. Looking at Horst's photograph of Dietrich wearing Dior's New Look, which was published in *Vogue* in 1947, we see an ultra-glamorous collaboration between a gay male photographer, a gay couturier, and a bisexual female celebrity.

In contrast to the spectacular styles they designed for wealthy and famous clients, the couturiers themselves tended to dress so as to fit invisibly into a heteronormative society that had become increasingly hostile to homosexuals. Even within the world of fashion, which, like the theater, had long included many LGBTQ individuals, greater discretion was now required. In his essay "Couture as Queer Auto/Biography," Christopher Breward observed:

> In the staged portrait photographs of Dior, Balmain, Hartnell, and Amies that frequently appeared in the pages of *Vogue* … during the 1950s (often in the company of muses and models), it is notable that all of the men adopted elegantly tailored English-style suits … described by journalists … as the Edwardian look, [which rejected, what historian Frank Mort called] "the voluminous tailoring associated with American mass culture" [in favor of] "the paradoxical attractions of dandyism".[8]

Edwardian style might have been acceptable in London and Paris, but its dandyish aspects were probably too unconventional for gay male designers in the United States, where psychoanalysts like Bergler fanned the flames of homophobia.

Meanwhile, in postwar France, Chanel attacked both Dior and Cristóbal Balenciaga as "queens" and "pederasts" who "want to be women." The sight of women in New Look styles acted on her as "a red flag to the bull," recalled Franco Zeffirelli. In his autobiography, he described Chanel loudly and angrily hissing at two girls:

> Look at them. Fools, dressed by queens living out their fantasies. They dream of being women, so they make real women look like transvestites .... They can hardly walk. I made clothes for the new woman. She could move and live naturally in my clothes. Now look what those creatures have done. They don't know women. They've never *had* a woman!⁹

Bergler attacked not only postwar women's fashions, but also the *garçonne* styles of the 1920s, which he predictably associated with gay male designers' attraction to androgynous young men—despite the fact that the leading designers of the 1920s were overwhelmingly women. Similarly, when Chanel repeatedly told journalists that

Figure 5.3 Jacques Fath with model Bettina, 1950. Photograph by Louise Dahl-Wolfe. Collection Center for Creative Photography. © Center for Creative Photography, Arizona Board of Regents.

"Men make dresses in which one can't move," she conveniently forgot that, during the interwar years, both male and female designers had created the same kind of loose, comfortable clothes. Accustomed to a fashion world filled with other women (whom, admittedly, she disliked), Chanel was now unhappy to see so many gay male designers. "Fashion is now in the hands of American Seventh Avenue and the pederasts," she tactlessly told Cecil Beaton.[10]

Even years later, these prejudices remained alive in many quarters. After Chanel's death in 1971, her old friend Paul Morand published his book *L'Allure de Chanel* (1976), in which he argued that "The invert is the enemy of woman ... Women are their designated victims." Using language reminiscent of the Nazis, he vilified "the cynical ... dirty fags [*pédérasts*]" who are "the microbes of this ravishing epidemic ... [of] unwearable dresses." "How many young women I have seen die under the subtle, intoxicating influence of the 'horrible queer' [*l'affreuse tapette*]."[11] Richard Nixon also made homophobic remarks in 1971, which were caught on the White House Watergate tapes. Echoing Bergler, Nixon said: "you know one of the reasons fashions have made women look so terrible is because the goddamned designers hate women."[12]

In 1954, the (married, bisexual) couturier Jacques Fath upheld an alternative stereotype, when he told a journalist: "Fashion is art ... and men are the creators ... The only role a woman should have in fashion is wearing clothes." Seeking to erase the history of women such as Chanel and Schiaparelli, he predicted that "someday all great designers will be men." American sportswear designer Clare McCardell countered that "someday all designers will be women. Men, I hope, will be busy with masculine things."[13]

Improved Skin, Minus the Frightening Genitals

"As for the normally heterosexual male, his interest in women's clothing, at least at first glance, seems obscure," wrote Bergler. Yet he quickly concluded that most heterosexual men (especially, the American "He-Man") feared the pre-Oedipal mother almost as much as homosexual men did. They suffered from what he called the "*septet of baby fears.*" Without acknowledging the work of Melanie Klein, he listed these as "*Fear of being starved, devoured, poisoned, choked, chopped to pieces, drained, castrated.*" Fashion mitigated the fears of heterosexual men with "a game of half-exposure, half-concealment, *gaining its power from a universal infantile experience*," presumably, the sight of a women's vagina. Bergler even made the hyperbolic claim that clothes, or at least women's clothes, were "a Masculine Invention."[14] Meanwhile, Freud had once suggested that women had invented weaving, so as to hide their defective genitals.

Bergler defined women's fashion as "improved skin, minus the frightening genitals." By concealing the genitals, feminine fashionable dress alleviated male castration fears, while encouraging other kinds of sexual "peeping." Echoing Flügel and Laver, he went on to argue that: "Stripped to its essentials, fashion is no more than a series of permutations of seven given themes, each theme being a part of the female body … One and then another part of the body is emphasized by succeeding styles."[15]

"What do women live out in their obsession with fashion?" Bergler asked rhetorically. Like male homosexuals, women expressed their neuroses and aggression in their clothes, he argued, but unlike homosexual men, most women had "bad taste." Defining good taste in terms of inconspicuous conformity to normative feminine dress, he claimed that "*conspicuous tastelessness in dress is mostly an unconscious pseudo-aggressive and defensive attack on the enshrined mother image*."[16] Significantly, Bergler never once suggested that women might actually take *pleasure* in fashion. Instead, he implied that, if women's neurotic inhibitions and repressed anger could be cured, they would dress better—and not annoy their husbands so much.

Already in 1947, conservative psychiatrist Marynia E. Farnham had co-authored a bestselling book entitled *Modern Woman: The Lost Sex*, in which she argued that "very large numbers" of women were "psychologically disordered" and socially destructive. Whether they were frigid housewives, failed career women, "overdoting, overstrict, or rejecting" mothers, they all "play[ed] the part of the Woman of Fashion," as advertisers exploited their neurotic fears. Worse, their "unhappiness" created an "epidemic" of neurosis. Most of Farnham's colleagues (and reviewers) seem to have agreed that women should avoid "the psychopathology of feminism" and concentrate on homemaking.[17]

In her book *The Woman of Fashion* (1949), dress historian Doris Langley Moore mocked "the psycho-analytical interpreters" of dress, for their "compulsion, almost religious in character, which constrains them to search incessantly for sexual implications." Pointing out that "the sexual tendencies of women's apparel have never been underestimated," she also rejected the idea that changing female fashions were "a meter of the prevailing feminine psychology which can easily be read by the expert equipped with a set of Freudian instruments."[18] Undaunted, Laver continued to repeat that driving forces behind fashion change was women's desire to attract men, while men's clothing was motivated by the desire to exhibit status.[19]

In postwar America, even straight, white, cisgender men experienced social pressure to conform to normative standards. There are undertones of Cold War paranoia in an advertisement warning them: "You're being watched! Dress Right—you can't afford not to!" Postwar films also fueled paranoia. The film *Spellbound* (1945), for example, contained a famous dream sequence by Salvador Dalí, featuring a multiplicity of huge eyeballs. Another motif involved the nightmare of being interrogated under a spotlight, whether by the police or a foreign enemy. A photograph of Ava Gardner on the set of *The Killers* (1946) appears to show her in just such a situation. Yet her seductive gaze, body language, and dress gave her an aura of dangerous power. Indeed, she was dressed to kill in a one-shouldered black gown created by Universal costume designer Vera West.

Figure 5.4 "Dress Right"™ advertisement. American Institute of Men's and Boys' Wear.

Figure 5.5 *Spellbound*, 1945, USA. Set design by Salvador Dalí. Directed by Alfred Hitchcock. Courtesy The Museum of Modern Art. © 2024 Salvador Dalí, Fundació Gala-Salvador Dalí, Artists Rights Society. Digital Image © The Museum of Modern Art/Licensed by SCALA/Art Resource, NY.

Psychoanalysis and Popular Culture

So influential was psychoanalysis in mid-century America, there was even a comic book titled *Psychoanalysis*. Published in 1955 and aimed at adults, it featured a fictional pipe-smoking psychiatrist, into whose "quiet, subdued, tastefully decorated consultation room come the emotionally disturbed [and] the mentally troubled." His three fictional patients were a problem teenager, Freddy Carter; an unhappy, insecure young woman, Ellen Lyman; and a fat TV writer, Mark Stone, who was "expensively-tailored, yet gave the appearance of being sloppily-dressed." The publishers had consulted with several psychiatrists, to ensure a degree of verisimilitude, although this fictional psychoanalyst frequently told his patients what was wrong with them, which he unfailingly traced back to their relationship with their parents. "But why would I want to kill my own father?" asked Mark.

Ultimately, the doctor told his patients that they needed to adjust to the realities of the world. "Psychoanalysis won't change the world. But it can help you deal maturely with your own problems." Interestingly, the back of the first issue featured an advertisement for body-building by Charles Atlas, implying that the American focus on self-improvement

Figure 5.6 Actress Ava Gardner on the set of *The Killers*, directed by Robert Siodmak. Photo by Sunset Boulevard/Corbis via Getty Images.

Figure 5.7 *Psychoanalysis* comic books, issues 1 and 2, 1955. EC Comics. Writers: Daniel Keyes, Robert Bernstein. Artists: Jack Kamen, Marie Severin. Photo courtesy © The Museum at FIT.

involved both psyche and soma. Although there were only four issues, they were reprinted as a book and inspired two television programs.[20] But this sanitized version of psychoanalysis, focusing on helping people achieve "peace of mind" was a far cry from the homophobic and misogynistic realities.

Psychoanalytic Homophobia

In addition to *Fashion and the Unconscious*, psychoanalyst Edmund Bergler was also the author of works such as *Frigidity in Women* (1936), *Neurotic Counterfeit-Sex* (1951), *Homosexuality: Disease or Way of Life?* (1956), and *One Thousand Homosexuals* (1959). With titles like these, he clearly hoped to reach both a general and a professional audience. Many of his biased assumptions were widely shared at the time. However, the term "homophobia" seems too mild for the vicious mixture of hatred and fear expressed by Bergler in 1956: "I have no bias against homosexuality [but] homosexuals are essentially disagreeable people ... [They are] subservient when confronted with a stronger person, merciless when in power, unscrupulous about trampling on a weaker person. The only language their unconscious understands is brute force."[21] Sandor Rado and Charles Socarides were also among the psychoanalysts who insisted most vehemently that homosexuality was inherently pathological. This type of thinking also dominated psychiatry, and influenced the *Diagnostic and Statistical Manual of Mental Disorders* (DSM-1, 1957), which listed homosexuality as "a sociopathic personality disorder."[22]

In *Cold War Freud: Psychoanalysis in an Age of Catastrophes*, Dagmar Herzog explored some of the reasons for this obsessive and incoherent hostility. Everyone thought psychoanalysts were the "experts" on sex. However, the influence of Christianity in the United States "had exacerbated ... analysts' ambivalence about how to handle the presumed centrality of sex." Already predisposed to regard homosexuality, the career woman, and "frigid" wives as problems, psychoanalysts increasingly stressed "conservative family values" in the name of mental "health."[23]

Since no one who was openly gay was permitted to practice psychoanalysis in the United States, homosexual men and women who entered into analysis were constantly told that they were developmentally arrested, gender-disordered, and perverse. Many psychoanalysts attempted to "cure" patients of their homosexuality. When this, predictably, failed, analysands had often wasted years of their lives. In *Cures: A Gay Man's Odyssey* (1991), Martin Duberman recalls the "abusive, scornful tone" that Bergler used to characterize homosexuals. "Yet Bergler's fellow therapists ... never once rebuked him for the transparent, disabling anger he freely vented against those who had entrusted themselves to his care." Duberman even admitted:

> I once wrote Bergler (I think it was after reading his 1956 best-seller *Homosexuality: Disease or Way of Life?*) asking for his help – a measure, I suppose of my

desperation. Bergler wrote back to say he would consider taking me on as a patient when and if I moved to the New York area. By the time I did, fortunately, I had accepted other (not necessarily more trustworthy) guides.[24]

Like many gay men at the time, Duberman couldn't help internalizing much of the overwhelmingly negative view of homosexuality that pervaded US society. But that was beginning to change.

The Erotic and the Political

The movement for gay liberation included progressives who regarded sex as an inherently emancipatory force, as well as those who favored strategic alliances with other oppressed groups. There had always been a minority of leftists within the psychoanalytic movement. Wilhelm Reich (1897–1957), for example, was a self-proclaimed "Freudo-Marxist," who was rediscovered in the 1960s and 1970s by a new generation. Young people identified with Reich's support for "the sexual revolution" and his attacks on the authoritarian family

Figure 5.8 Vietnam War protests, 1966. Photo by Fairfax Media via Getty Images/Fairfax Media via Getty Images via Getty Images.

in his book *The Mass Psychology of Fascism*. Reich's open hostility toward homosexuals was as yet hardly noticed.[25]

Herbert Marcuse's *Eros and Civilization: A Philosophical Inquiry into Freud* ([1955] 1966) also found a response among "the new youth," "the new bohème, the beatniks and hipsters," who were "in protest against repression" and in "solidarity with the wretched of the earth." Marcuse (1898–1979), a German-American philosopher, wrote: "Can we speak of a juncture between the erotic and political dimension?" While he saw the need for "strengthened defense against destruction," he argued that modern civilization would benefit from abandoning its "surplus-repression." Thus, he perceived a deep "significance in the buttons worn by … demonstrators … against the slaughter in Vietnam: MAKE LOVE, NOT WAR."[26] Although the work of psychoanalytic leftists did not *directly* influence fashion, it contributed to the rise of a generational counterculture that rejected traditional hierarchies in favor of "liberation" and "equality," both within western society and globally. This manifested itself sartorially in more-or-less bohemian or "revolutionary" styles.

Black Skin, White Masks

Racism, antisemitism, homophobia, and misogyny are among the most ubiquitous types of group hatred. They have shared features, but there are also historical differences. Frantz Fanon (1925–61) was probably the single most influential Black psychiatrist of the twentieth century. Born in Martinique, then a French colony, he studied medicine in France, specializing in psychiatry. His book *Black Skin, White Masks* (1952, English translation 1967) became a key text in the anticolonial and civil rights movements. According to Fanon, "only a psychoanalytical interpretation" could explain the "alienation of the black man," his rage, despair, and "the internalization—or, better, epidermalization—of this inferiority [complex]," which develops in response to white racism. Under the white gaze, Black people were hyper-visible, yet invisible as individuals. Wearing European clothes could provide a temporary "feeling of equality with the European for Africans," he suggested, but also an identification with the oppressor and/or a form of deliberate parodic "mimicry." Fanon had read Lacan, and he addressed the psychology of the white racist in relation to the mirror stage: "There is no longer any doubt that the true other for the white man is and remains the black man."[27]

African American writers, such as Richard Wright and Ralph Ellison, also embraced the emancipatory potential of psychoanalysis in the fight against racism. The Lafargue Clinic in Harlem promoted antiracist psychiatry, linking psychic wellbeing and the struggle for social justice.[28] In 1968, African American psychiatrists William Grier and Price Cobbs published *Black Rage*, which conceptualized rage as one of "the psychic adaptation[s] to the trauma of oppression." Black psychoanalysts have continued to investigate the effects of white racism, including the ways in which the Black racial other is the object of degrading and destructive fantasies, which, like racist speech and behavior, are usually disavowed by white racists.[29]

The Black Panther Party for Self Defense, founded in San Francisco in 1966, was associated with a sartorial style that owed nothing to the respectability politics of the early civil rights movement. Instead, the Black Panthers developed a deliberately "revolutionary" look that combined rebel chic with military styling. Men wore black leather jackets and black berets as a type of quasi-military uniform, not unlike those adopted by many anticolonial liberation movements. They also carried weapons. Self-fashioning by Panther women was also militant but less uniform, often emphasizing "Afro" hairstyles.

Other African Americans, who consciously identified with their stolen heritage, increasingly adopted African garments, such as the dashiki, and/or western garments featuring African iconography. For example, Harlem-based fashion designer Madame Willi Posey, who had created elegant fashions in the 1950s, now gravitated toward Afrocentric looks. Posey was the mother of artist Faith Ringgold and the grandmother of Michele Wallace, Black feminist scholar and author of *Black Macho and the Myth of the Superwoman* (1979).

Adjusting to the Normal Feminine Role

In her book *Wife Dressing: The Fine Art of Being a Well-Dressed Wife* (1959), fashion designer Anne Fogarty argued that "wife-dressing" in girdles and feminine dresses would help women's *husbands* get ahead in their careers. Like most American ready-to-wear designers, Fogarty's clothes echoed those created by Parisian couturiers, although they were more cheaply made. Her book also reads like a reverse mirror image of Simone de Beauvoir's feminist text *The Second Sex*. Fogarty cited an unnamed child psychologist who had interviewed a little girl about what she thought of her mother: "a dust mop," said the child. Fogarty concluded from this the necessity for "complete femininity" at all times, warning: "Don't look like a steam-fitter or a garage mechanic when what you are is, purely and simply, a wife."[30]

In 1959, the same year that *Wife Dressing* was published, the "Therapy of Fashion" program was introduced as a pilot study at Napa State Hospital in California. Over the next decade, members of The Fashion Group mounted fashion shows in hospitals and instructed patients in appropriately "feminine" makeup, hairstyles, and fashions. Some of these patients later said that they had benefitted from the Therapy of Fashion program. It was preferable to the typical situation in mental hospitals, where patients usually had to wear cheap, often dirty, institutional uniforms. Yet there is no question that these women were being pressured to perform "normality, as defined by male medical authorities and female fashion experts."[31]

"I talked to women who had spent years on the analyst's couch, working out their 'adjustment to the feminine role'," wrote Betty Friedan in *The Feminine Mystique* (1963), a key text in second-wave American feminism.[32] Friedan's subjects were primarily dissatisfied being limited to the roles of housewife and mother, although, the "feminine role"

Figure 5.9 Stokely Carmichael reading Fanon, 1967. © John Haynes. All rights reserved 2024/ Bridgeman Images.

Figure 5.10 Panther Party members, 1969. Photo by David Fenton/Getty Images.

Figure 5.11 Willi Posey, ensemble, c. 1970. Photo © The Museum at FIT.

Figure 5.12 Anne Fogarty, August 1951. Nina Leen/The LIFE Picture Collection/Shutterstock.

Chapter 5 Bitter Enemies

also involved sex—and if a woman were "frigid" or if she had clitoral rather than the approved vaginal orgasms, that was regarded as a problem. It was a serious problem if women rejected "femininity" in favor of looking or behaving like men. Lesbianism was widely viewed as a perversion, although straight male psychoanalysts sometimes harbored fantasies about "saving" feminine lesbians. Friedan herself actively tried to exclude lesbians from the National Organization of Women, arguing that "the lavender menace" would damage the reputation of the feminist movement.

Historically, lesbians have received much less attention than gay men in psychoanalytic theory and practice. In "The Psychogenesis of a Case of Female Homosexuality" (1920), Freud attributed the patient's lesbianism to her "masculinity complex," originating in the Oedipal relationship with her father.[33] Significantly, Freud also conflated "feminism" with "lesbianism," which may have contributed to the fearful hostility to lesbians expressed by feminists such as Betty Friedan. Indeed, even "feminist psychoanalysts" have tended to perpetuate the idea of normative heterosexuality by minimizing attention to lesbian desire.[34]

Women's experiences of psychanalysis varied, of course. When Mexican Surrealist painter Remedios Varo fled fascist Spain for Paris, she became acquainted with both Surrealism and psychoanalysis. After the Nazis invaded France, Varo escaped to Mexico, where she joined a community of artists, including Leonora Carrington. Varo described her painting *Woman Leaving the Psychoanalyst's Office* (1960) in the following terms: "This lady leaves the psychoanalyst tossing her father's head into a well (as is proper upon leaving the psychoanalyst). In the basket she carries other psychological waste: a clock, symbol of the fear of arriving late, etc. The doctor's name is Dr. FJA (Freud, Jung, Adler)." According to Varo, the painting depicted a friend, whose psychoanalysis had liberated her, at least partly, from her father fixation.[35]

Varo and Carrington shared an interest in magic and witchcraft, as well as in Jung, especially his ideas about alchemy, archetypes, and esoteric symbolism. Among Varo's unpublished writings, we find a surreal recipe "to provoke erotic dreams," including dreams of rape and incest.[36] In 1960, Varo painted another picture of a woman trying to hide her large nose under a handkerchief, while she enters a building, where the display window features a woman with multiple breasts. *Visit to the Plastic Surgeon* could be regarded as a companion piece to *Woman Leaving the Psychoanalyst's Office*. If so, Varo may have meant to imply that society always believes there is *something* about women that needs to be fixed.

"I am a Homosexual. I am a Psychiatrist"

In the early to mid-1960s, when gay and lesbian activists in the United States protested against discrimination, they almost always wore respectable, gender-conforming attire—skirts for women, jackets and ties for men. But by 1969, when police raided the Stonewall Inn, riots broke out. The police were shocked when the queers fought back, and especially

Figure 5.13 Remedios Varo, *Woman Leaving the Psychoanalyst's Office*, 1960. Museo de Arte Moderno, Mexico City. © 2024 Remedios Varo, Artists Rights Society (ARS), New York/VEGAP, Madrid.

Figure 5.14 Kay Tobin Lahusen, Barbara Gittings protesting at Independence Hall, Philadelphia, PA, July 4, 1966. Photo by Kay Tobin © Manuscripts and Archives Division, The New York Public Library.

shocked that some of the fiercest fighters were the "drag queens." Known in the medical world as "transvestites" and "transsexuals," they were a despised minority even within the LGBTQ+ community. Despite divisions within the community, in 1970, the New York chapter of the Gay Liberation Front marked the anniversary of Stonewall with a poster, urging brothers and sisters to "COME OUT!!" It featured a photograph by Peter Hujar showing casually dressed young men and women marching down the street.

In 1972, at the annual convention of the American Psychiatric Association, a man in disguise had been smuggled into the building to speak on a panel entitled "Psychiatry: Friend or Foe to Homosexuals—a Dialogue." When he emerged onstage wearing a Nixon mask, an oversized tuxedo, and a fright wig, the audience gasped. Speaking through a voice-distortion microphone, he began: "I am a homosexual. I am a psychiatrist." The man, known as "Henry Anonymous, M.D.," went on to describe the secret world of gay psychiatrists. The other members of the "Gay P.A." (closeted members of the American Psychiatric Association) had finally convinced him to speak, arguing that this would be more effective than picketing the convention. "All of us have something to lose," he told the audience. Their licenses could be revoked, their careers ended; they could even be arrested, since sodomy was still a crime in forty-two states. "We are taking an even bigger

Figure 5.15 Peter Hujar, *COME OUT!!*, 1970. Black and white poster. © 2024 The Peter Hujar Archive/Artists Rights Society (ARS), New York.

risk, however, in not living fully our humanity," he said. "This is the greatest loss, our honest humanity."³⁷

The audience gave him a standing ovation, and John Ercel Freyer (1938–2003), the man in the mask, "felt a … great sense of freedom." The following year, in 1973, the American Psychiatric Association announced that homosexuality was *not* a mental illness. A "complicated conjunction of reasons" lay behind this decision but psychiatrists were listening to the scientific evidence that homosexuality was simply a "common behavior variant."³⁸ In 1987, when the DSM eventually agreed, the legal basis for many discriminatory practices was removed. But it was not until 1988 that the more conservative American Psychoanalytic Association finally followed suit.

Meanwhile, Dr. Freyer told few people that he had been the masked man. He had already been forced to resign from his residency in 1964, when his chairman learned that he was gay, and in 1973 he lost another job, when a hospital administrator told him that because he was "both gay and flamboyant, we cannot keep you." "As this person who was in disguise, I could say whatever I wanted," recalled Dr. Freyer years later. "I did this one isolated event, which changed my life, which helped change the culture in my profession, and then I disappeared." Dr. Freyer eventually received tenure, but it would be a long time

Figure 5.16 Barbara Gittings, Frank Kameny, and Dr. John Fryer as Dr. H. Anonymous at the American Psychiatric Association's 1972 convention. Photo by Kay Tobin © Manuscripts and Archives Division, The New York Public Library.

before people recognized that his speech had been a moment comparable to the 1969 Stonewall riots.[39]

Homosexuality was never a mental disorder, of course. The *real* problem was and still is "homophobia." The term, coined in the 1960s, emphasizes the fear and dislike of homosexuals and homosexuality. As psychoanalysts David Goldenberg and Patrick Vierson Brown put it, since homophobia was for many years "the norm," the vast majority of psychoanalysts failed to recognize that, like misogyny and racism, homophobia itself was (and is) a "pathological symptom" involving the projection, not only of one's own repressed libidinal desire, but even more, the projection of one's own aggression, hatred, and envy. Partly a defense against the individual's developmental traumas, homophobia is also closely related to socially structured power relations and forms of hatred.[40] As Kenneth Lewes wrote: "The discourse on homosexuals from the second world war until the 1980s was a neurotic symptom that … served to discharge disowned sexual and sadistic impulses. It helped bolster the fragile self-esteem and cultural identity of psychoanalysts; and it was maintained irrationally in the face of experience and obvious historical fact."[41]

Penis or Phallus?

"The greater part of the feminist movement has identified Freud as the enemy,' wrote Juliet Mitchell in her influential book *Psychoanalysis and Feminism* (1974). As women and sexual "minorities" began to emancipate themselves from the medicalized discourse of "experts," the cultural authority of Freudian psychoanalysis declined. However, Lacanian psychoanalysis became increasingly influential after 1970, as Lacan began focusing on desire and sexual difference. Although Mitchell acknowledged that there were serious problems with current psychoanalytic practice, she went on to argue that the "rejection of psychoanalysis and of Freud's works is fatal for feminism. However it may have been used, psychoanalysis is not a recommendation *for* a patriarchal society, but an analysis *of* one. If we are interested in understanding and challenging the oppression of women, we cannot afford to neglect it."[42] In particular, Mitchell drew attention to the situation in contemporary France, where psychoanalytic discourse was changing rapidly, as Lacan rejected Freud's emphasis on anatomy.

Unlike Freud, Lacan almost never mentioned penis envy. He also distinguished between the penis, a part of the male anatomy, and the phallus, an ancient classical representation of the erect penis and testes, which has long been the symbol of generative and sovereign power. When he lectured on "The Signification of the Phallus" in 1958, Lacan argued that what distinguishes the sexes was not the "anatomical distinction between the sexes" (that is, the presence or absence of the penis), but the subject's "relation" to the "phallus," which Lacan called the "signifier of desire": "If the mother's desire is for the phallus, the child wants to be the phallus in order to satisfy her desire." (In other words, the child wants to be whatever the mother wants.) The phallus is not to be confused with the anatomical penis, Lacan warned. No one "has" the phallus; although Lacan suggested that men are more likely to *think* they "have" the phallus, while most women try to "be" the phallus.[43]

Because Lacan seemed to herald the end of "biological essentialism," his work attracted a number of educated feminists, who were understandably tired of being told that anatomy is destiny. "The importance of the phallus is that its status in the development of human sexuality is something which nature *cannot account* for," wrote Jacqueline Rose.[44] Mitchell drew the conclusion that: "In 'penis-envy' we are talking not about an anatomical organ, but about the ideas of it that people hold ... within human society." Women might sometimes experience "penis envy," she implied, but if so, this was directed *not* toward the anatomical organ, but rather toward the male power and privilege that are symbolized by the phallus.[45]

Although Lacan flatly rejected this sociologically oriented interpretation of his work, it nonetheless influenced many English-speaking feminists. Meanwhile, in 1974, Viennese émigré psychoanalyst Heinz Kohut told his American colleagues that he could see no significant difference between the little girl's "narcissistic injury" when she realized that she had no penis and the little boy's discovery that his penis was "very small" compared with that of "a grown man." Faced with his colleagues' criticism, Kohut insisted that the mere fact of having no penis had no lasting psychological effect on women. If "penis envy" existed at all among adult women, it was only those who, as girls, did not experience "mirroring acceptance" of their bodily selves.[46] It took more than a decade, however, before many other American psychoanalysts agreed.

The phallus still reigned supreme at the center of the symbolic order, which, in Lacanian theory, institutes language and makes subjectivity possible. Yet although Lacan was in many ways as phallocentric and patriarchal as Freud, he influenced the members of an important women's liberation group, *Psychoanalyse et Politique*. Luce Irigaray, for example, critiqued not only Freud's repression of the mother–daughter relationship, but also Lacan's concepts of the law of the father and the phallic signifier. She criticized the way human subjectivity had been masculinized, arguing in favor of a different, *feminine* subjectivity.[47]

Sonia's Clothes

Women like Luce Irigaray, Julia Kristeva, and Hélène Cixous became deeply engaged with Lacanian thought, deconstructing "Western philosophical and literary discourse," and even suggesting that there could be "no revolution without the disruption of the symbolic order."[48] Although most of these women refused to identify themselves as "feminists," their critical use of psychoanalysis would indirectly influence the 1970s feminist critique of fashion—and fashion itself. Hélène Cixous is famous for her essay "The Laugh of the Medusa" ([1975] 1981), in which she ruthlessly mocks Freud and Lacan: "Too bad for them if they fall apart upon discovering that women aren't men, or that the mother doesn't have one. But isn't this fear convenient for them?"[49]

Cixous also directly intervened in the discourse on fashion when she wrote about her experience wearing clothes designed by Sonia Rykiel: "I go to Sonia Rykiel as one goes to a woman, as one goes home. As one goes to a closet-friend; which is to say, I go inside, eyes closed. With my hands, with my eyes in my hands, with my eyes groping like hands. I see—touch the body hidden in the body."[50]

Rykiel was one of the first women in France to find success in the modern field of *prêt-à-porter*, at a time when haute couture was dominated by men. She started her business in 1968, and was soon known for her close-fitting knit separates. It is significant that Cixous zeroed in on the sense of *touch*. These are not clothes that *look* dazzling or that function like armor; these are clothes that *feel* good on the female body.

> Sonia's clothes never turn back against the body, never attack it, never seek to put it in one's place. They don't conceal, don't forbid. There are shield-clothes, mirror-clothes, shimmering, dazzling clothes, clothes that both attract and repel the gaze, clothes of the armor species, clothes that remold the body to a precise measure ... I have had some. Few. I never liked them. I donned them to go to war.
>
> Sonia's clothes are for peace. For skin which breathes ... Not loving the gaze. They give themselves to be lived ...
>
> I enter the garment. It is as if I were going into the water ... which envelops me and, without effacing me, hides me transparently.
>
> And here I am, dressed at the closest point to myself. Almost in myself.[51]

Women around the world increasingly adopted a wardrobe of separates, including trousers. However, it was not only female designers, like Rykiel, who created comfortable, functional clothes for liberated women. In Paris, young gay designer Yves Saint Laurent drew on the masculine wardrobe, inspired, he said, by Marlene Dietrich. Clients, such as the actress Catherine Deneuve, praised the way his clothes empowered working women, while not neglecting the element of seduction.

Figure 5.17 Sonia Rykiel, striped wool pant set, c. 1975. Photo © The Museum at FIT.

Meanwhile, in the realm of feminist theory, Laura Mulvey's important essay "Visual Pleasure and Narrative Cinema" (1975) drew on psychoanalytic ideas about castration anxiety, scopophilia, and Lacan's concept of the mirror stage to analyze films in terms of a "male gaze" that objectifies and fetishizes women. According to Mulvey, the camera takes the same voyeuristic position as the male protagonist, while producing representations of the female protagonist as a surface image, fetish, or mask of femininity. Mulvey's essay has been criticized for exaggerating the unique power of the white, heterosexual, male gaze, ignoring the role of fantasy and reflexivity.[52] But her essay has been immensely influential, and thanks to her, we are better equipped to perceive the male gaze at work, not only in films, such as *Peeping Tom* (1960) or *Blow-Up* (1966), but also in fashion photography. Some of the most memorable fashion photographs of the late twentieth century were the controversial products of a voyeuristic and fetishizing male gaze, such as the work of Helmut Newton and Guy Bourdain.

The combination of sexual liberation and women's liberation in the 1960s and 1970s resulted in a variety of different styles of fashion and fashion imagery. If "Sonia's clothes" were tactile and freeing, "for peace," as Cixous put it, Vivienne Westwood's punk styles were deliberately fierce and confrontational.

Vivienne Westwood and the Punks

In 1970s London, members of the punk subculture developed a "style in revolt" that was a deliberately "revolting style."[53] The punks wore torn or damaged clothing, pierced their flesh, and incorporated into their look various offensive or threatening objects, such as safety pins, razor blades, swastikas, chains, and tampons. In particular, they drew on the iconography of sexual fetishism and political rebellion. Beginning as a do-it-yourself phenomenon, punk entered the fashion system when designer Vivienne Westwood opened a boutique, successively named Let It Rock, Sex, and Seditionaries. Her partner Malcolm McLaren began promoting a punk rock band called the Sex Pistols.

Both as a music genre and a look, punk was aggressive, anarchic, and abject. Psychoanalyst Julia Kristeva had developed her concept of the abject as "something that disgusts you … you see something rotting and it makes you want to vomit." She associated this with the individual's need to "cut the instinctual dyad of the mother and child."[54] Abjection has played a significant role in contemporary avant-garde art and photography, including fashion photography, such as the 1990s vogue in fashion photography for "heroin chic." But abjection has been much less prevalent in fashion, per se.

Punk was one of the first styles to emphasize abjection, as well as "deviant" sex and aggression. Young people who adopted punk styles seemed flagrantly antisocial to most middle-class adults, almost certainly including conservative psychoanalysts, who tended to regard youthful rebellion against society as Oedipal acting out, and body modification as self-mutilation. In fact, there was a nihilistic quality to the punk slogan, "No future!"

Figure 5.18 A pinstriped trouser suit by Yves Saint Laurent, 1967. Photo by Reg Lancaster/Daily Express/Hulton Archive/Getty Images.

Figure 5.19 Publicity still from the 1966 film *Blow-Up*. MGM/Photofest.

Yet punk style can also be interpreted as a generational revolt against feelings of hopelessness, as well as a search for an alternative community and a sense of empowerment.

Westwood's notorious bondage suit in shiny black sateen became an influential icon of punk anti-fashion, or as she called it, "confrontation dressing." The look consisted of trousers, based on US Army trousers, but featuring straps between the knees, which alluded to the practice of bondage and discipline. Westwood had researched fetish clothing, adding zippers on the legs and at the crotch, as well as a bum flap. The trousers were worn with a parachute shirt that also featured straps and rubber buckles. Based in part on combat gear, the shirt also referenced the straitjackets traditionally utilized in mental hospitals to restrain violent patients.

Johnny Rotten, singer in the Sex Pistols, was photographed wearing the prototype bondage suit in 1976, when the band went on their Anarchy Tour. "The bondage clothes are ostensibly restricting, but when you put them on they give you a feeling of freedom," said Westwood, who demonstrated how she could turn cartwheels while wearing them.[55] Although fashion professionals were initially horrified by this deliberately revolting style, it was quickly assimilated into fashion. Indeed, punk anti-fashion has not only proved to be one of the most resilient subcultural styles, it has also had a powerful impact on the entire fashion system.

Figure 5.20 Johnny Rotten, dressed in the prototype black sateen bondage suit. Heathrow, 1976. Photograph © Ray Stevenson.

6
Desire and Sexual Difference

When the actress Elizabeth Hurley wore Gianni Versace's notorious safety pin dress to a film premiere in 1994, her dress was slit almost to the hip, and as she moved, glimpses of her inner thigh flashed into sight. Her shoulders and arms were bare, and a deep décolletage partially exposed her breasts. A slice of naked skin was visible along her torso, where safety pins conspicuously failed to hold the dress completely closed. Did the dress look sexy, because it exposed so much of her naked body? Many people would say so.

But, as "Freud showed us," human sexuality is not just a "natural" instinct. "Sexual desire is replete with conflict, longing and fantasy," writes feminist psychoanalyst Susie Orbach. "In our epoch," she continues, "the body itself has grown as complicated a place as sexuality was for Freud's. It too is shaped and misshaped by our earliest encounters with parents and carer, who also contain in themselves the forces and imperatives of our culture, with its panoply of injunctions about how the body should appear."[1] Whatever fears and fantasies we may have about our bodies, contemporary fashion tends to reveal a great deal of the female body. Therefore, exposure, per se, fails to explain why this *particular* dress triggered such a media frenzy.

Figure 6.1 Elizabeth Hurley in Versace's safety pin dress with Hugh Grant, 1994. Photo by Gareth Davies/Mission Pictures/Getty Images.

Figure 6.2 1992 Versace collection. Photograph by Irving Penn. © The Irving Penn Foundation. Image courtesy of Versace.

"Just a boring old punk classic," said Versace about the dress that made front-page news. He was being ironic: There is nothing "boring" about the dress, which was the most revealing of several variants in Versace's 1994 "punk" collection. But its erotic allure involved far more than selective body exposure. Safety pins are central to the power of Versace's dress, in large part because they alluded to the transgressive punk subculture of the 1970s. Safety pins had pierced the punks' skin, as well as their clothes; now Versace's safety pins pierced and pinned together the skin-tight fabric of the dress, threatening or promising to come apart.

"There was never any danger," Versace insisted afterwards. "That's why you call them *safety* pins."[2] But neither the brand nor the style was particularly safe. Indeed, each of the safety pins featured the strange Versace logo: the Medusa, a monstrous female from Greco-Roman mythology, with snakes as hair, whose look turns men to stone. Freud famously interpreted the Medusa as a symbol of castration, although she could certainly convey other meanings. The safety pin dress also recalled Versace's 1992 "bondage" collection, which brought sexual fetishism and sadomasochism into high fashion. Was it "Chic or Cruel?" asked *The New York Times*. "The dominatrix's straps and stilettos will not be denied," joked *Harper's Bazaar*. Versace himself recalled that fifteen years before, he had presented a "similar collection" in Dallas, "and they turned the lights up on us. They said these clothes belonged only in a leather bar. And now, last night, there were 200 socialites in bondage."[3] As his reference to a leather bar implied, one source for the collection was the queer leathersex community.

Versace's reputation was also an issue. In his article "Gianni Versace's Anti-Bourgeois Little Black Dress," which analyzed the safety pin dress, Richard Martin argued that the designer was notorious for having reinserted "the voluptuous" and "the body" into "modern dress"—in this case by associating his version of the "little black dress" with the mediatized image of "the prostitute." When the Metropolitan Museum announced that the Costume Institute was organizing a posthumous exhibition of Versace's work, Martin received "violently contrasting responses," including "hate mail."[4]

Meanwhile, actor Hugh Grant, Hurley's date at the film premiere, wore a tuxedo, conventional masculine formal attire. According to academic John Harvey, Euro-American "men have been shy of uncovering their bodies." (Is shy a synonym for anxious, afraid, or ashamed?) Men, like women, may wear minimal clothing on casual occasions, such as a vacation at Miami Beach. Yet in contrast to women's greater situational body exposure on *formal* occasions, men have usually preferred to "show the body through its covering ... while never finally exposing more than face and hands."[5] Women on the red carpet are also routinely asked, "Who are you wearing?" But no one cared who made Hugh Grant's tuxedo.

Fashion history includes many examples of spectacular male dress, of course, from the codpiece to tight leather jeans. But in most cases, men's fashions have emphasized the body through padding, tightness, and/or sexual (phallic) symbolism. (A well-tailored suit combines all three.) Even today, the actual *exposure* of men's naked skin on most social occasions remains quite rare, although this has begun to change. Timothée Chalamet, for example, wore a custom-made red halter-top jumpsuit by Haider Ackermann at the 2022 Venice Film Festival, which has encouraged a few other men to expose more skin. What does psychoanalysis tell us about men's and women's fashion in the late twentieth and early twenty-first centuries?

The Phallic Woman

As Freudian ideas were increasingly overshadowed by Lacanian psychoanalysis, there were changes in the interpretation of sexual fetishism and phallic symbolism. The classic Freudian concept of sexual fetishism involves the male fetishist's choice of a substitute for the "missing" maternal penis/phallus. This idea is not absent from Lacan's "return to Freud," but the emphasis has shifted to the "feminine" subject's willingness to embody the phallus. In 1968, American psychoanalyst Robert C. Bak famously described "the phallic woman" as "the ubiquitous fantasy in perversions."[6] By the late twentieth century, I would argue, she was also one of the most ubiquitous fantasies in fashion. Her body hard and erect, the phallic woman has a look of such sexual power and glamour that she is one of the commonest male sexual fantasies. But why does she also appeal to women?

In his 1985 photograph for *Paris Vogue*, Peter Lindbergh depicts a tall blonde woman wearing a dark and austerely elegant tailored ensemble by the *enfant terrible* of French fashion, Jean Paul Gaultier. Cool and glamorous, she smokes a cigarette, while pushing a baby carriage down the street. In their book *Women and Fashion: A New Look* (1989), Caroline Evans and Minna Thornton compared the work of different fashion photographers, exploring how women looking at fashion magazines might perceive images like this. Drawing on Flügel's interpretation of "stiffness and tightness" in tailoring as "overdetermined by phallic symbolism," they interpreted Lindbergh's photograph as giving the fashion model "a hard, lean edge" and "a phallic presence." Yet rather than being a "hackneyed male fantasy" of the fetishized phallic woman, they saw the photograph as a "witty" presentation of the female subject that combined "the entirely contradictory attributes of the dandy and the mother."[7] The dandy, of course, is the archetype of the man of fashion. As French poet Charles Baudelaire observed, the dandy is not just a fop or a conventionally well-dressed, ruling-class male, but a creature of artifice, unlike most other men. By the beginning of the twentieth century, if not before, there were also female dandies, such as Chanel.

When I was writing *Fetish: Fashion, Sex and Power* (1996), I had the opportunity to show various fashion photographs to a group of psychoanalysts in New York City. When I showed them Lindbergh's photograph, they immediately exclaimed: "The phallic mother!" Like Evans and Thornton, they also identified her as "the bad mother," holding a lit cigarette over the pram, which she wheels in the street, instead of safely on the pavement. Both the psychoanalysts and the feminist visual scholars recognized that representations of the good, loving mother and the bad, sexy, fashionable woman are often sharply distinguished in people's minds.

To imagine the powerful, sexual, glamorous (phallic) mother goes against modern society's predominantly sentimental and desexualized image of maternity. Indeed, so deeply repressed is the common children's fantasy of the phallic mother, who is desired and desiring, that many men have trouble seeing their own wives as lovers once they have had children together. Women also often feel deeply ambivalent, even hostile, toward the maternal image. Certainly, in the world of fashion, glamorous maternal imagery is exceed-

Figure 6.3 Peter Lindbergh for *Vogue Paris*, August 1985. © Condé Nast.

ingly rare, apart from Lanvin's Art Deco mother–daughter icon. Gaultier was unusual among contemporary fashion designers in as much as he did not invariably privilege the daughter over the mother, often featuring older women in his advertisements and runway shows. In their analysis of Lindbergh's photograph, Evans and Thornton showed how opposites were brought together in this image of a fashionable, *dandiacal* mother. They drew attention to details that the analysts missed, such as the gold chain attached to two points on the front of the model's tailored jacket, right over where her nipples would be.

Cone Bras and Corsets

Vivienne Westwood and Jean Paul Gaultier pioneered the concept of underwear as outerwear. Already in her Fall/Winter 1983 collection, Westwood showed 1950s-style structured brassieres worn over clothes, thus violating the longstanding taboo on exposing "hidden" clothing. Taboo or not, visible lingerie was quickly assimilated into both avant-garde and high fashion. Westwood's research into historic garments inspired her to create corsets and bustiers shaped like eighteenth-century stays. Gaultier also emphasized and exaggerated the size and shape of women's breasts with his brassieres, bustiers, and corsets. His 1984 cone bra dress, sometimes described as a "corset dress with a torpedo brassiere," was immediately famous. Gaultier also occasionally dressed men in brassieres and corsets, although he later decided that putting a man in a brassiere was a travesty.

Breasts are interesting for psychoanalysts, because they are central to the infant's oral stage and pre-Oedipal attachment to the mother figure. Freud emphasized the pleasure that the infant obtained from nursing, and Melanie Klein thought that small children of both sexes envied their mother's ability to grow babies in her uterus and feed them from her breasts. Klein also distinguished between the infant's fantasies of the "good" and "bad" breasts. Does everyone, male and female, have a pre-Oedipal attachment to breasts? Or can breasts also function in the unconscious as phallic symbols?

Already in 1936, Freud's colleague Otto Fenichel had published "The Symbolic Equation: Girl = Phallus," in which he argued that "penis-girls" cause male sexual desire by idealizing the "castrated" sexual object.[8] In other words, a woman can often assuage male castration fear by fetishizing herself, or allowing herself to be fetishized, often through fashion. Her entire body can be fashioned into a phallus, or a particular body part and/or a related item of dress may be fetishized. One of Bak's case studies, for example, described a young heterosexual man who was aroused by "*big breasts, sticking out*." He also fetishized brassieres and corsets, both of which highlight the breasts, and he enjoyed pulling a woman's breasts out of her brassiere, because of what Bak called "the breast–penis equation."[9] As in the accounts of Krafft-Ebing and Freud, a man's fetishistic fantasy focuses on part of a woman's body and dress. Notice also how both Fenichel and Bak slip back and forth between describing a "penis" and a "phallus," as though they were synonymous.

Figure 6.4 Vivienne Westwood, brassiere as outerwear, *Nostalgia of Mud* collection, Fall/Winter 1983. Photograph by Niall McInerney, © Bloomsbury Publishing Plc.

Figure 6.5 Jean Paul Gaultier showing a bra from his 1984 *Barbès* collection. Photo by: Photo12/Universal Images Group via Getty Images.

Figure 6.6 Jean Paul Gaultier, cone bra dress, also described as a corset dress with a torpedo brassiere, Fall 1984. Photo by Daniel SIMON/ Gamma-Rapho via Getty Images.

By the last quarter of the twentieth century, women's fashionable dress increasingly incorporated elements from the iconography of sexual fetishism, including corsets and pointy brassieres, extremely high heels, leather, and elements of bondage. Such fashions have been widely interpreted in terms of the phallic woman, usually defined as a woman who is in possession of the/a phallus, although it might be more accurate to say that she embodies the phallus. Indeed, Lacan seems to have "added something new to Freudian theory" with his concept of "being the phallus."[10]

Such is the Woman behind her Veil

"*Such is the woman behind her veil: it is the absence of the penis that makes her phallus, object of desire*,"[11] wrote Lacan. Drawing on Riviere's idea of the feminine masquerade, he called attention to male display, *parade* [show]. In her Lacanian study of dress, *La robe: Essai psychoanalytique sur le vêtement* (1983), Eugénie Lemoine-Luccioni observed that "the masquerade … serves to show women what they do not have (a penis), by making a display of other things." She went on to add:

> To tell you the truth, if the penis were the phallus, men would not need plumes or cravates or medals … The *parade*, like the masquerade, betrays a lack: No one

has the phallus. And if the penis were the phallus, the Bororos would not have invented the penis sheath, their first and only clothing, as Levi-Straus tells us. *The penis only becomes the phallus when it is exhibited and hidden at the same time.*[12]

Suddenly the codpiece (the penis sheath of European fashion) makes sense. But we can also see why such an obvious strategy of hiding yet exhibiting the penis might eventually be rejected in favor of more nuanced sartorial strategies.

Lacan defined the difference between the sexes in terms that are neither biological nor cultural; instead, he argued that it is the individual's *relation to the phallus* that determines what he calls "sexuation." This is complicated, but, fortunately, Lacanian psychoanalyst Anouchka Grose has a succinct explanation that can throw light on fashion. Whereas men usually believe (or pretend to believe) that they have the phallus, that is, that their penis *is* the phallus, "women's relationship between the mask and whatever's behind it is more ambiguous," writes Grose: "It's as if women hold up the mask as a mask and say, 'Isn't this a charming disguise and I bet you can't guess what's behind it?' The façade is held up in order to instigate the search, to make people curious, whereas with men the idea would actually be to fool people." Grose admits that this may seem "to reduce men, yet again, to the generic position of 'the basic sex'." But she leaves open the possibility that *sometimes* a man's "macho performance" can give "the impression that he may be hiding something *more*, rather than less, behind the spectacular exterior."[13] I take this to mean that, while women often try to masquerade as the phallic "object of desire," this is also *sometimes* the case for men. Perhaps especially for (some) gay men? In addition, I suspect that certain designers may propose sartorial strategies for both men and women, which are intended to make certain that other people are curious about what is behind the mask.

Jean Paul Gaultier and the Male Object of Desire

Jean Paul Gaultier (1952–) violated many fashion taboos—about age, body size, and social class—but he is best known for challenging sex/gender norms. His tailored suits and jackets for men were often colorful and decorative, in contrast to the "unmarked" look of normative heterosexual masculinity. One 1988 jacket, for example, has a bright orange back, further decorated with stripes, diamonds, tassels, rhinestones, fleurs-de-lis, and a large medal mounted with a crown and featuring the initials JPG. Surely this style qualifies as phallic *parade*? A garment like this was not entirely new to modern menswear, of course. During the "peacock revolution" of the 1960s and early 1970s, young men often wore spectacular, colorful fashions, just as they grew their hair long as an expression of their opposition to "establishment" values.

More radically, Gaultier began putting men in skirts. The very phrase "men in skirts" is an implicit attack on longstanding western gender binaries, where trousers are associated with masculinity and skirts or dresses with femininity. Even during the peacock

Figure 6.7 Jean Paul Gaultier Homme, jacket, 1988. Photo © The Museum at FIT.

revolution, apart from certain performers, such as David Bowie and Mick Jagger, few men adopted skirts or dresses. Meanwhile, women had long since adopted trousers. But as early as his Spring/Summer 1985 collection, Gaultier told journalists: "Among … the young generation of men, the codification of masculinity has changed a lot. You don't wear your masculinity. You are masculine or you are not – it is not the clothes that make you masculine or feminine."[14]

Significantly, Gaultier's skirts did not look particularly "feminine." Indeed, they were usually styled with overtly macho materials and accessories, such as heavy work boots—a style that gay men had pioneered during the 1970s. The Scottish kilt had always been the exception to the rule that western men do not wear skirts, and due to its hyper-masculine associations, it helped pave the way for a gradual acceptance of skirts for men, at least among fashion's avant-garde.

It may be useful briefly to compare Gaultier with another, more mainstream designer, Giorgio Armani (1934–). When Richard Gere wore Armani's clothes in the film *American Gigolo* (1980), both the actor and his Armani wardrobe were widely perceived as sexy. The camera lingered over Gere's naked torso, as well as his Armani-clad body, and an entire scene was devoted to his clothes being laid out on the bed. Although Armani's jackets and suits retained many of the characteristics of conventional men's tailoring, they were much more lightly structured and made from soft, luxurious materials in ambiguous

Figure 6.8 Richard Gere, on the set of the film *American Gigolo*, Paramount Pictures, 1980. Glasshouse Images/Alamy Stock Photo.

colors such as taupe and "greige." Flügel would probably have loved the easy fit and tactile appeal of Armani's menswear. Unlike, say, a structured suit in tightly woven navy-blue wool, the Armani suit could not easily be read as a display of phallic "masculinity." But it was also not obviously coded as "feminine," since it was neither brightly colored nor decorative. When Armani began designing women's fashions, he also drew on this somewhat "androgynous" appeal, although he rejected the term.

Gaultier, of course, went much further than Armani. In 1998, Gaultier showed a pink silk halter-top jumpsuit, much like the one Timothée Chalamet wore in 2022. Yet even a provocateur like Gaultier showed it on the runway worn over a button-down shirt, and with the model carrying a jacket over his arm. Naked back exposure was apparently still a step too far, perhaps because it implied sexual access from behind.

In his advertising imagery, even more than his runway shows or the design of his clothes, Gaultier played with sexual fantasies, utilizing the homoerotic imagery of sailors, for example, or depicting tiny men sucking the teats of a ferocious giant woman, who is nude except for her sunglasses. Some of the men pictured in that advertisement wore conventional dark suits, characterized by phallic symbolism, such as strict tailoring and rigid verticality, but other men were depicted with elements of body exposure and vulnerability.

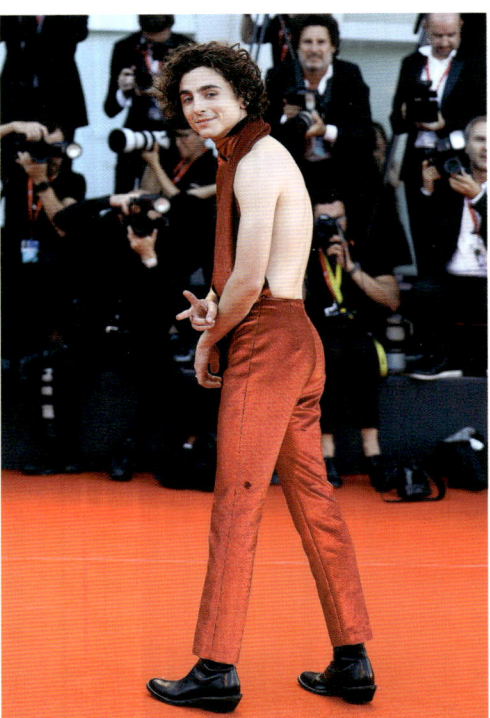

Figure 6.9 Timothée Chalamet wearing Haider Ackermann at the 2022 Venice Film Festival. Photo by Maria Moratti/Getty Images.

Figure 6.10 Jean Paul Gaultier, pink halter-top jumpsuit, Spring 1998 collection. Photo by Giovanni Giannoni/Fairchild Archive/Penske Media via Getty Images.

Figure 6.11 Jean Paul Gaultier, man's jumpsuit, Spring 1998. Photo © The Museum at FIT.

From Nana to Madonna

Lionel Vermeil, who worked with Gaultier for more than twenty years, had himself been in Lacanian analysis, and on at least one occasion, before Gaultier arrived for an interview, Vermeil shared his "vision" of the designer with a journalist, warning, "You might find it too psychoanalytic." "Gaultier wanted to remain a child. His grandmother adored him," the journalist duly wrote. "Too much, in my view," added Vermeil. Gaultier himself often recalled seeing his beloved Nana, his maternal grandmother, a hairstylist and tarot reader, in her old-fashioned corsetry, one of the "sartorial incidents" (as Vermeil put it) of the designer's childhood—as though his childhood foretold his career.[15]

As a small child, Jean Paul had made breasts and a brassiere for his teddy bear Nana (which is also a French word for grandmother). When Gaultier finally arrived for the interview, he provided more subtle insights into his beliefs and creative process, recalling that it was through talking with his grandmother that "I learned about the psychology of human beings—that fashion is about people's desires, however unformulated." He also emphasized that designers look for inspiration in the outer world, not just in their own fantasies. For example, he once knew a girl who liked to expose a bit of bra strap. "It's not

Figure 6.12 Madonna wearing Jean Paul Gaultier conical bra corset, *Blonde Ambition* world tour, Feyenoord Stadion, De Kuip, Rotterdam, Holland, July 24, 1990. Photo by Gie Knaeps/Getty Images.

my fantasy," he said. "It's about looking, spotting desires and being seduced by those desires themselves."[16]

Certainly, for a designer to be successful, the clothes they create must appeal to other people; their fantasies must mesh. Gaultier famously designed the corsets for Madonna's Blonde Ambition tour in 1990, which helped transform the corset from a symbol of women's oppression to one of female sexual power. He described Madonna as a "liberated woman who still *played the game of femininity* while being so strong she was almost macho."[17] Throughout his career, including when he designed for the luxury company Hermès, Gaultier explored fantasies of androgyny and gender fluidity, as well as hyper-femininity and masculinity.

Thierry Mugler: Making Women Feel Powerful

"I have always worked to make women feel powerful," said Thierry Mugler (1948–2022), a designer known for fashions that evoke both fetish and fantasy. Even more than Gaultier, Mugler created many fashions based on the hard body. One of the earliest in 1980 was a "gladiator bustier" made of form-fitting leather. He also made exoskeleton designs in metal; one corset even morphed into a motorcycle. Admitting that some of his corsets

Figure 6.13 Jerry Hall modeling in Thierry Mugler, 1980. Photo by Allan Tannenbaum/Getty Images.

were "very structured … even restrictive," he nevertheless insisted: "We demand comfort, but what about confidence?" Asked by French *Vogue* if he had ever had psychoanalysis, he said: "No, but … I devoted fifteen years to psychosynthesis, which makes the link between body, memory, and soul." And he added, "I look for the best way to give life to a fantasy."[18]

Although mainstream feminists were often horrified by Mugler's "fembot" fashions, which transformed women into angels, insects, mermaids, and sexy cyborgs, Linda Nochlin, the great feminist art historian, argued: "It's so extreme that these women aren't sex objects, they're sex subjects … this is a kind of artifice—it's a performance." In 1994, when journalist Holly Brubach conducted an interview with Nochlin and Mugler for *The New York Times*, unexpected synergies were revealed. Nochlin said that she agreed with Joan Riviere that

Figure 6.14 Thierry Mugler, evening set, *Les Atlantes* collection, Spring 1989. Photo © The Museum at FIT.

femininity is a condition of disguise. You learn how to be feminine – it's not something natural, ever. So I would say that the great designer of clothing is always providing additional disguises to create new forms of the feminine … clothes tell you something about the choice of the woman who's wearing them, but they don't tell you anything about the quote-unquote real woman, because I don't think there is a real woman. There's a real person, but I don't think it's a woman.

"Very true," replied Mugler. "There is only the person who chooses to play the feminine role." If he sometimes chose "transsexuals" as models, he explained, this was "because no one wants to be more feminine than a transsexual."[19] The term "transgender" began to appear in the early 1990s, encompassing and gradually replacing earlier terms such as transvestite and transsexual.

The game of "being masculine" was also open to everyone, argued Mugler, who designed for men, as well as women. Indeed, his broad-shouldered suits for men, like his curvy suits for women, were among his most popular designs. "It's the turn of the man to be the sexual object," added Mugler. There are also different *types* of male sexual objects, he added, some more "macho" than others. Nochlin mentioned both Baudelaire's dandy and contemporary gay culture as contributing to the game of fashioning different types of masculinity.[20] Hold that thought! Can there be a masculine masquerade?

Figure 6.15 Connie Girl modeling at the Thierry Mugler Spring/Summer 1992 fashion show. Photo by Pierre Vauthey/Sygma/Sygma via Getty Images.

Figure 6.16 Thierry Mugler, Spring 1985 ready-to-wear collection. Photograph by Niall McInerney, © Bloomsbury Publishing Plc.

Figure 6.17 John Galliano, *Suzy Sphinx* collection, Autumn/Winter 1997. Photo by Niall McInerney, © Bloomsbury Publishing Plc.

John Galliano: *petit objet a* and *jouissance*

In *Fashion and Psychoanalysis: Styling the Self* (2012), cultural critic Alison Bancroft used Lacanian concepts, such as *petit objet a* and *jouissance* to interpret the work of John Galliano (1960–) and Lee Alexander McQueen, arguing that their respective fashions represented very different ideas of femininity. Galliano's fashion "positions woman (or woman-clothed-in-his-gowns) as *objet a*, the object of desire for men." In support of this, Bancroft quotes Galliano saying: "My goal is really very simple. When a man looks at a woman wearing one of my dresses, I would like him basically to be saying to himself: 'I have to fuck her' … I just think every woman deserves to be desired."[21]

Lacan's concept of *objet a* or, more precisely, *objet petit a* [the small other object] is usually translated, not as the object of desire but as the object (cause) of desire, with the emphasis on *cause*. It is related to Freud's lost object, Klein's partial object, and Winnicott's transitional object. However, it is not an actual object: it is not the mother of infantile memory, or the "good" breast, or the teddy bear. Nor is it the fetish object, although it is often fetishized. Lacan's object-cause of desire is not *what* we desire. It is closer to what causes us to desire something.

In ordinary speech, when we talk about the "objects of desire," we tend to think of desirable things, such as an Hermès handbag, which is beautiful, expensive, and difficult to

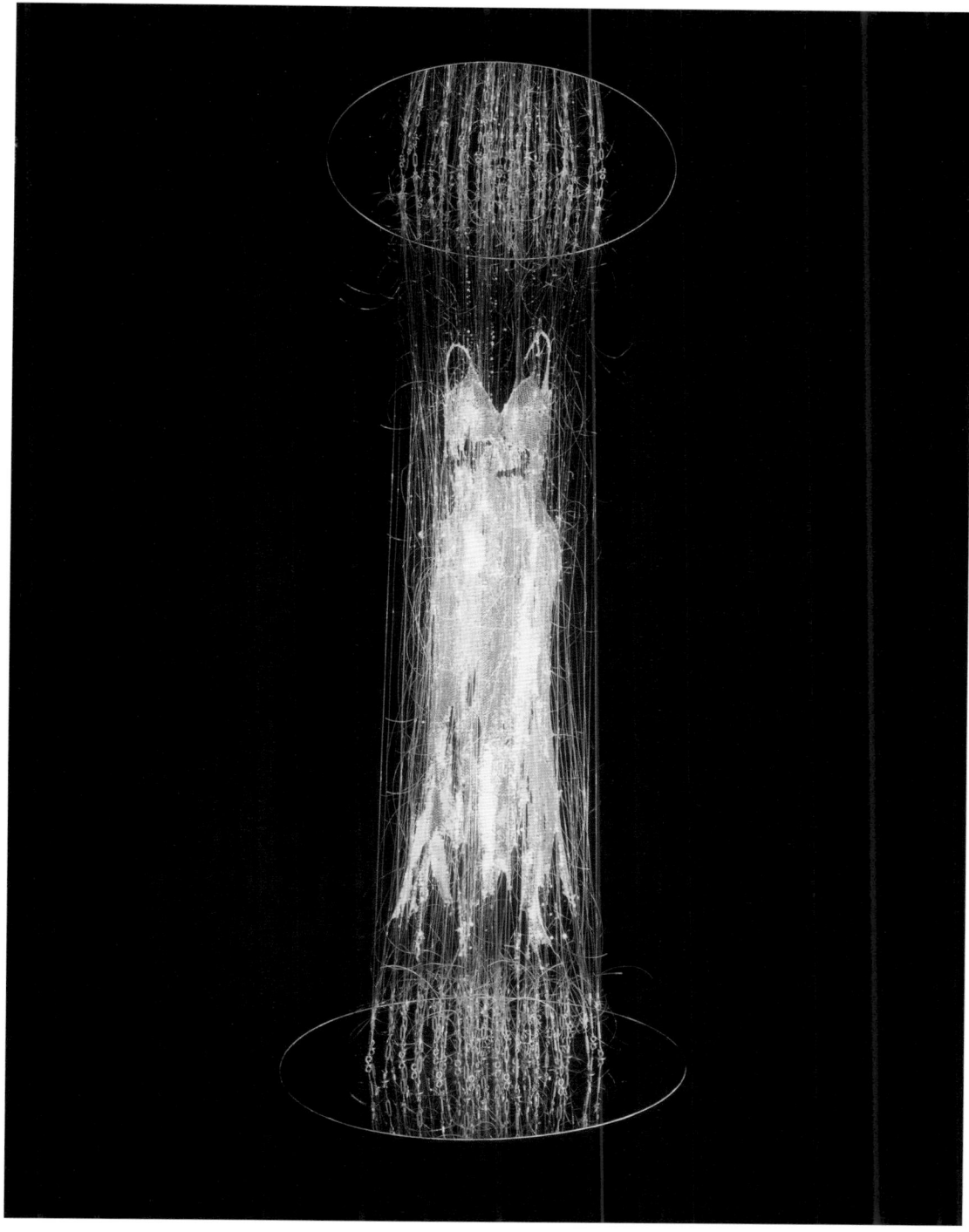

Figure 6.18 E.V. Day, *Transporter*, 2000, from the "Exploding Couture" series. Photo courtesy E.V. Day Studio.

obtain. But we also acknowledge that a person can be the object of desire. For Lacanians, the object (cause) of desire is always a lost and unobtainable object, because the lack is really in the subject. The object that is *substituted* for it can be a thing such as an Hermès handbag or a person (glamorous arm candy), but what makes this object desirable is that it is desired by others.

Many of Galliano's fashions, such as his body-worshipping, bias-cut evening gowns, do seem to position the woman who wears them as the object of desire for heterosexual men. In addition, Galliano has often represented women as sexually accessible, reflecting the popular male fantasy of the omnisexual woman. According to Bancroft, Galliano's fashions express "a male fantasy of feminine jouissance." The French word *jouissance* can be defined as "enjoyment," but for Lacanians, it also takes on a range of other meanings, including lust and a powerful orgasmic feeling.

Lacan envisioned feminine *jouissance* in the form of Bernini's statue of Saint Teresa. Contemporary artist E.V. Day attempts something similar with her installation piece, *Transporter*, 2000, part of her "Exploding Couture" series. It features a silver sequined dress by Stephen Sprouse, which is suspended between two mirrored disks and stretched by hundreds of monofilaments. "It's not about someone violently destroying a dress," says Day, "but rather something orgasmic—a celebratory expansion of energy."[22] *Jouissance*, for Lacanians, does *not* refer to the feeling of pleasure. If, for Lacan, desire signifies lack, then *jouissance*, especially feminine *jouissance*, signifies something more, something beyond pleasure that borders on pain.[23]

McQueen, Castration, and the Real

By contrast, Lee Alexander McQueen (1969–2010) said he wanted his fashions to "empower" women and provoke fear in men. A woman wearing his clothes, he argued, would look "so fabulous you wouldn't dare lay a hand on her." According to Bancroft, this untouchable fabulousness was "the castration threat, the slipping of the veil of femininity that is couture to reveal the terrifying maw of castration." McQueen's work was often perceived during his lifetime as "an assault on the figure of woman," but Bancroft argued: "On the contrary, by facilitating a display of the feminine as something other than a veiled nothing, he provides a site of resistance in which the disruptive potential of feminine jouissance can make its appearance (in the Symbolic)."[24] In McQueen's collection *La Poupée*, for example, "the violence of castration is writ large, and on the body too, by clothing that more usually veils, covers, screens off." Or, as was said of artist Orlan's work: "it shows the copresence of the phallic and the castrated."[25]

Although Bancroft insists that the "explicit savagery" of McQueen's work more openly resists projections of male desire, she goes on to admit that Galliano's fashions also sometimes act as the "interjection of the Real" into the Symbolic. In Lacanian terminology, the Real is definitely *not* reality, but rather the inexpressible and unimaginable. In contrast

Figure 6.19 Alexander McQueen, *La Poupée* collection, Spring/Summer 1997. Photo by Niall McInerney, © Bloomsbury Publishing Plc.

to the visual and phenomenal register of the Imaginary or the register of the Symbolic, which is associated with language and law, the Real is associated with the other, with sexual difference, trauma, and the unbearable bodily intensity of *jouissance*.[26]

Although Bancroft's analysis is dense, it can be enlightening if you are already familiar with the work of these two great designers. But she seems oddly unaware that it is very common for designers to say that fashion is about sexual desire, almost as common as it is for them to say that their designs "empower" women. During his lifetime, McQueen was often accused of being misogynistic, and no wonder when so many of his collections had deliberately provocative titles, such as *Jack the Ripper Stalks His Victims*, *Highland Rape*, and *Bellmer La Poupée*. His *Eclect Dissect* collection (for Givenchy) was about a mad scientist mutilating women.

While the accusation of misogyny cannot entirely be discounted, I would argue that McQueen's often brutal imagery was as much or more about *himself* than about women. As he once said: "My collections have always been autobiographical, a lot to do with my own sexuality and coming to terms with the person I am – it was like exorcizing ghosts in my collections."[27] McQueen's work was often about beauty and terror. *The Hunger* (Spring/Summer, 1998) was about vampires, sex, mortality, and decay. *Joan* (Autumn/Winter, 1998–99), inspired by Joan of Arc, portrayed her as a heretic-martyr. As McQueen said: "Anyone can be a martyr for their cause. Maybe I was a martyr for homosexuality when I was six."[28] Many of his collections addressed death and dissolution. *Dante* (Autumn/Winter 1997) also featured images from a "blind colony" of Native Americans. Blindness is a highly unusual subject for a fashion designer. Although the classic psychoanalytic reading of blindness associates it with castration (Oedipus blinds himself when he realizes his crimes of incest and patricide), blindness can also be associated with inner vision. McQueen had tattooed on his arm the words: "Love looks not with the eyes."

I agree with Brancroft that McQueen's vision of the feminine seems to have been a genuine site of resistance to patriarchal power. But she provides no clear evidence that he took the "feminine" position, or what that means in the context of her rather rigid Lacanian approach. It is also problematic that she ignores men's fashion entirely. She did later write an article titled "Masculinity, Masquerade and Display: Some Thoughts on Rick Owens's Sphinx Collection and Men in Fashion" (2016). But here, too, she insisted that "Fashion is inherently feminine, and thus always feminizing." Fashion is invariably "a feminine cultural form, regardless of the anatomy of the wearer." Owens' collection (which included several ensembles that permitted the audience to glimpse limp penises) is probably *not* an example of virile display in fashion. Indeed, I suspect that Owens' *Sphinx* collection

Figure 6.20 Alexander McQueen, *The Hunger* collection, Spring/Summer 1996. Photo by Niall McInerney, © Bloomsbury Publishing Plc.

Figure 6.21 Alexander McQueen, *Joan* collection, Autumn/Winter 1998. Photo by Niall McInerney, © Bloomsbury Publishing Plc.

Figure 6.22 Alexander McQueen, *Joan*, Autumn/Winter 1998 collection. Photo: firstVIEW.

Chapter 6 Desire and Sexual Difference   **157**

deliberately pulled back the veil surrounding male illusions. I believe that Bancroft is too dogmatic when she dismissed the idea that there can ever be a "masculine masquerade" or that fashion can ever serve as a "signifier of masculinity."[29] More problematic is the way Lacan's theory of sexuation is limited to the binary of masculine and feminine, although one could envision a spectrum running from one to the other. Meanwhile, Freud continues to inspire designers including Galliano.

Freud or Fetish

"I believe Monsieur Christian Dior was the first true fetishist designer," said John Galliano. "He had an Oedipus complex, he was in awe of his mother, and his New Look was full of fetish symbolism. You have only to look at the high heels, the corsets which emphasized the bust and the waist, the big skirts which emphasized the hips."[30] Galliano had been appointed artistic director at the House of Dior in 1997, exactly fifty years after Christian Dior transformed fashion with his 1947 "New Look" collection. Three years later, he shared his thoughts about Dior with New Zealand-born British journalist Hilary Alexander. It was the night before Galliano would present his latest couture collection, entitled *Freud or Fetish*.

Christian Dior was almost certainly *not* the first true fetishist designer. He was probably not a sexual fetishist at all, except in the sense that many psychoanalysts believe that "Fetishizing is the norm for males."[31] On the other hand, Dior's ultra-feminine New Look fashions, "the high heels, the corsets," certainly *do* evoke the iconography of sexual fetishism, although few people at the time, apart from psychoanalysts, would have had the specialized knowledge to recognize this.

When Galliano said that Dior "had an Oedipus complex" and felt "awe" for his mother, it is not clear to what extent he understood what the Oedipus complex is supposed to mean, or that postwar psychoanalysts believed that gay men had not successfully resolved their Oedipus complex by separating from the mother, identifying with the father, and choosing another female love object. Galliano may just have meant that Dior loved and admired his mother. He may also have intended to imply, correctly, that Dior's New Look fashions were inspired by the Belle Époque fashions that his mother had worn when he was young. It is probably not accidental that many male (and some female) designers have spoken of how their mothers represented for them an ideal of beauty and elegance, to which they often returned.

When the fashion crowd arrived at the École des Beaux-Arts for Dior's Autumn/Winter 2000 Haute Couture collection, they found on their seats copies of an imaginary letter from Sigmund Freud to Carl Jung: "Recently I glimpsed an explanation for the case of fetishism. So far it concerns only clothes, but it is probably universal."[32] Someone on Galliano's team had done enough research to know that fetishists do not only fixate on clothing objects such as high-heeled shoes; they may also be obsessed, for example, with

Figure 6.23 Model wearing Christian Dior ballgown, Spring-Summer 1950. Photograph by Louise Dahl-Wolfe. Collection Center for Creative Photography. © Center for Creative Photography, Arizona Board of Regents.

particular body parts, such as feet or hair, types of people, such as redheads or chauffeurs, and/or ritualized sexual scenarios.

Freud or Fetish opened with the appearance of a Felliniesque bishop wearing a lavishly embroidered and padded New Look robe, walking down the runway, swinging a thurible and bowing to members of the audience. He was followed by models representing the "bride and groom." The bride's white satin bias-cut wedding gown drew applause from the audience, but most viewers didn't seem to notice that the groom's hands were tied behind his back with a pearl necklace. He was also wearing a green carnation, made notorious by Oscar Wilde as an emblem of homosexuality.

The wedding party followed, aristocratic and Edwardian, in corseted dresses, diamond chokers, and huge feather-decked hats. Marisa Berenson played the mother of the bride, accompanied by other models of a certain age, such as Carmen dell'Orefice and Benedetta Barzini, each paired with a younger man. The first few couples were elegant, but the figures soon became more bizarre, as white tie and top hats gave way to twisted military uniforms and garish makeup.

After the "wedding" came the "nightmare." Or rather a series of nightmares, accompanied by scary music, including what seem to be children's nightmares, as well as more adult sexual fantasies. There was a horse-woman in grey leather with a saddle and tail—perhaps a reference to Freud's case study of Little Hans with his horse phobia? She was followed by a sexually ambiguous figure in a chauffeur's uniform, and a nurse with a huge hypodermic needle. According to Galliano, this section evoked "that feeling of this young child looking through the keyhole and seeing what the real world was about, that mummy was sleeping with the chauffeur and the chauffeur was having it off with papa, and this, well, this is one of his nightmares."[33]

To the sound of moaning, the dancer Anne-Sophie Balsing appeared as a "kinky barrister" in a corset and satin gown, with a noose around her neck. Sophie Dahl appeared as a bejeweled French maid wearing a red corset under her uniform. Lots of fetishes there: corsets, jewels, glitter, uniforms. A black-and-white Leigh Bowery-like figure (shades of Galliano's youth in London's club scene) led in on a leash by a woman dressed all in scarlet including her corset top hat by Stephen Jones.

There was also a terrifying crocodile woman, draped in crocodile skin, wearing crocodile boots and one long scaly glove, with bones around her neck, crowned with the head of a stuffed crocodile penetrated by an arrow. In Lacanian terms, this would surely constitute an incursion of the Real. Where does she fit in the family romance? Freud saw the Mother and Son as a loving dyad, rudely interrupted by the Father's greater claim. Lacan, however, viewed the Father (or "The Name-of-the-Father") as the necessary third element, barring the way to the seductive but dangerous Mother. As Lacan put it:

> The mother is a big crocodile and you find yourself in her mouth. You never know what may set her off, suddenly making those jaws clamp down. That is the mother's desire. … There is a roller, made of stone, of course, which is potentially there at the level of the trap and which holds and jams it open. That is what we call the phallus. It is a roller which protects you should the jaws suddenly close.[34]

Galliano's crocodile woman was certainly at least as terrifying as McQueen's creations.

"I am trying to symbolize what fetishism evokes in the psychology of clothing," Galliano told Suzy Menkes after what she described as a "powerful but disturbing show." The veteran fashion journalist admitted that "As an exercise of the imagination, the show … was exceptional. And if Britpop artists can explore the dark recesses of sexual

Figure 6.24 Chauffeur, John Galliano for Dior Haute Couture Autumn/Winter 2000. Photo by Victor VIRGILE/Gamma-Rapho via Getty Images.

Figure 6.25 John Galliano for Dior Haute Couture Autumn/Winter 2000–2001, crocodile woman. Photo by Victor VIRGILE/Gamma-Rapho via Getty Images.

fantasy, why not a couturier?" Yet she wondered whether the "hard-porn" imagery symbolized women's "degradation." As the headline put it: "Fetishism on the runway: chic or sick?"[35]

Fashion scholar Caroline Evans interpreted the Dior fashion show very differently, suggesting that Galliano's references to sexual fetishism and "perversion" simply "masked the real form of fetishism that was paraded in this collection, that of the commodity."[36] Of course, sexual fetishism and commodity fetishism are not necessary mutually exclusive. Artist Sylvie Fleury implicitly addresses the idea of commodity fetishism when she goes on shopping expeditions and then makes art works out of the luxury goods she has purchased. Her art may take the form of videos (of a woman trying on shoes, for example) or installations. Yet Fleury also emphasizes the *pleasure* that she and many other women obtain from fashion and luxury goods.

In her 2009 article "*Filles fétiches, femmes fétichistes*" ("Fetish Girls, Fetishist Women"), psychoanalyst Geneviève Morel described how "normal" masculine fetishism typically functions: There is a male subject, an Eye, facing the female genitals. "Between the two is a screen. The fetish is painted on this screen, which enables him not to see the female genitals nude, by veiling them … Isn't this the structure of fashion? One finds there the same

Figure 6.26 Sylvie Fleury, *Untitled*, 1994, from the exhibition *Spring* at Galerie Philomene Magers in Cologne (March 21–April 19, 1997). Art & Public Geneva. © Sylvie Fleury, Courtesy the artist and Sprüth Magers.

Figure 6.27 VVB35 Vanessa Beecroft Performance, 1998. Solomon R. Guggenheim Museum, New York © 2024 Vanessa Beecroft.

pairs of signifiers … nude/dressed or veiled/unveiled calling forth the phallic woman."[37] As an example of this phenomenon in the art world, she uses one of Vanessa Beecroft's performances, in which about a dozen nearly naked female models stand in the atrium of the Guggenheim Museum; in the center of the group are a few women who are naked … except for their high heels.

What, then, is the unconscious appeal of fashion for women? Most psychoanalysts agree that female fetishism is either very rare or does not exist, *at least not as fetishism functions for men*. As Morel puts it: "If you understand the Freudian structure of masculine fetishism, you understand that there does not exist a feminine fetishism that functions in an identical or symmetrical way." While acknowledging there may nevertheless be some female fetishists, Morel places more emphasis on the wider social phenomenon of "fétichisme féminin de masse," whereby women's "fetishization" of their own bodies serves to give their bodies a "phallic value" that attracts men.[38] This is not dissimilar to the conclusion I came to in my book *Fetish: Fashion, Sex & Power*. However, I believe that this phenomenon is *not* just about women fetishizing themselves to attract men. Nor does women's love of, say, "sexy girl shoes" mean that they want a closet of phallic symbols. It is certainly possible that women have their own type of female fetishism, perhaps deriving from the perception of the mother's body as the "lost" object of desire.

In her article "Self-Fashioning, Gender Display, and Sexy Girl Shoes: What's at Stake—Female Fetishism or Narcissism?," Lorraine Gamman suggests that "fetishism and narcissism are constellatory interarticulations that inform the masquerade." Commodity fetishism is often a factor in female self-objectification, but women may also experience pleasure in their self-fashioning. She concludes by observing that "there has yet to be a useful or systematic analysis of the role of narcissism."[39] I agree, and suggest, in turn, that that embodied experience of fashion may well appeal to women's fetishism and narcissism, both in the sense of reassurance for loss and in confident self-love.

7
To Touch the Gaze

"Vulnerability is foreign to me," said Karl Lagerfeld. Yet in the same interview for *Le Figaro*, the famous designer recalled growing up with a mother who was often harshly critical. This was a theme to which he returned in many interviews, explaining, for example, that he wore gloves, because his mother said his hands were ugly and he spoke rapidly, because she was impatient with the "stupid" things he said. Later in the interview, former model Carla Bruni started to ask him about passion and love, "Some girls say, '*That man, I have him under my skin* … '" But Lagerfeld interrupted her: "Then let them consult a dermatologist! There is another expression I detest: 'Love makes you blind'. There are glasses for that."[1] His words led contemporary French psychoanalyst Pascale Navarri to think about "the fragility" we sometimes feel when other people look at us.[2] And also, we might add, the vulnerability we feel when people "get under" our skin, penetrating our defenses.

Fashion is often described as a "second skin," a phrase that usually carries the implication that dress functions primarily to display our sexual allure and/or our personal identity. Yet novelist J.G. Ballard suggested otherwise when he defined fashion as "*a recognition that nature has endowed us with one skin too few.*"[3] Most dress theorists (myself included) have tended to downplay the protective function of clothing, seeing it as something primitive that has been largely superseded in modern society, where neither warm furs nor magic amulets are necessary. But psychoanalysts know that the primitive parts of our psyche

Figure 7.1 Karl Lagerfeld wearing sunglasses. Photo by Bertrand Rindoff Petroff/Getty Images.

continue to play a powerful role long after we have become adults. In recent years, a number of psychoanalysts have begun to explore fashion's unconscious relationship with issues such as vulnerability and trauma.

The Look of Fashion

"What the look of fashion exposes is, simultaneously, our vulnerability about being seen and not being seen," argues Navarri in *Trendy, sexy et inconscient: Regards d'une psychoanalyst sur la mode* (2008). We use fashion both "to call attention to ourselves and to protect ourselves." Fashion makes us "visible" to an indifferent world, while also providing us with "protective dark glasses" that hide our vulnerability.[4] Lagerfeld was always impeccably and distinctively dressed, making him immediately visible and recognizable, and he almost always wore dark glasses. Indeed, he once compared his dark glasses to a burqa, evoking an Islamophobic stereotype for a garment that conceals a woman's body and face. Since the eyes are often perceived as windows to the soul, people who habitually wear dark glasses may be suspected of hiding their feelings. But, especially with famous people, the message conveyed by dark glasses may be a "double discourse." As Roland Barthes wrote: "The hiding must be seen: *I want you to know that I am hiding something from you* ... I advance pointing to my mask."[5]

Lagerfeld was notorious for making hostile remarks about fat people; this was probably in large part a projection of his own body dysmorphia. He recalled that, growing up, he had such problems with binge eating that his mother would tie him to the bed at night. As a young man, he was hyper-muscular and showed off his body, but when he stopped working out, he became fat and hid his body under voluminous Japanese suits. In 2001, he went on a diet and lost almost 100 pounds, saying he did it because he wanted to fit into the slim suits that Hedi Slimane designed for Dior.

You may recall that Alessandra Lemma described how, if the mother's gaze fails to hold up a "benignly distorting mirror," she cannot help her child "install internally a pair of 'rose tinted glasses'." Internalizing "a more persecutory gaze," the individual "may become overly reliant on image and mirrors in order to feel whole and may also feel compelled to modify the body in order to achieve an idealized form."[6] Indeed, Navarri wondered whether Lagerfeld's mother might have influenced, not only his self-image, but also his career, if "behind each new collection of the master, there [hid] a ferocious maternal eye."[7]

The Gaze of Narcissus

Is there something about the fashion system that encourages narcissism? Certainly, people in the fashion world are unusually concerned with external appearance, physical beauty, and sartorial style. The ancient myth after which narcissism was named described how a beautiful young man fell in love with his reflection, and ignoring the nymph, Echo, eventually died of thirst. Both Freud and Lacan placed narcissism at the center of human sexuality,

Figure 7.2 Caravaggio, *Narcissus*, c. 1600. Galleria Nazionale d'Arte Antica. Wikimedia Commons.

but whereas for Freud, primary narcissism was merely a phase in childhood, Lacan saw it as the foundation of the subject via the mirror stage. According to Ovid, when Narcissus caught sight of himself reflected in a pool of water, he exclaimed "Then let me look at you and feed my wretched frenzy on your image." Lacan, more than Freud, grasped the importance of the gaze of Narcissus and his emotion at the sight of this delusory image.[8]

Freud had associated narcissism (self-love) with biological women and homosexual men. But in Lacanian psychoanalysis, "femininity" and "masculinity" are only *very* loosely connected to biological sex and sociocultural ideas about gender. The Freudian concept of "female narcissism" has often been used to explain why so many women are so attracted by fashion. Indeed, it was psychoanalytic dogma in the United States from the 1930s through the 1980s that: "Female narcissism as it is expressed in clothing and jewelry is usually interpreted as a displacement from the penis, i.e. *girls treat their whole bodies as a penis to exhibit.*"[9]

However, the historically situated narrative linking female narcissism and penis envy was increasingly rejected. Already criticized in the 1920s, by the 1990s, progressives in the United States tried to address the perceived female "lack" with counternarratives, like the children's song "Boys are fancy on the outside, girls are fancy on the inside." However, at least one little girl allegedly responded indignantly: "No, that's not true. When I get dressed up, I'm fancy all over." Recounting this anecdote in 1996, a female psychoanalyst interpreted the girl's statement as "an expression of whole-body narcissism and pleasure." Penis envy, she suggested, is "a male fantasy of what his experience would be if he were deprived of the penis."[10]

Already by the 1980s, English-speaking psychoanalysts increasingly believed that "a working level of narcissism is inseparable from self-esteem."[11] The "defining qualities" of the "pathological" narcissist, whether male or female, were said to be "vanity, exhibitionism, and arrogant ingratitude." Such a person "is developmentally stuck between 'the mirror and the mask'—a reflected appraisal of himself, or a disguised search for one." Behind his "grandiose self," there is concealed "a hungry, enraged, empty self."[12] Today, most analysts agree that for complex social reasons, there are more narcissistic patients than formerly, and fewer hysterical, sexually repressed patients.

For English-language psychologists who focus on personality research, "narcissists are more likely to wear expensive, flashy clothes"—especially "brand-name" fashions that reinforce their high status and make them "the center of attention." Narcissists are preoccupied with "good looks" and spend time on grooming; if female, they tend to wear makeup and show off their cleavage. They rank high on extraversion and low on agreeableness. Some psychologists even claim that "narcissism does have a distinct physical signature, and can be detected from physical appearance alone."[13]

Psychoanalysts, whether Freudian or Lacanian, tend to dismiss these claims as oversimplified. They do believe that a new fashion may provide a temporary sense of wellbeing: "I look good." But this quickly wears off, because fashion can also be an aggressive force that destabilizes and fragments the self, in part by constantly demanding a new and better appearance. The narcissist's apparent "vanity" is really a defensive self-enhancement, although to some degree, this is true for everyone. As psychoanalyst Eve Golden puts it, when people feel "narcissistically deficient," they "may seek clothes as a way to make good the lack, relying on them at once for proud display and for concealment of shame."[14]

The Gaze of the Medusa

Another Greek myth recounts how the sight of the female monster Medusa, with her hair all snakes, turned men to stone. Medusa was originally a nymph, who was raped by

Neptune in Athena's temple. Athena took out her rage on Medusa, turning her into a monster. The hero Perseus defeated Medusa by making her see herself in the reflective surface of his shield, while he turned his own eyes away, as he stabbed her to death with his sword. Following Freud, most psychoanalysts have interpreted the terrifying image of Medusa in terms of castration anxiety.[15]

However, the fears expressed here are probably even more primitive, or, in psychoanalytic terms, pre-Oedipal. As Claudia Benthien writes: "What we are dealing with is the archaic fear of the magical, possession-taking gaze of the other … and at the same time

Figure 7.3 Caravaggio, *Medusa*, 1595–98. Galleria degli Uffizi, Florence. Photo by Fine Art Images/Heritage Images/Getty Images.

with the fear of being fascinated and blinded by what is seen, the desire for possession and incorporation."[16]

Many people fear the "penetrating" or "judgmental" gaze of other people, and they consciously try to dress in such a way as to camouflage themselves or ward off this type of gaze. We are not just referring to the sexually objectifying "male gaze." There are T-shirts depicting Medusa's face surrounded by hissing snakes, with the caption "The Female Gaze," which may indicate an awareness that the gaze of Medusa is not just about voyeurism and sex. It is more like the ancient concept of the "evil eye"—a look that can wither and kill. As Benthien points out, on nudist beaches, there is greater "regulation of looking"—and not just in the sense of restricting sexualizing looking. Looks that reduce another person to "a fragile, aging, fleshy body are [also] taboo … For the uncovered skin is not only an erotic surface, but also the defenseless state of being in its most elemental form."[17]

Nudity is both "feared and desired," because it can expose us to "the gaze that shames," but also to "the gaze of desire," writes psychoanalyst Paul-Laurent Assoun. As he points out, society's "vestimentary norms" are first enforced by the mother, who dresses the little child and inculcates the belief that nakedness is shameful. One of the functions of clothing is thus as protection against shame, a "shame-guard" (*pare-honte*). However, "clothing does not just cover nudity, it [also] designates [the wearer's] sex, as well as

Figure 7.4 Versace, purse, c. 1992. Photo © The Museum at FIT.

exploring ambiguity." Clothing can thus function unconsciously both as the "signifier of desire" and as a "castration-guard" that prevents the viewer from experiencing fear and/or overexcitement at the sight of the other's body.[18]

Versace's choice of the Medusa as a brand logo is brilliant, because she was a special kind of monster. The incarnation of fear, "the forbidden vision," and "the void of death," her role is apotropaic. Like the ferocious deities of Tibetan Buddhism, it is precisely her terrifying aspect that makes her such a powerful protector for the person who owns an object "that carries her effigy." To protect ourselves from the maleficent gaze, we must cover ourselves with a special "magical" skin that can repel the gaze or reflect it back from the surface of our body onto the hostile viewer.[19]

A Skin for Thought

Psychoanalyst Didier Anzieu (1923–99) first articulated his theory of "the skin ego" in 1974, publishing the first edition of his book *Le Moi-peau* in 1985. However, it is only recently that his work has inspired a new approach to thinking about fashion, one which emphasizes the skin's role as the surface of the body, where it functions both as a boundary and as an interface between the self and the world. Anzieu built on Freud's statement that "The ego is first and foremost a bodily ego," which is also "the projection of a surface."[20] But he also drew on his family's intergenerational trauma. For just as it was the death of Freud's father that led to Freud's self-analysis and the rise of psychoanalysis, so also did the tragic life of Anzieu's mother contribute to his conception of the skin ego as a metaphor based on the biological skin, and also on the "phantasy" of a common skin belonging to both mother and child.

Marguerite Pantaine was born in 1892, two years after her sister, the first Marguerite Pantaine, died in a tragic accident, when, too lightly dressed, she came too close to the fire and was burned to death. Conceived as a replacement for the dead child, Anzieu's mother grew up to be creative and intelligent, but emotionally fragile. In 1917, she married René Anzieu, but their first child, a little girl, died at birth, strangled by the umbilical cord. A year later, when a son, Didier, was born, he was another replacement child. Suffering from psychotic postpartum depression, Marguerite left her family. In 1931, she was arrested in Paris for attacking a famous actress with a knife. Incarcerated in an asylum, she became known to history as Lacan's famous patient "Aimée."

In 1949, Didier Anzieu entered analysis with Lacan. When he resumed contact with his mother and discovered her connection with Lacan, Anzieu terminated his analysis—and tried without success to get Lacan to return his mother's writings. Many years later, he said that Marguerite's tragic life had contributed to his decision to become a psychoanalyst—to take care of people like his mother. He also talked about the impact of intergenerational trauma on his childhood. His parents, especially his mother, were determined to protect him, and perceived even the slightest draft as a threat: "I was not

Figure 7.5 Didier Anzieu and his wife Annie Péghaire Anzieu, 1976. Photo courtesy Christine Anzieu-Premmereur.

allowed to risk myself in the outside air without being smothered under several layers of clothing: sweater, overcoat, beret, and scarf." Clothes represented "envelopes of care, concern, and warmth," but also the weight of parental anxiety, and he "carried their load on [his] back."[21] Looking back, he realized that these experiences had contributed to the birth of his theory of the skin ego.

Sometimes described as "the other French Freud," Anzieu has often been contrasted with Jacques Lacan.[22] Whereas Lacan's approach to human subjectivity was disembodying in its extreme emphasis on the linguistic, Anzieu focused on the role of sensorimotor experiences and emotional functioning that come *before* language and thought. Among these very early sensations, those on the skin are especially important. Anzieu's emphasis on the skin and on touch built on Freud's concept of the "bodily ego," and also seem to complement Lacan's emphasis on the eye and the gaze. Lacan stressed image and language, while Anzieu stressed embodiment and emotion, which have an even more primary relationship to the development of the mind.

Anzieu's wife, Annie Péghaire Anzieu, was also a psychoanalyst. When I asked their daughter, Dr. Christine Anzieu Premmereur, about her father's sartorial style, she told me:

> My father had no clue of what he should wear, apart from what was professional. My mother, shown with him in this 1976 photograph, helped him choose his suits. But he was very sensitive to the appreciation of others, and could be, on a few occasions when he had to pay attention to clothes, independent and unconventional in his choices. He appreciated my mother's attention to feminine stylish clothes. And when I had my first evening dress, an Yves Saint Laurent gown that was a gift from my grandparents, my father knew that was meaningful to his adolescent daughter. His appreciation was important for me, but he was also interested in the dress's fabric and the style of that time.[23]

The Skin Ego: To Hold and Protect

The skin ego functions "as a containing, unifying envelope for the Self," wrote Anzieu. It develops as the infant "experiences the contact of its body with that of the mother, and within the framework of a secure relationship with her," thus acquiring a sense of "the integrity of its bodily envelope." Anzieu believed that as children internalize parental care, this is associated with the fantasy of a "shared maternal skin" and a "psychic envelope," which become the seed for the child's developing self.[24] His ideas recall Winnicott's descriptions of how the "good enough" mother confidently handles the baby, facilitating emotional containment when the infant becomes overstimulated or agitated.

Anzieu's work was grounded in findings from infant observation and child analysis, which are widely accepted today. Esther Bick, for example, studied the function of the skin in early object relations, arguing that it helped hold together "parts of the [infant's] personality, not as yet differentiated from parts of the body." Observing "the infant trembling and quivering when the nipple is taken out of his mouth, but also when his clothes are taken off," Bick hypothesized a primal terror of "falling to pieces." Normally, this terror was assuaged by the "optimal object," that is "the nipple in the mouth, together with the holding and talking and familiar-smelling mother." Typically, "the infant introjected the mother's 'containing' role, which was then experienced as its own skin." But if "disturbances" occurred, the infant might develop "second-skin" formations, such as an aggressive "hippopotamus skin" or the "sack of apples" skin, a "thin-skinned, easily-bruised"

Figure 7.6 Romeo Gigli, cocoon coat, Fall 1991. © The Museum at FIT.

persona.²⁵ Problems in mother–infant interaction and/or mind–body integration may also manifest themselves as feeling like "a crab without a shell."²⁶

Anzieu seldom explicitly mentioned clothing in relation to the skin ego, but his ideas can fruitfully be applied to the study of dress. I think we can imagine how some items of clothing, such as a cocoon coat, may serve to help hold and contain a person who feels as though they are "falling apart." Indeed, a number of designers, such as Alber Elbaz, have mentioned their belief that certain clothes feel reassuring, in part because they gently "hold" or "hug" the wearer.

Just as the skin offers some protection against physical trauma, external "aggression," and "penetration," Anzieu argues that the skin ego functions as "a protective barrier for the psyche."²⁷ Initially, of course, it is the caregiver's bodily surface that serves as a shield, protecting the infant against external aggression and/or stimuli that would be overly exciting. Protected this way, children have less need to build up a "crustacean" or "muscular" ego, sometimes known by the Reichean term as "character armor." If necessary, clothing can also provide a protective second skin.

Japanese designer Yohji Yamamoto once said: "I make clothing like armor. My clothing protects you from unwelcome eyes."²⁸ Comme des Garçon's black hooded dress deliberately exaggerates the idea of protective, concealing dress. But many styles of dress can be protective. A biker's padded leather jacket, for example, is *physically* protective, but it can also be psychologically protective by making the wearer look and feel tough. A chic little black dress is often described as armor to face the world, but an expensive suit can also provide emotional armor against hostile or contemptuous looks or even just an intimidating environment, like a job interview. "*I weaponize glamour*," says British artist Alice Channer. "*I see clothes as a kind of armour that can change and mutate.*"²⁹

When an individual's skin ego is not strong and flexible enough, writes Anzieu, "the slightest narcissistic wound makes a tear in it." It is sometimes necessary then to reinforce the outside of the skin ego "with a symbolic maternal skin, analogous to the aegis [shield] of Zeus, or those stunning, showy rags in which young female models, often anorexic, drape themselves, the splendor of which re-narcissizes them temporarily in the face of the constant threat that the psychical container may disintegrate."³⁰

Anzieu's reference to anorexic young female models brings up an important issue. Fashion does not "cause" anorexia, the radical refusal to eat, but it contributes to eating disorders such as anorexia, bulimia, and obesity. Clinical evidence indicates that anorexia also usually involves psychological issues, such as the refusal "to grow up and become a sexual adult." Like other types of extreme body modification, anorexia can also be a way of reclaiming ownership of one's body from an intrusive, internalized mother.³¹ Not withstanding these issues, many fashion models have testified to the pressure exerted on them to stay very thin, and some, like the Brazilian model Ana Carolina Macan,

Figure 7.7 Comme des Garçons, hooded dress, Spring 2017. Photo: firstVIEW.

Figure 7.8 Azzedine Alaïa, hooded evening dress, Winter 1986. Photo © The Museum at FIT.

have died of anorexia. Body dysmorphia also seems to be widespread in the fashion world.

Can anything be done about women's issues with "body image" and "body projects"? In their article "The Deceptive Mirror," Lucia Ruggerone and Renate Strauss argue for more emphasis on "the embodied dimension of dressing" and on "the materiality of making and wearing clothes." Rather than focusing so much on how we look in clothes, we might think more about how clothes feel—and how they make us feel.[32] The experiences of one model may be relevant.

Veronica Webb and Azzedine Alaïa

African American model and actress Veronica Webb worked with many fashion designers, but she was especially close to Tunisian-born, Paris-based Azzedine Alaïa, whose "second-skin" designs were renowned for displaying and enhancing a woman's figure. "Some of my very first memories are of my mother making clothes for me," Webb recalled. "So I was uniquely suited for going to Paris [where] … Azzedine and I worked very closely together, and spent hours and hours doing fittings, and we talked and made dinners for everyone." Notice how she associates making clothes (and food) with warm feelings. But how did she feel about the way clothes made her look?

Azzedine believed that his fashions made women more powerful," recalled Webb. "But I come from a conservative background, so when I started working at age 19, I felt very conflicted about wearing sexy clothes … It wasn't until I was 27 or 28 that I really felt comfortable wearing something that screamed supermodel."

> When I wore [Alaïa's snakeskin ensemble] on my 30th birthday, it made me feel like my childhood vision of what a model would look like. It's an amazing feeling, because we grow up looking through the window at fashion, and wearing fashion has an Alice in Wonderland effect. You know, when I put this on, what rabbit hole will I fall down? Being a model is not just about the way you look. There is a deep sensuality to it, because the job is so tactile. You feel the material against your skin—and no one was more maniacal than Alaïa about cutting the material to fit your body exactly and also to give your body freedom. Alaïa once said to me, 'Fabric is sometimes just as important if not more than the people who we love, because we spend more time being held by the fabric than those who are closest and dearest.' He was saying that fashion can be a substitute for being with the person you love.[33]

Figure 7.9 Supermodel Veronica Webb, wearing an Azzedine Alaïa snakeskin bustier and skirt at El Teddy's restaurant, NYC, 1995. DMI/The LIFE Picture Collection/Shutterstock.

Sexualization

A very important function of the skin ego is "sexualization," which involves treating the skin as an erogenous zone. One of the most iconic fashions of our era is the green Versace dress that Jennifer Lopez wore to the Grammy Awards in 2000. The dress, with its tropical green print of leaves and bamboo, had already appeared on the catwalk, where it was worn by Amber Valetta, as well as in Versace advertisements. Donatella Versace herself had worn it at the Met Gala in 1999, but it was only when Lopez wore it at the Grammys that the internet crashed, because so many people were watching. Celebrities often wear daring outfits, but it is rare that the celebrity and the dress have such synergy. Lopez was an extremely popular Latina celebrity with a voluptuous figure, which the dress dramatically highlighted. Lisa Armstrong of *The Times* choose it as Dress of the Year in 2000, because she thought it represented "some kind of water mark in the current symbiosis between fashion and celebrity."[34]

"The dress was provocative enough I guess to make people really interested," Lopez told *Vogue* twenty years later. "When it blew open, everybody was like 'What's going to happen next?' Nothing. It's all taped shut."[35] The dress was, indeed, provocative: Not only

Figure 7.10 Jennifer Lopez wearing Donatella Versace at the 42nd Grammy Awards, 2000. Photo by Jeff Vespa/WireImage.

was the fabric diaphanous, the skirt was slit up the front, while the plunging neckline reached below the navel where it looked barely held together by a jeweled pin. But it was the anticipation of a wardrobe malfunction, when the skirt blew open, exposing the thighs and bejeweled crotch, and the breasts threatening to burst out, barely restrained by invisible tape, that really ratcheted the excitement up. Of course, her body was attractive, but it was her body moving within the dress and the anticipation that all would be revealed, as in a striptease, that caused pandemonium. Or as French writer Roland Barthes put it: "Is not the most erotic portion of a body where the garment gapes? There are no 'erogenous zones.' It is intermittence, as psychoanalysis has so rightly stated, which is

Figure 7.11 Bach Mai, Look 16, Spring 2023. Photo by Amber Gray, © Bach Mai.

erotic: the intermittence of skin flashing between two articles of clothing; it is this flash itself which seduces, or rather: the staging of an appearance-as-disappearance."[36]

Sexualization of the skin ego might also mean using a textile with a shiny reflective surface and/or one that feels soft and silky. New York designer Bach Mai chose to use silver couture-quality silk velvet, which gives his evening dress visual and tactile appeal, while its cut exposes atypical parts of the body, "framing" areas of naked skin and thereby sexualizing them. The use of transparent or semi-transparent materials that lightly veil the skin can also be erotic, as with Helmut Lang's chiffon and horsehair evening dress.

Figure 7.12 Helmut Lang, evening dress, Fall 2004. Photo © The Museum at FIT.

Skin Surfaces

Like Freud's "mystic writing pad," Anzieu's skin ego also functions as "a filter of exchanges and a surface of inscription." It is a palimpsest with layers of inscriptions or scars. Tattooing and other forms of body modification are more or less permanent means of inscribing messages on the skin, while fashion is a temporary and easily replaceable system of communicating, whether directly, as with message T-shirts and brand logos, or obliquely via social and sartorial codes.

Tattoos are fashionable, even ubiquitous. Yet many psychoanalysts still regard body modification in terms of mutilation, although the wider public has come to accept tattooing and piercing as a matter of individual choice and self-adornment. Anzieu himself recognized that body modifications, such as cutting, can represent an attempt to hold oneself together by "inflict[ing] a real envelope of suffering on oneself" and "restricting the unbearable pain to a fixed place."[37] It is probably necessary to think of these practices on a continuum, exploring their causes, as well as the specific messages conveyed.

Although the human skin can be smooth and soft, it can also be damaged or defaced. French fashion designer Olivier Rousteing suffered severe burns across his body when the gas fireplace in his home exploded in October 2020. The "entire front" of his body became engulfed in flames," and his left eye was "so badly damaged that [he] could barely see out of it." He recalled the slow recovery process: "My skin was returning, but it was

Figure 7.13 Viktor & Rolf, "I'm Not Shy I Just Don't Like You" dress, Spring/Summer 2019 haute couture. Photo by Thierry Chesnot/Getty Images.

white, due to a lack of melanin, and it contrasted with my darker skin. This tonal difference was particularly evident on my fingers, which I decided to hide by covering each with a multitude of rings." The accident would ultimately inspire his Spring/Summer 2022 collection for Balmain, which featured dresses that appeared to be made out of white gauze bandages: "I noticed that my collection's bandages were – just like my fears and obsessions – loosening themselves, little by little, and finally, falling away, as they elegantly dangled from the collection's key pieces."[38]

Looking at dress as a metaphoric second skin can be especially revealing when interpreting avant-garde fashion. Martin Margiela, one of the most radical and influential

Figure 7.14
Balmain, Spring 2022 collection. Photo by Dominique Charriau/Getty Images.

designers of our era, often deconstructed garments and repurposed cast-off objects, processes that evoke destruction and rag-picking. His famous Spring/Summer 1997 collection featured a sleeveless linen tunic/jacket, which mimics the look of a standarized Stockman dress form. It does not look anything like a "normal" finished garment. Confusing to observers unfamiliar with avant-garde fashion, Margiela's tunic was exciting to fashion connoisseurs and inspiring to other designers. As a knowledgeable journalist for *Le Monde* wrote: "under their unfinished aspect, [the clothes in this collection] offer … a definition of the *métier* [the craft of fashion]: the sense of line, the hand workmanship, and the secrets of an exactingness, to the millimeter."[39]

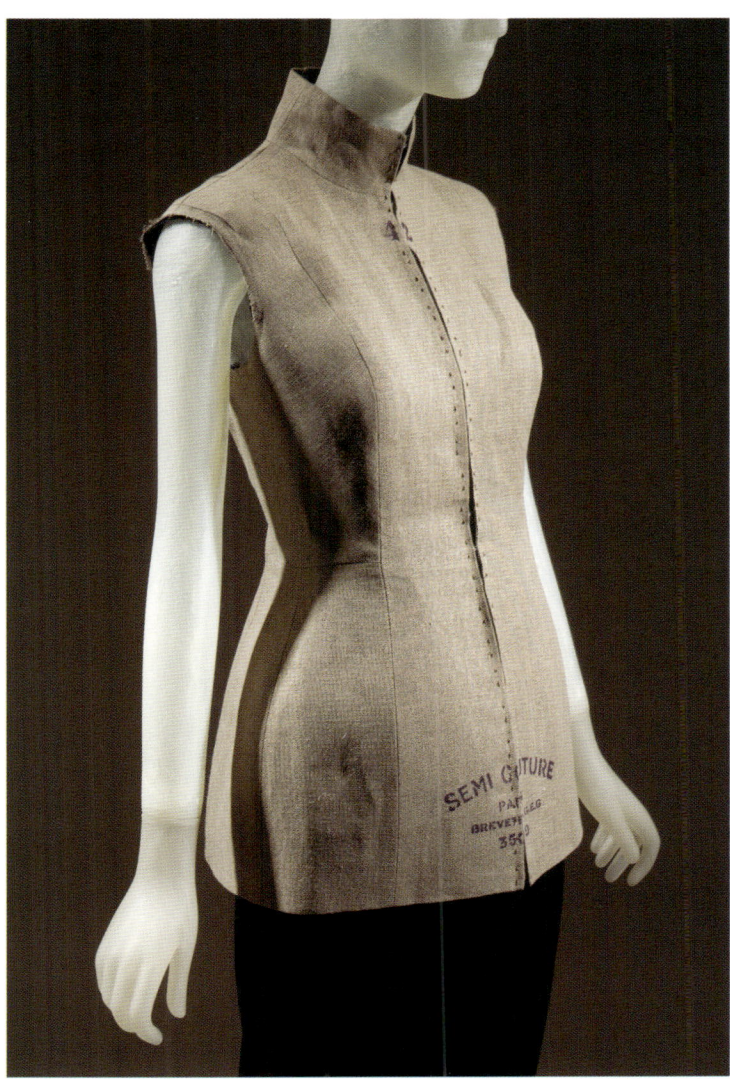

Figure 7.15 Maison Martin Margiela, Linen dress form tunic, Spring 1997. Photo © The Museum at FIT.

Other experimental fashions also violate accepted ideas about the need for a unified and legible surface for the embodied self. Designer Bernard Wilhelm, for example, created a white deconstructed jumpsuit (2021) that is frayed, fringed, and paint-spattered, with an oversized bodice, knee-length pants, and multiple rows of drawstring cords; the ensemble looks more like a pile of rags than a designer garment. Conventional ideas about beauty are not necessarily important to avant-garde designers, who may look instead for strong ideas or emotions. Rei Kawakubo of Comme des Garçons has always pursued alternative ideas about beauty, perhaps most strikingly with her 1997 "Body Meets Dress, Dress Meets Body" collection, better known in the press as the "Lumps and Bumps" collection, for the way that it flagrantly rejected the traditional idealized feminine silhouette.

Figure 7.16 Rei Kawakubo of Comme des Garçons, dress, *Body Meets Dress, Dress Meets Body* collection, Spring 1997. Photo © The Museum at FIT.

A Replaceable, Updateable Skin

"Clothing is the skin of the skin," writes psychoanalyst Patrick Avrane.[40] Marc Lafrance goes further, emphasizing that Anzieu saw "the body's surface—its skin—as a crucial constituent of the mind's structures and functions."[41] And because "all human bodies have skin," Naomi Segal goes on to argue that

> The skin-ego offers us ... a theory centred on the body metaphor which removes castration from the position it holds in all other psychoanalytic theories ... The penis-phallus is no longer the leading organ, and thus we are not divided by our possession or non-possession of it, however nuanced, politicized, or symbolic. ... If human beings are able to feel and think, it is not by means of a genital organ that some have and others lack—or even that everyone lacks but everyone desires—but by means of the universal human organ, our skin.[42]

Stella North has even mapped out a construct that she calls "the clothing ego," which she believes to be "implicit within [Anzieu's] theory of the skin ego." As she traced "the surfacing of the self" across skin and clothing, she argued that "clothing extends the skin ego schema." What she calls our "first and second skins" are certainly in a reciprocal relationship, and her metaphor of "thinking through clothes" is appealing. Yet I remain unconvinced when she writes: "The body thus becomes an interface of inter-implicating skins: clothing-ego facing skin-ego and skin-ego facing body-ego." Anzieu famously wrote: "to be oneself is first of all to have a skin of one's own." But does this require (as North insists) "the acceptance of one's intersituation with clothing?" And what does this even mean?[43]

Clothing is certainly "a replaceable surface for the self." It may even be, in North's words, "*a replaceable, updateable skin.*" I love that phrase, although I take it metaphorically. North's essay is a serious and important attempt to describe how each of us constructs "a particular clothing-skin-body interface," a specific "face to the world."[44] Yet clothing, however material, is not an integral part of us, the way our skin is. Perhaps because North seems to confuse clothing made of cloth with "dress" (which includes tattooing, muscle-building, hairstyles, and other ways of fashioning the body), I believe that she oversimplifies the sheer liminality and artificiality of dress and fashion. Therefore, I prefer to try to draw on Anzieu's concept of the skin ego, rather than the clothing ego, to elucidate our experiences of dress.

Freud's theories are now thought to have anticipated new findings in brain research, which emphasize the role of the brainstem and the influence of emotions on higher order cognition. Contemporary neuroscience thus also supports Anzieu's belief that *feeling*—in the sense both of touch and emotion—precedes and leads to the ability to think. The thinking ego develops on the foundation of the skin ego.

Fashion certainly arouses emotions, and psychoanalytic ideas about unconscious defense mechanisms, can be extremely useful in understanding how negative emotions, such as anxiety, envy, or shame, influence people's beliefs and behaviors. For example, when we experience

Figure 7.17 Viktor & Rolf, Autumn/Winter 2020 haute couture. Photo by Casper Kofi, courtesy Viktor & Rolf.

uncomfortable feelings, like envy, and "want to get rid of" the feeling, we may "project envy into the other person." The envious person will usually be unaware of why they "flaunt … possessions or attributes … in such a way as to provoke envy." Alternatively, "because success can bring with it the fear of envy," a person might "dress down … so that no one would want to envy poor little us."[45]

Many designers deliberately work with emotions. During the COVID-19 pandemic, for example, Dutch designers Viktor & Rolf created an extraordinary couture collection in 2020 focusing on the emotions that many people were experiencing. As each look appeared in the filmed fashion show, a voice commented on the style, as was customary in fashion shows of the past. For example, when a model appeared wearing a long black coat covered with large spikes, the voice said: "You're angry, you have a right to be angry." Another flowing pink dress was covered with different emojis, signifying anger, sadness, happiness, and shock.

Figure 7.18 Viktor & Rolf, Autumn/Winter 2020 haute couture. Photo by Casper Kofi, courtesy Viktor & Rolf.

Feelings, such as anxiety or fear, can be symbolically represented, when artists or designers imagine bodies in need of extra protection. Anouk Wipprecht's Spider Dress 2.0 for INTEL is programmed to protectively extend spider-like appendages whenever someone comes too close. A dress by avant-garde Japanese designer Kei Ninomiya of Noir is covered with many sharp plastic spikes, like a porcupine or a rose. Common in nature, this defensive mechanism can present an extremely aggressive visual impression.

Figure 7.19 Spider Dress 2.0, dress created by Anouk Wipprecht for INTEL (2015) collaboration with Philip H. Wilck. Photography by Jason Perry.

Figure 7.20 Noir Kei Ninomiya, dress, Fall 2021. Photograph courtesy Comme des Garçons

The metaphor of the skin ego may be especially relevant to modern fashion because it seems that "the skin in itself has never been so intensely, libidinally figured as in our era." This is partly related to the ubiquity of exposed skin, but also perhaps "because of the multiplication of skin surfaces [and] signifying screens."[46] In recent years, Anzieu's work has attracted increased attention within the field of psychoanalysis, as well as in other disciplines, from cultural studies to design, where the proliferation of artificial and digital skins has led us to think more about the multiple meanings of skin. Personal fashion blogs, for example, offer "a tool for potential self-representation [that] many women have appropriated." As Agnès Rocamora observes, in many cases "the screen/mirror shows an idealized self the viewer can identify with and therefore appropriate to work on her own identity construction, whilst also indulging in the pleasure of voyeurism that her status as a spectator grants her."[47]

Figure 7.21 Issey Miyake, bustier, 1983. Photo © The Museum at FIT.

8

Bodies to Wear

Fashion has become increasingly "gender-fluid" in the twenty-first century. This development is almost certainly related to growing public awareness of transgender and non-binary individuals, together with a corresponding paradigm shift in thinking about gender and sexuality. Many people today increasingly question the binary system (male/female, homosexual/heterosexual), replacing it with a spectrum that is also fluid. In 2014, Laverne Cox, star of the popular Netflix series *Orange is the New Black*, was featured on the cover of *Time* magazine, where she was described as "one of the estimated 1.5 million Americans who identify as transgender." Cox recalled having been bullied, assaulted, and put into therapy for acting feminine. But when she gave a public speech in San Francisco, "I stand before you as a proud African-American trans woman," the audience erupted in cheers.[1] Yet trans visibility has also triggered renewed hostility in a politicized environment. In 2023, Cox was horrified by the "ferocious … backlash against trans."[2]

Contrary to popular belief, the concept of psychosexual "gender" (as opposed to biological "sex") was *not* a feminist idea that emerged in the 1970s. It actually originated in the mid-1950s, along with the new technology of sex/gender reassignment surgery. This was the period when Christine Jorgensen's 1952 "sex change" made headlines around the world. John Money, professor of medical psychology at Johns Hopkins University, used the term "gender roles" as early as 1955. Money is a controversial figure, because he surgically modified many intersex children, as well as boys whose genitals had been damaged.[3]

Figure 8.1 Laverne Cox wearing a vintage Thierry Mugler jacket from the A/W 1990 collection. Photography by Sequoia Emmanuelle @sequoiaemmanuelle. Photo assistant: @mariaqphotography. Makeup: @theladydeja. Hair: @kiyahwright1. Styled by: @christinajpacelli.

Gender entered Freudian psychoanalysis about a decade later, via the work of Robert Stoller, whose idea of "core gender identity" developed from Money's hypothesis that "sex and gender are not necessarily in a relation of symmetry." Stoller argued that "although the penis contributes to the sentiment of being male, it is not essential."[4] Many feminists subsequently adopted the idea of gender as socially constructed and extremely malleable. The longevity of the term "gender" and its strategic importance for women, queer, and transgender people favor its use, although the medical origins and deployment of the concept of gender remain problematic.

"Beyond pink and blue, dolls and cars … how does a child begin to identify unconsciously as a girl or a boy?" asked Lacanian psychoanalyst Patricia Gherovici in her book *Please Select Your Gender* (2010).[5] According to Gherovici:

> Sexual difference is neither just the body (as biological substrata) nor the psychic introjections of the social performance of gender (a socially constructed role). Neither the perspective of biological essentialism nor that of social constructivism have been able to solve the problem of unconscious sexual difference. Since sexual difference is neither sex nor gender, sex needs to be symbolized, and gender needs to be embodied.[6]

Fashion provides *one* way in which this happens, she argues. Narrative is another.

In her 2024 lecture "Bodies to Wear," Gherovici said: "Thirty years after Judith Butler's *Gender Trouble* … fashion is no longer just a question of clothes; it is also about bodies."[7] We have always fashioned our bodies, of course, through practices ranging from tattoos to plastic surgery. But transgender people make the artificiality of this self-fashioning crystal clear, because they seek to live in a body that is gendered differently from the one they were "assigned at birth." As Kate Bornstein put it in her book *Gender Outlaw: On Men, Women, and the Rest of Us*: "My identity as a transsexual lesbian whose female lover is becoming a man is manifested in my fashion statement; both my identity and fashion are based on collage. You know—a little bit from here, a little bit from there? Sort of a cut-and-paste thing."[8]

"Gender-Fluid Fashion is Gaining Traction"

The fashion system includes many LGBTQ+ people, and has long featured gender-bending fashions and even trans models. In his review of Gucci's Fall 2015 menswear collection, the first designed by Alessandro Michele, fashion journalist Tim Blanks emphasized its "blurred gender divide" and "very deliberate sissiness." The male models were "lank-haired ephebes" wearing chiffon blouses with "pussy bows."[9] Both male and female models wore fur-lined mules and carried handbags. Five years later, fashion writers have tended to see Michele's first fashion show for Gucci in 2015 as having launched a gender-bending fashion revolution. This is an oversimplification. Already in 2013, Jonathan W. Anderson

Figure 8.2 Alessandro Michele for Gucci, man's ensemble, Spring 2017. Photo © The Museum at FIT.

put male models in leather dresses and ruffled hot pants, which used "patterns drafted for women." Dismissed by some as "ridiculous," his "radical, unisex designs" also received serious attention.[10] Other designers, such as Rick Owens, have long designed dresses for men, along with other gender-fluid styles, like high-heeled platform boots. Yet Michele's take on maximalist gender-fluidity had a definite impact on fashion.

"They call me the ruler of gender fluidity, but, to me, I was just pulling out beauty," said Michele in 2020, adding that he preferred hybrids, "male-but-female; female-but-male," to more "conventionally beautiful people."[11] In the fashion industry, there are also commercial reasons to focus on novelty and transgression, which tend to appeal to younger customers. From the beginning, young people bought a lot of Gucci. As Ken Downing, then the fashion director of Neiman Marcus, told *The New York Times* in 2015: "What we're seeing now is a seismic shift in fashion, a widening acceptance of a style with no boundaries, one that reflects the way young people dress." Trend forecaster Lucie Greene also argued that "the whole perception of sexual orientation is being challenged by the millennials. Among the cohort of 12-to-19-year-olds, defining Generation Z, the lines between male and female are becoming increasingly blurred."[12]

Some of the recent popularity of gender-bending style may have reflected fashion's perennial fixation with rock stars of the past, such as David Bowie. "My clothes are very influenced by the clothes worn by men like David Bowie," says fashion designer Bella Freud, great-granddaughter of Sigmund Freud. "I'm interested in the way a girl looks boyish—not mannish or masculine." Her trouser suits for women "bring out their femininity," she says, while also making them "look like hot guys." Freud sees "people being less constrained by their roles," and recognizes similarities between the fashion situation in the 2020s, the 1920s, and the 1970s, periods of "a lot of freedom," and gender fluidity in modern fashion.[13] Gender-bending style is also evidence of the fashion world's delight in whatever is opposed to the normal or conventional. ("Normal is a setting on the dryer.")

For her podcast *Fashion Neurosis*, Bella Freud invites guests such as Rick Owens to lie on the couch and free-associate. Owens mused that his childhood body dysmorphia may

Figure 8.3 David Bowie wearing a dress designed by Michael Fish at his home, Haddon Hall, Beckenham, Kent, 1971. Trinity Mirror/Mirrorpix/Alamy Stock Photo.

have contributed to the way his designs often distort the human figure. "Distortion and exaggeration is always what I'm going for," he says. Freud herself wrote on Instagram: "If I had had a perfect body, I would never have become a designer. My insecurities and self-doubt are what propelled me into the world of creating clothes as a foil for my dissatisfaction and frustration with my appearance."[14]

Although the fashion system has traditionally tended to ignore how bodies, sex, and gender intersect with race, ethnicity, and class, there are individual designers who explore this area. Among them are Grace Wales Bonner, a designer of Caribbean heritage

Figure 8.4 Grace Wales Bonner, man's suit, Spring 2017. Photo © The Museum at FIT.

based in London, whose work explores beautiful representations of Black masculinity. Mexican artist and fashion designer Bárbara Sánchez-Kane also creates extraordinary clothes that deconstruct clichéd ideas about body, sex, and gender within the context of a Catholic and macho culture.

"Gender-fluid fashion is gaining greater traction," reported the *Business of Fashion* in 2022. Women have long adopted styles "outside of their gender identity," but now young men are also increasingly shopping "across gender boundaries," wearing dresses and nail

Figure 8.5 *Mamado* pantsuit by Bárbara Sánchez-Kane as featured in "Amantes Encontrados" for *Vogue Italia*, 2019. Photo by Paola Vivas. Styling by Chino Castilla. Models: Emiliano and Samuel for GUERXS AGENCY MX.

polish.[15] Gender-bending fashion has not only become increasingly visible on fashion runways and in the media, but also some fashion writers have adopted a new vocabulary, derived from cultural and trans studies. In 2019, for example, Wren Sanders wrote an online article for *British Vogue*, in which she argued that: "More than ever, the gender-bending we've grown accustomed to seeing on the runway is accompanied by a growing awareness of and sensitivity to the experiences of trans and gender nonconforming individuals – people for whom the bending of gender is not merely a style, but an identity."[16] Perhaps not coincidentally, this article appeared the year that Laverne Cox became the first transgender model to be featured on the cover of the September 2019 issue of *British Vogue*.

The fashion world tends toward self-congratulation, and critics argue that "there is a risk in theorizing gender fluidity and the inclusion of trans and gender non-conforming bodies in fashion as inherently transgressive." Fashion is a business, and, as Veronica G. Llamas puts it: "Conflating an aesthetic preference for 'gender fluidity' with the language of gender identity can seem like a form of commodification." The mere presence of trans and non-binary models on fashion runways and in fashion media can be a type of "tokenism."[17]

Even as the visibility of trans models and actresses has increased, there have been "wins and shortcomings" on "the new diversity frontier." Obviously, modeling jobs provide opportunities for some trans individuals, who have the preferred physiognomy. But, according to trans model Valentijn de Hingh, the "cisgender gaze" that operates the cameras "has a huge impact on how trans people are represented." The fashion industry also "has a tendency to congratulate itself" for being "the first" to feature a particular model or style, even if they have already been pioneered within "marginalized communities." Is it really so "revolutionary" in 2020 to feature Harry Styles in a Gucci dress on the cover of *American Vogue*?[18]

Looking back at transgender media representation in US fashion periodicals such as *Vogue*, *Harper's Bazaar*, and *Women's Wear Daily*, from 2013 to 2020, Enrique Zhang also saw "the promise and limits of transgender visibility in fashion media." Among the "competing discourses," there was "a growing acceptance of non-normative gender identities," but this seemed to hinge on "trans people's ability to conform to normative gender expression." Yet fashion journalists also, paradoxically, often argued that trans models "subvert" gender norms. Consider this description of Andreja Pejić, who began modeling as an androgynous "male" model and later came out as a transgender woman: "There is nothing masculine about her … [She] is as feminine as my sister, as my mother, as my biologically female friends. This is, of course, the product of extreme effort … not to mention … phenotypic luck. She engages – and dismantles – all one's visceral perceptions of gender."[19]

According to Zhang, fashion magazines also employ a "neoliberal logic of visibility" and "empowerment," which positions trans women, particularly trans women of color, as "role models," while also "depoliticizing" trans activism. Although the promise of "positive representation" does little or nothing to help most trans people, Zhang also identifies "a recent shift towards a social justice framework as trans activists of color are given greater voice in the pages of fashion magazines."[20] Trans designer Pia Davis of No Sesso put it this way: "Let's make sure that real change is happening—that it's not just clickbait."[21]

The Monster Speaks

The fashion world has problems, but the situation is much worse in the field of psychoanalysis, where many practitioners appear to have learned nothing from the profession's egregious history of misogyny, homophobia, and transphobia. It is no wonder that trans people are reluctant to deal with psychoanalysts, unless they have to go into therapy to get letters of recommendation, which are often required in order to access transgender medical care—from puberty blockers to hormones and surgery. Although there are important exceptions, many psychoanalysts continue to pathologize transgender individuals.

In 2019, Paul B. Preciado was invited to speak to an audience of 3,500 psychoanalysts affiliated with the École de la Cause freudienne. When he asked if there were any gay, trans, or non-binary psychoanalysts present, "there was silence, broken by wild laughter." When he said that the field of psychoanalysis needed to deal with new ideas about sexuality and gender, "half the room laughed, while the others cursed or demanded that he leave." One woman shouted, "Don't let him speak, he's Hitler!"[22] Comparing himself to the talking ape Red Peter in a story by Franz Kafka, Preciado said:

> I address myself to you from my 'cage' of a trans man … my body marked by medical and legal discourse as a 'transsexual,' characterized by the majority of your psychoanalytic diagnostics as the subject of an 'impossible metamorphosis' … beyond neurosis, at the edge of or even in psychosis … Oh well, it is starting from this position as mentally ill, where you have sent me, that I address myself to you as the monkey-human of a new era … I am the monster who speaks to you. The monster that you have constructed with your discourse and your clinical practice. I am the monster who has risen and taken speech, not as your patient, but as a citizen, as your monstrous equal.[23]

The room descended into pandemonium, and Preciado was unable to finish his speech, which he later published in a small book dedicated to Judith Butler.

"The trans crisis is upon us," declared Jacques-Alain Miller, Lacan's powerful son-in-law. The year was 2021, and Miller blamed "*La Butler* and her maenads." He boasted that he had "never" read Judith Butler, "not me," but he knew that Butler and "her" frenzied followers had unleashed terrible ideas about "gender." Butler's deliberate "misuse" of Lacanian language had also turned the field of sexuality into a "bordello."[24] Many French Lacanians refuse to use the word "gender" in its "American" sense, and many of them regard transsexuality as a psychosis, caused by a failure of the paternal function. Conservative French Lacanians even predicted a civilizational catastrophe if lesbian or homosexual couples were allowed to marry and have children, insisting that children need to have both a father and a mother. But attitudes like this extend far beyond France.

After 1945, most psychoanalysts "approached the body as bedrock" and "unequivocally located gender as a factual truth residing in anatomical difference." Traditionally, a successful analytic outcome required trans patients to "accept" their "natal sex" and give up their "wish for bodily modification." However, as psychoanalyst Avgi Saketopoulou observed in 2014, a small but growing number of analysts agreed with gender theorist Gayle Solomon that "For all genders … the experience of the body is mediated through fantasy, but it is only in trans bodies that the work of fantasy is observable, as it doesn't fluidly map itself into the flesh."[25]

In an emotionally powerful article, Saketopoulou wrote about her experiences with a little trans girl:

> My six-year-old patient Jenny and I worked together in analytic play therapy two or three times weekly for a year and a half before she was able to share with me something I had known all along from her parents: Jenny had been born male. One day, Jenny confided worriedly: 'I don't want you to think I've been lying to you, but there is something I haven't told you: Dad thinks I'm a boy.' She paused shortly, scanning my face for a reaction to her revelation, then added sadly, 'sometimes I wear boy clothes so his heart doesn't keep breaking'.

Significantly, Saketopoulou did *not* pressure Jenny to accept that she was "really" a boy. She did help Jenny gain insight into her feelings about her body, that, like her father, "she too was confused about how she could be a girl when she had a penis." Eventually, Jenny was able to develop her own positive stories about her personal journey of transformation.[26] She was luckier than most trans patients.

In 2021, Saketopoulou discussed adolescent trans patients with another psychoanalyst, David Bell. When Saketopoulou pointed out that adolescent bodies will irrevocably change without gender-blocking drugs, Bell insisted that adolescents still needed to wait until "they could be helped to become more able to express a less stereotyped version of gender identity, or maybe … accept their homosexuality without undergoing medical and surgical treatments."[27] Saketopoulou would later compare this attitude to "passing off transphobia as psychoanalysis and cruelty as 'clinical logic'."[28]

All children experience developmental conflicts, and all children need to feel seen and validated by their loved ones. Yet LGBTQ+ children have often *not* been "seen" favorably, which can result in deep feelings of shame. Children who grow up to be homophobic or transphobic also struggle with toxic feelings, and any deficits in their emotional development may be triggered by the sight of "out" LBGTQ+ people. According to psychoanalysts David Goldenberg and Patrick Viersen Brown: "Within the context of the 'watch me' aspect of development, we can hypothesize that the freedom of the 'out' homosexual activates resentment in the person with homophobia. The 'out' homosexual or LGBTQ person has retained the pride and self-esteem that derives from ... being seen and appreciated by a parent." Even if they were wounded in childhood, when they grow up, LGBTQ+ people often find a "chosen" family whose members will see and affirm them.

In their article "Fashioning Hate: Driving the Runway of Desire," Goldenberg and Brown write:

> Part of mythological 'gay culture' is the ubiquitous runway, reified in camp and drag, where an 'out' LGBTQ person struts their stuff, walking a runway of display. This display may be merely performative or defiant but can be internally transformative. Exaggerated expressions of sexuality and gender nonconformity ... provide space, through distance, to work through shame and to ... experience the pleasure of a voyeuristic/exhibitionistic dynamic ... that is, [to] be seen, recognized, and securely held.[29]

Tiresias, Patron Saint of Psychoanalysis

Lacan once said that Tiresias, the man-woman seer of Greek mythology, "ought to be the patron saint of psychoanalysis." In her book *Transgender Psychoanalysis: A Lacanian Perspective on Sexual Difference* (2017), Gherovici argues that trans people are not marginal figures suffering from gender trouble. Like Tiresias, they have much to tell us about the different relationships that people have with their bodies. "I think how nice it would be to unzip my body from forehead to navel and go on vacation. But there is no escaping it, I would have to pack myself along," wrote Leslie Feinberg. "All I wanted was liberation ... to live as myself, to clothe myself in a more proper body," wrote Jan Morris. "If I were trapped in that cage again nothing would keep me from my goal ... not even the prospect of death itself."[30]

Gherovici uses Lacanian theory and especially his concept of the *sinthome* as a framework for rethinking sexual difference in terms of creativity, rather than pathology. Lacan had used this archaic term for "symptom" to explore the work of the writer James Joyce. Gherovici takes up this idea and develops a new narrative about the validity of transgender people's desire to live and dress in accordance with their inner sense of self. It is not that they are trapped in the "wrong" body. Rather, like everyone, they are trapped in a *mortal* body that they need to make their own.

Mortality, the prospect of death, is a real issue for trans people. They sometimes feel such an urgent need to take charge of their bodies that they may commit suicide if prevented from doing so. Yet transitioning itself can sometimes feel like death—while also facilitating a rebirth. As Gherovici writes: "Ultimately, the most radical discovery of psychoanalysis is that sex is tied to the death drive ... Reproduction does not guarantee immortality through replication but rather shows the uniqueness (and death) of each individual." What lives on, suggests Gherovici, is "beauty as a denial of death."[31]

Fashion is also a denial of death, since fashion evokes the medieval idea of the king's two bodies, one mortal, the other undying. Thus, the tradition of presenting new fashions every fall and spring implicitly proclaims, "Fashion is dead! Long live fashion!" We find the idea that death is necessary for rebirth expressed repeatedly across time, from Giacomo Leopardi's "Dialogue of Fashion and Death" (1842) to Chanel's statement that: "Fashion must die and die quickly, in order that it can begin to live." Philosopher Walter Benjamin also observed that: "Fashion mocks death."[32]

Figure 8.6 Undercover, dress, Fall 2020, Japan. Photo © The Museum at FIT.

In *Beyond the Pleasure Principle* (1920), Freud proposed that the human mind is torn between Eros (love and life) and Thanatos (death and destruction). Barbara Vinken has argued that, traditionally: "Fashion tried to deny death, but now it teaches us to live beautifully with death. Through fashion, one tries on one's own mortality, [revealing] the irreducible individuality of each person in the face of death."[33] Traditionally, most fashion designers have tried to deny anything that conflicts with a seamless ideal of beauty. Only a few, such as Schiaparelli, dared to play with the imagery of mortality. However, just as many

Figure 8.7 Noir Kei Ninomiya, Spring/Summer 2023 collection.
Photo courtesy Comme des Garçons.

artists have argued that destruction is necessary for creation, so also, in recent years, have a number of avant-garde designers associated fashion with images of death, destruction, and decay. In one of his collections for Undercover, for example, Jun Takahashi juxtaposed roses and razor blades on many of the garments. Knowing his work, it is possible to interpret this as symbolic of the creative struggle between Eros and Thanatos.

Fashion also helps individuals create narratives of transformation. Laverne Cox recalled how she was attracted by the tailoring of a 1988 Mugler jacket, whose hourglass silhouette appealed to her. "This is such a good example of what a Mugler blazer does for the body, being a trans woman and not very shapely. The construction, the architecture of it all, is really what excites me." Soon she had not only acquired an extraordinary collection of vintage Mugler, she had also become a true expert on fashion.[34] In their article "The Deceptive Mirror," dress scholars Ruggerone and Strauss also emphasize the experience of *wearing* clothes. Drawing on the work of Gilles Deleuze and Félix Guattari, they argue that: "We do not desire clothes as objects we lack, but as bodies we want to couple with to go out in the world."[35]

If the body is not a given, fixed entity, but rather involves a process of embodiment or "a becoming of the body," then the "gender trouble" presumed to affect transgender people is actually a universal condition. Using the Lacanian concept of the sinthome, which ties together the Imaginary, the Symbolic, and the Real, Gherovici argues that trans people identify not with the body into which they were born, but with the art of artifice. Yet it is not only transgender individuals who have an artificial and contingent relationship with their bodies. All human beings are the opposite of "natural." We are not born, but rather *become* who we are, and that becoming continues throughout our lives. By exploring the development of our individual subjectivity, psychoanalysis gives us greater insight into the art of living.

NOTES

Introduction

1. Peter Gay, *The Freud Reader* (New York: W.W. Norton & Company, 1995).
2. Sherry Turkle, *Psychanalytic Politics: Jacques Lacan and Freud's French Revolution* (London: Guilford Press, 1992), 210–11.
3. Adam Phillips, "The Interested Party," in *The Beast in the Nursery* (New York: Pantheon Books, 1998), 8.
4. Lynn Hunt, "Psychology, Psychoanalysis, and Historical Thought," in *A Companion to Western Historical Thought*, ed. Lloyd Kramer and Sara Maza (London: Blackwell Publishers, 2002), 337–9.
5. Janine-Chassaeguet-Smirgel, *The Body as Mirror of the World*, translated by Sophie Leighton (London: Free Association Books, 2005), xiv.
6. Hunt, "Psychology, Psychoanalysis, and Historical Thought," 345–7.
7. Valerie Steele, *Fashion and Eroticism: Ideals of Feminine Beauty from the Victorian Era to the Jazz Age* (Oxford: Oxford University Press, 1985), 9.
8. Hervé Mazurel, *L'inconscient ou l'oubli de l'histoire. Profondeurs, metamorphoses et revolutions de la vie affective* (Paris: Éditions La Découverte, 2021), 15.
9. Valerie Steele, "The F Word," *Lingua Franca: The Review of Academic Life* (April 1991): 17, 20.
10. Joanne Entwistle, *The Fashioned Body: Fashion, Dress and Modern Social Theory* (Cambridge: Polity, [2000] 2015), 1.
11. Mary Ellen Roach-Higgens and Joanne B. Eicher, "Dress and Identity," in *Dress and Identity*, ed. M.E. Roach-Higgens, J.B. Eicher, and Kim K.P. Johnson (New York: Fairchild Publications, 1995), 7–18. See also J. Entwistle, "The Dressed Body," in *Body Dressing*, ed. Joanne Entwistle and Elizabeth Wilson (Oxford: Berg, 2001).
12. Eve Golden, "Clothes, Inside Out," in *I Shop, Therefore I Am: Compulsive Buying and The Search for Self*, ed. April Lane Benson (Norvale: Jason Aronson, 2000), 149.
13. *The Oxford English Dictionary*, quoted in Carolyn Mair, *The Psychology of Fashion* (New York: Routledge, 2018), 3.
14. Rachel Mesch, *Before Trans: Three Gender Stories from Nineteenth-Century France* (Stanford: Stanford University Press, 2020), 8–9.
15. Elizabeth Grosz, "The Body," in *Feminism and Psychoanalysis: A Critical Dictionary*, ed. Elizabeth Wright (Oxford: Blackwell, 1992), 36.
16. Sigmund Freud, *The Ego and the Id*, S.E. vol. 19, 26.
17. C. Baerveldt and P. Voestermans, "The Body as a Selfing Device," cited in Anne Boultwood and Robert Jerrard, "Ambivalence, and Its Relation to Fashion and the Body," *Fashion Theory* 4, no 3 (2000): 303.
18. Suzy Menkes, "The Freud of Fashion," *International Herald Tribune* (February 11–12, 2012): 14–15.
19. Victoria Kelley, "A Superficial Guide to the Deeper Meanings of Surface," in *Surface Tensions: Surface, Finish, and the Meaning of Objects*, ed. Glenn Adamson and Victoria Kelley (Manchester: Manchester University Press, 2013), 13.

20. Jacques Lacan, "Seminar on 'The Purloined Letter'," in *Écrits*, Jacques Lacan, translated by Bruce Fink (New York: W.W. Norton, 2006).
21. Dani Cavallaro and Alexandra Warwick, *Fashioning the Frame: Boundaries, Dress and Body* (New York: Berg, 1998), xxiii.
22. Elizabeth Wilson, *Adorned in Dreams: Fashion and Modernity* (Berkeley: University of California Press, 1985), 11.
23. Janice Miller, "Sigmund Freud: More than a Fetish: Fashion and Psychoanalysis," in *Thinking Through Fashion: A Guy to Key Theorists*, ed. Agnès Rocamora and Anneke Smelik (New York: I.B. Tauris, 2016), 46.
24. Gillian Rose, *Visual Methodologies: An Introduction to the Interpretation of Visual Materials* (London: Sage, 2001), 150.
25. Stella North, "The Surfacing of the Self: The Clothing-Ego," in *Skin, Culture and Psychoanalysis*, ed. Sheila L. Cavanagh, Angela Failler, and Rachel Alpha Johnson Hurst (New York: Palgrave Macmillan, 2013), 82.

Chapter 1

1. Deborah P. Margolis, *Freud and His Mother: Preoedipal Aspects of Freud's Personality* (Northvale: Jason Aronson, 1996), 3–6, 17, 117, 152, 156–7.
2. Sigmund Freud, *The Complete Letters of Sigmund Freud to Wilhelm Fliess 1887–1904*, translated and edited by Jeffrey Masson (Cambridge: Harvard University Press, 1985), 272.
3. Sigmund Freud, *Letters to Wilhelm Fliess*, 267–9.
4. Peter Gay, *Freud: A Life for Our Time* (New York: W.W. Norton, 1988), 11–12.
5. David Kuchta, *The Three-Piece Suit and Modern Masculinity, England, 1550–1850* (Berkeley: University of California Press, 2002), 2.
6. Jonathan C. Kaplan, "The Man in the Suit: Jewish Men and Fashion in fin-de-siècle Vienna," *Fashion Theory: Journal of Dress, Body and Culture* 25, no 3 (2020): 339–66.
7. Catherine Joubert and Sarah Stern, *Déshabillez-moi: Psychanalyse des comportements vestimentaires* (Paris: Fayard, [2005] 2012), 9–10.
8. Martin Freud, *Glory Reflected: Sigmund Freud – Man and Father* (London: Angus and Robertson, 1957), 25.
9. Christopher Oldstone-Moore, *Of Beards and Men: The Revealing History of Facial Hair* (Chicago: University of Chicago Press, 2016), 196–7.
10. Ernst L. Freud, ed. *The Letters of Sigmund Freud* (New York: Basic Books, 1975), 233.
11. Ernst Freud, *The Letters of Sigmund Freud*, 27.
12. Janet Stewart, *Fashioning Vienna: Adolf Loos's Cultural Criticism* (New York: Routledge, 2000), 125.
13. Adolf Loos, "Men's Fashion" (1898) in *The Rise of Fashion: A Reader*, ed. Daniel Leonhard Purdy (Minneapolis: University of Minnesota Press, 2004), 94–5.
14. Ernst Freud, *The Letters of Sigmund Freud*, 102.
15. Ernst Freud, *The Letters of Sigmund Freud*, 91.
16. Ernst Freud, *The Letters of Sigmund Freud*, 58–9.
17. Ernst Freud, *The Letters of Sigmund Freud*, 132, 143–4, 146.
18. Ernst Freud, *The Letters of Sigmund Freud*, 148–9.
19. Ernst Freud, *The Letters of Sigmund Freud*, 6.
20. Ernst Freud, *The Letters of Sigmund Freud*, 79.
21. George Makari, *Revolution in Mind: The Creation of Psychoanalysis* (New York: Harper Perenial, 2009), 9.
22. Robert A. Nye, "The Medical Origins of Sexual Fetishism," in *Fetishism as Cultural Discourse*, ed. Emily Apter and William Pietz (New York: Cornell University Press, 2005), 14–15.
23. Quoted in Georges Didi-Huberman, *Invention of Hysteria: Charcot and the Photographic Iconography of the Salpêtrière*, translated by Alisa Hartz (Cambridge: MIT Press, 2003), 80.
24. Asti Hustvedt, *Medical Muses: Hysteria in Nineteenth-Century Paris* (New York: W.W. Norton & Company, 2011).
25. Anouchka Grose, "Reclaiming Hysteria," in *Hysteria Today*, ed. Anouchka Grose (London: Karnac, 2016), xxiv, xxvii.
26. Ernst Freud, *The Letters of Sigmund Freud*, 195, 193.
27. Ernst Freud, *The Letters of Sigmund Freud*, 187.
28. F.T. Vischer, "Fashion and Cynicism" (1879), in *The Rise of Fashion: A Reader*, ed. Daniel Leonard Purdy, 156–9, and quoted in Frederich Wendel, *Weib und Mode* (Dresdin: Paul Aretz Verlag, 1928), 173–5.
29. Anthony Shelton, "The Chameleon Body: Power, Mutilation and Sexuality," in *Fetishism: Visualising Power and Desire*, ed. Anthony Shelton

30 Rosalind C. Morris and Daniel H. Leonard, *The Returns of Fetishism: Charles de Brosses and the Afterlives of an Idea* (Chicago: Chicago University Press, 2017), 45.

31 Karl Marx, *Economic and Philosophic Manuscripts of 1844*, in *Marx-Engels Collected Works* (Moscow: Progress, 1975), 312.

32 Karl Marx, *Capital*, vol. 1, translated by Ben Fowles (New York: Penguin, [1967] 1976), 165.

33 Alfred Binet, *Le Fetichisme dans l'Amour* (Paris: FV Éditions, [1887] 2014), 4–7.

34 Beth Archer Brombert, *Edouard Manet: Rebel in a Frock Coat* (Boston: Little Brown, 1996), 384, quoted in Valerie Steele, *The Corset: A Cultural History* (New Haven: Yale University Press, 2003), 113.

35 Martin Freud, *Sigmund Freud: Man and Father* (New York: Vanguard, 1958), 125.

36 Ernst Freud, *The Letters of Sigmund Freud*, 176.

37 Brett Kahr, "Letter from London: Four Unknown Freud Anecdotes," *American Imago* 67, no. 2 (2010): 307–8.

38 Rosalind Minsky, *Psychoanalysis and Culture: Contemporary States of Mind* (New Brunswick: Rutgers University Press, 1998), 185–211, 185, 198.

39 Barry Richards, *Disciplines of Delight: The Psychoanalysis of Popular Culture* (London: Free Association Books, 1994), 1, 90–7, 109–10.

40 Helga Dittmar, "The Role of Self Image in Excessive Buying," in *I Shop, Therefore I Am: Compulsive Buying and The Search for Self*, ed. April Lane Benson (Northvale: Jason Aronson, 2000), 107–11.

41 Alison Clarke and Daniel Miller, "Fashion and Anxiety," *Fashion Theory* 6, no. 2 (2002): 192.

42 Werner Muensterberger, *Collecting: An Unruly Passion* (Princeton: Princeton University Press, 1994), 9, 235, 242. See also Janine Burke, *The Sphinx on the Table: Sigmund Freud's Art Collection and the Development of Psychoanalysis* (New York: Walker and Company, 2006).

Chapter 2

1 Eli Zaretsky, *Secrets of the Soul: A Social and Cultural History of Psychoanalysis* (New York: Alfred A. Knopf, 2004), 5.

2 Sigmund Freud, *An Outline of Psycho-analysis*, Standard Edition, vol. 23 (1940), 286.

3 Jonathan Lear, *Open Minded: Working Out the Logic of the Soul* (Cambridge: Harvard University Press, 1998), 27.

4 Eric Kandel, *The Age of Insight: The Quest to Understand the Unconscious in Art, Mind, and Brain, from Vienna 1900 to the Present* (New York: Random House, 2012), 14.

5 Sigmund Freud, *The Interpretation of Dreams*, S.E., vol. 5, 354–6, 373, 377. See also Freud, "Fragment of an Analysis of a Case of Hysteria," S.E. vol. 7, 1–22.

6 Sigmund Freud, "Contribution à la theorie du rêve," in *Les Premiers Psychanalystes* (Paris: Gallimard, 1979), quoted in Patrick Avrane, *Quands les vêtements nous déshabillent* (Paris: Presses Universitaires de France, 2024), 90–1.

7 Mario Perniola, "Between Clothing and Nudity," in *Fashion: Critical and Primary Sources*, vol. 1: *Late Medieval to Renaissance*, ed. Peter McNeil (New York: Berg, 2009), 95–7.

8 Dvora Miller-Florsheim, "Family Secrets as a Component of Disturbances in Gender Identity Formation," *Clinical Studies: International Journal of Psychoanalysis* 1, no. 2 (1995): 72.

9 Claire Pajaczkowska and Ivan Ward, ed. *Shame and Sexuality: Psychoanalysis and Visual Culture* (New York: Routledge, 2008), 9.

10 Philippa Levine, "States of Undress: Nakedness and the Colonial Imagination," *Victorian Studies* 50, no. 2 (2008): 189–90, 192.

11 Ruth Barcan, *Nudity: A Cultural Anatomy* (Oxford: Berg, 2004), 16.

12 M.J. Rantala, "Evolution of Nakedness in *Homo sapiens*," *Journal of Zoology* 273 (2007): 1.

13 Winfried Menninghaus, "Caprices of Fashion in Culture and Biology: Charles Darwin's Aesthetics of Ornament," in *Philosophical Perspectives on Fashion*, ed. Giovanni Matteucci and Stefano Marino (London: Bloomsbury, 2017), 146–7.

14 Sigmund Freud, *Totem and Taboo* (1912–1913), *The Standard Edition of the Complete Psychological Works of Sigmund Freud*, translated and edited by James Strachey et al. (London: The Hogarth Press and the Institute of Psychoanalysis, 1953–1975), 24 volumes, vol. 13.

15 Adeline Masquelier, *Dirt, Undress, and Difference: Critical Perspectives on the Body's Surface* (Bloomington: Indiana University Press, 2005), 8.

16 Freud, *The Interpretation of Dreams*, S.E. vol. 4, 244.

17 Freud, *The Interpretation of Dreams*, S.E. vol. 4, 242–3, 238–9.

18 Elana Shapiro, "Adolf Loos and the Fashioning of 'the Other': Memory, Fashion, and Interiors," *Interiors* 2, no. 2 (2011).

19 Didier Anzieu, *Freud's Self Analysis*, translated by Peter Graham (London: The Hogarth Press, 1986), 224–6.

20 Eugenie Lemoine-Luccioni, *La robe: Essai psychanalytique sur le vêtement* (Paris: Le champ freudien aux Editions du Seuil, 1983), 49.

21 Kenneth Clark, *The Nude* (New York: Doubleday, 1959).

22 Elizabeth Wilson, *Adorned in Dreams: Fashion and Modernity* (Berkeley: University of California Press, 1985), 14.

23 Wayne A. Myers, "The Traumatic Element in the Typical Dream of Being Naked," *Journal of the American Psychoanalytic Association* 37, no. 1 (1989): 121.

24 Pajaczkowska and Ward, *Shame and Sexuality*, 3.

25 Freud, "Hysterical Phantasis and their Relation to Bisexuality" (1908), S.E. vol. 9, 166.

26 Freud, "Introductory Lectures in Psychoanalysis," S.E. vol. 15 (1915–16), 153–9.

27 Daniel Pick and Lyndal Roper, "Psychoanalysis, Dreams, History: An Interview with Hanna Segal," *History Workshop Journal* 49 (1999): 165–6.

28 Cathleen Chaffee, ed. *Marisol: A Retrospective* (New York: DelMonico Books, 2023), 174.

29 Carl Jung, *Man and His Symbols* (New York: Dell, 1968).

30 Carl Jung, *Memories, Dreams, Reflections*, edited by Aniela Jaffé (New York: Pantheon, 1963), 394.

31 Catherine Bronniman, *La robe de psyche: Essai de lien entre psychanalyse et vêtement* (Paris: L'Harmattan, 2015), 121, 123–8.

32 Bronniman, *La robe de psyche*, 136–44.

33 New Orleans Museum of Art, *A Queen Within: Adorned Archetypes* (Barrett Barrera Projects, 2018).

34 Freud, *Three Essays on the Theory of Sexuality* (1905), S.E. vol. 7, 135–56, 191, 169.

35 E.V. Welldon, cited in Deanna Holtzman and Nancy Kulish, "Female Exhibitionism: Identification, Competition, and Camaraderie," *International Journal of Psychoanalysis* 93, no. 2 (2012): 276.

36 Freud, "Instincts and Their Vicissitudes," S.E. vol. 14, 127–9.

37 Robert de Montesquiou, *La Divine Comtesse* (Paris, 1913), 203.

38 Freud, *Three Essays on the Theory of Sexuality*, 156.

39 Freud, *"Civilized" Sexual Morality and Modern Nervous Illness*, S.E. vol. 9.

40 Robert Musil, *The Man Without Qualities*, translated by Eithne Wilkins and Ernst Kaiser (London: Secker and Warburg, 1960), vol. 1, 331–2, 337.

41 Freud, *Jokes and Their Relation to the Unconscious*, S.E. vol. 8, 98.

42 Freud, *Jokes and Their Relation to the Unconscious*, S.E. vol. 8, 98.

43 Karl Kraus, "The Eroticism of Clothes" (1906), in *The Rise of Fashion*, ed. Daniel Leonard Purdy (Minneapolis: University of Minnesota Press, 2004), 241–2.

44 "Freud and Fetishism: Previously Unpublished Minutes of the Vienna Psychoanalytic Society," edited and translated by Louis Rose, *Psychoanalytic Quarterly* 57 (1988): 155–6.

45 "Freud and Fetishism," 155–6.

46 Freud, "Fetishism," S.E. vol. 21, 129, 154.

47 Freud, *Three Essays*, S.E. vol. 7, 153–5.

48 Jann Matlock, "Masquerading Women, Pathologized Men: Cross-Dressing, Fetishism, and the Theory of Perversion, 1882–1935," in *Fetishism as Cultural Discourse*, ed. Emily Apter and William Pietz (Ithaca: Cornell University Press, 1993), 33.

49 Gaëtan Gatian de Clérambault, 'Passion erotique des etoffes chez la femme" (1908), in *La passion des etoffes chez un neuro-psychiatre*, ed. Yolande Papetti et al. (Paris: Solin, 1990), 34–6.

50 Joan Copjec, "The Sartorial Superego," in *Read My Desire: Lacan Against the Historicists* (London: Verso, 2015), 80–2, 87, 106–9.

51 See Lorraine Gamman, "Self-Fashioning, Gender Display, and Sexy Girl Shoes: What's at Stake – Female Fetishism or Narcissism?," in *Footnotes on Shoes*, ed. Shari Benstock and Suzanne Ferriss (New Brunswick: Rutgers University Press, 2001),

93, 99; and Lorraine Gamman and Merja Makinen, *Female Fetishism* (New York: New York University Press, 1994).

52 Freud, "On Narcissism: An Introduction," S.E. vol. 14, 74, 88–9.

53 Freud, *Three Essays on the Theory of Sexuality*, S.E. vol. 7, 145, note 1; and Freud, "On Narcissism," S.E. vol. 14, 67–102.

54 Freud, "On Narcissism," S.E. vol. 14, 74, 88–9.

55 Freud, "Three Essays," S.E. vol. 7, 195.

56 Freud, "Femininity," S.E. vol. 22, 132.

57 Freud, "Some Physical Consequences of the Anatomical Distinction between the Sexes," S.E. 19.

58 Elizabeth Lunbeck, *The Americanization of Narcissism* (Cambridge: Harvard University Press, 2014), 139.

59 Sylvia Bliss, "The Significance of Clothes," *American Journal of Psychology* 27 (1916): 221.

Chapter 3

1 Mary Louise Roberts, *Civilization Without Sexes: Reconstructing Gender in Postwar France, 1917–1927* (Chicago: University of Chicago Press, 1994), 19–20.

2 Valerie Steele, *Fashion and Eroticism: Ideals of Feminine Beauty from the Victorian Era Through the Jazz Age* (Oxford: Oxford University Press, 1985).

3 Maude Bass-Krueger, "Fashion, Gender, and Anxiety," in *French Fashion, Women & the First World War*, ed. Maude Bass-Krueger and Sophie Kurkdjian (New Haven: Yale University Press and the Bard Graduate Center, 2019).

4 Eli Zaretsky, *Secrets of the Soul: A Social and Cultural History of Psychoanalysis* (New York: Alfred A. Knopf, 2004), 144, 150.

5 Christine Bard, *Les Garçonnes: Modes et fantasmes des Années folles* (Paris: Flammarion, 1998), 7–14.

6 Ivan Crozier, "(De-)Constructing Sexual Kinds Since 1750," in *The Routledge History of Sex and the Body, 1500 to the Present*, ed. Sarah Toulalan and Kate Fisher (New York: Routledge, 2013), 142, 157.

7 Nicole G. Albert, *Lesbian Decadence: Representations in Art and Literature of Fin-de-siècle France*, translated by Nancy Erber and William Peniston (New York: Harrington Park Press, 2016).

8 Bard, *Les Garçonnes*, 11.

9 Robert McAlmon, quoted in Allen Ellenzweig, *George Platt Lynes: The Daring Eye* (Oxford: Oxford University Press, 2021), 36.

10 Tamara Chaplin, "'A Woman Dressed Like a Man': Gender Trouble at the Sapphic Cabaret, Paris, 1930–1960," *French Historical Studies* 44, no. 4 (2021), 711–16.

11 Cocteau, quoted in François Buot, *Gay Paris: Une histoire du Paris interlope entre 1900 et 1940* (Paris: Fayard, 2013), 71.

12 Kit Heyam, *Before We Were Trans: A New History of Gender* (New York: Seal Press, 2022), 3.

13 James Steakley, "Cinema and Censorship in the Weimar Republic: The Case of Anders an Die Andern," *Film History* 11, no. 2 (1999): 183.

14 Sigmund Freud, "Anonymous (Letter to an American Mother)," in *The Letters of Sigmund Freud*, ed. Ernst Freud, 423–4.

15 Freud, *Three Essays on the Theory of Sexuality*, footnote added in 1915, 146n.

16 Rubén Gallo, *Freud's Mexico: Into the Wilds of Psychoanalysis* (Cambridge: MIT Press, 2010), 15–17, 20, 50.

17 Gallo, *Freud's Mexico*, 50–1, 53.

18 Jessica Schmidt, "Subversion in Style: Clothing, Identity, and Social Change in 1920s Paris," *Footnotes* 2 (2009): 26.

19 Susan B. Kaiser, *The Social Psychology of Clothing: Symbolic Appearances in Context* (New York: Fairchild, 1997), 539.

20 Georg Simmel, "Fashion," *American Journal of Sociology* 62, no. 6 (1957): 552.

21 Paul Morand, *L'Allure de Chanel* (Paris: Hermann, 1904), quoted in Valerie Steele, *Women of Fashion: Twentieth-Century Designers* (New York: Rizzoli, 1991), 40.

22 Salvador Dalí, *The Unspeakable Confessions of Salvador Dalí* (New York: Quill, 1981), 212.

23 Christopher Bollas, *Being a Character: Psychoanalysis and Self Experience* (New York: Hill and Wang, 1992), 39, 71, 272.

24 Madeleine Pelletier, quoted in Whitney Chadwick and Tirza True Latimer, *The Modern Woman Revisited: Paris Between the Wars* (New Brunswick: Rutgers University Press, 2003), 6.

25 Athol Hughes, "Joan Riviere and the Masquerade," *Psychoanalysis and History* 6, no. 2 (2004): 165.

26 Quoted in Stephen Heath, "Joan Riviere and the Masquerade," in *Formations of Fantasy*, ed. Victor Burgin et al. (New York: Methuen, 1986), 47.

27 Athol Hughes, "Joan Riviere: Her Life and Work," in *The Inner World and Joan Riviere: Collected Papers 1920–1958*, ed. Athol Hughes (London: Karnac Books, 1991), 10–16; Heath, "Joan Riviere and the Masquerade," 45–6.

28 Eli Zaretsky, *Secrets of the Soul: A Social and Cultural History of Psychoanalysis* (New York: Alfred A. Knopf, 2004), 149, 151.

29 Joan Riviere, "Womanliness as a Masquerade," in *Formations of Fantasy*, ed. Victor Burgin, James Donald, and Cora Kaplan (New York: Methuen, 1986), 356. See also "Womanliness as a Masquerade," in *The Inner World and Joan Riviere: Collected Papers: 1920–1958*, ed. Athol Hughes (London: Karnac Books, 1991).

30 Joan Riviere, "Womanliness as a Masquerade," in *Formations of Fantasy*, Burgin et al., 35–9.

31 Heath, "Joan Riviere and the Masquerade," 47.

32 Athol Hughes, *The Inner World and Joan Riviere* (London: Karnac Books, 1991), see especially "Joan Riviere: Her life and Work"; Athol Hughes, "Personal Experiences—Professional Interests: Joan Riviere and Femininity," *The International Journal of Psychoanalysis* 78 (1997): 899–911; Athol Hughes, "Joan Riviere and the Masquerade," *Psychoanalysis and History* 6 no. 2 (2004): 161–75.

33 Riviere, "Womanliness as a Masquerade," in Burgin, 38.

34 J.C. Flügel, "Clothes Symbolism and Clothes Ambivalence," *International Journal of Psycho-Analysis* 10 (January 1, 1929): 205–17. See also J.C. Flügel, *The Psychology of Clothes* (London: Hogarth Press, 1930), 20–2.

35 Flügel, *The Psychology of Clothes*, 160–1.

36 James Laver, *Taste and Fashion from the French Revolution until Today* (London: George G. Harrap, 1937), 252–4.

37 James Laver, *A Concise History of Costume and Fashion* (New York: Scribner's, 1969), 241.

38 Flügel, *The Psychology of Clothes*, 208–9. See also 203–4, 210–13.

39 Quoted in Michael Carter, "J.C. Flügel and the Nude Future," in *Fashion Classics from Carlyle to Barthes* (New York: Berg, 2003) 97.

40 Barbara Burman, "Better and Brighter Clothes: The Men's Dress Reform Party, 1929–1940," *Journal of Design History* 8 no. 4 (1995): 287, 275.

41 Flügel, *The Psychology of Clothes*, 110.

42 Chloe Chapin, "Masculine Renunciation or Rejection of the Feminine? Revisiting J.C. Flügel's *Psychology of Clothes*," *Fashion Theory: The Journal of Dress, Body and Culture* 25, no. 7 (2022): 983–1008.

43 Marion Bower, *The Life and Work of Joan Riviere: Freud, Klein and Female Sexuality* (New York: Routledge, 2019), 121.

44 Flügel, *The Psychology of Clothes*, 189.

45 Flügel, *The Psychology of Clothes*, 208–9. See also 203–4, 210–13.

46 Flügel, *The Psychology of Clothes*, 234–7. See also Michael Carter, *Fashion Classics from Carlyle to Barthes* (New York: Berg, 2003).

47 Flügel, "Clothes Symbolism and Clothes Ambivalence, 205–17.

48 Flügel, *The Psychology of Clothes*, 147.

49 Grace Q. Vicary, "Visual Art as Social Data: The Renaissance Codpiece," *Cultural Anthropology* 4, no. 1 (1989): 3. See also Peter Ucko, "Penis Sheaths: A Comparative Study," *Royal Anthropological Society Proceedings* (1969): 58; and Susan J. Vincent, *The Anatomy of Fashion: Dressing the Body from the Renaissance to Today* (New York: Berg, 2009), 103.

50 Will Fisher, *Materializing Gender in Early Modern English Literature and Culture* (Cambridge: Cambridge University Press, 2006), 59–82.

51 Will Fisher, "'Had it a codpiece,' 'twere a man indeed': The Codpiece as Constitutive Accessory in Early Modern English Culture," in *Ornamentalism: The Art of Renaissance Accessories*, ed. Bella Mirabella (Ann Arbor: University of Michigan Press, 2016), 102, 123–4.

52 Flügel, "Clothes Symbolism and Clothes Ambivalence," 216.

53 Diego Semerene, "Tailoring the Impenetrable Body All over Again: Digitality, Muscle, and the Men's Suit," in *The Routledge Companion to Fashion Studies* (New York: Routledge, 2022), 167–74.

Chapter 4

1. Valerie Steele, *Women of Fashion* (New York: Rizzoli, 1991), 66.
2. Elsa Schiaparelli, *Shocking Life* (New York: E.P. Dutton & Co., 1954), 59, 64, 67.
3. Schiaparelli, *Shocking Life*, 9–10, 124–5.
4. Caroline Evans, "Masks, Mirrors, and Mannequins: Elsa Schiaparelli and the Decentered Subject," *Fashion Theory* 3, no. 1 (1999): 14.
5. Salvador Dalí, *The Secret Life of Salvador Dalí* (New York: Dial Press, 1942), 167.
6. See David Lomas, *The Haunted Self: Surrealism, Psychoanalysis, Subjectivity* (New Haven: Yale University Press, 2000).
7. Dalí, *The Secret Life of Salvador Dalí*, 122.
8. Schiaparelli, *Shocking Life*, 97.
9. Sherry Turkle, *Psychoanalytic Politics: Jacques Lacan and Freud's French Revolution* (London: Free Association Books, 1992), xiv, 13, 16–18. See also Marion Michel Oliner, *Cultivating Freud's Garden in France* (London: Jason Aronson, 1988).
10. Jacques Lacan, *Écrits*, translated by Bruce Fink (London: W.W. Norton & Company, 2006), 3.
11. Elisabeth Roudinesco, *Jacques Lacan: An Outline of a Life and a History of a System of Thought*, translated by Barbara Bray (Cambridge: Polity Press [1997] 2007), 7–8, 13–14, 242.
12. Roudinesco, *Jacques Lacan*, 7–8, 13–14, 242.
13. Roudinesco, *Jacques Lacan*, 31.
14. Jacques Lacan, "On My Antecedents," in *Écrits*, 51.
15. Jacques Lacan, *De la psychose paranoïaque dans ses rapports avec la personalité* (Paris: Éditions du Seuil, 1975), see especially "Le Cas 'Aimée'," 153–206.
16. Roudinesco, *Jacques Lacan*, 51.
17. Martin Jay, *Downcast Eyes: The Denigration of Vision in Twentieth-Century French Thought* (Berkeley: University of California Press, 1993), 341.
18. Mark Pendergrast, *Mirror Mirror: A History of the Human Love Affair with Reflection* (New York: Basic Books, 2003), 362–9.
19. Jacques Lacan, "The Mirror Stage as Formative of the *I* Function as Revealed in Psychoanalytic Experience" (1949), in *Écrits*, 75–81.
20. Lacan, "On My Antecedents," *Écrits*, 55.
21. Donald Winnicott, *Playing and Reality* (London: Tavistock Publications, 1971), 111–18.
22. Alessandra Lemma, *Under the Skin: A Psychoanalytic Study of Body Modification* (New York: Routledge, 2010), 60–1.
23. Schiaparelli, *Shocking Life*, 17.
24. Paul Schilder, *The Image and Appearance of the Human Body* (London: Routledge, [1935] 1999), 13, 11.
25. Lacan, "The Mirror Stage," 76–8.
26. Amy Lyford, *Surrealist Masculinities: Gender Anxiety and the Aesthetics of Post-World War I Reconstruction in France* (Berkeley: University of California Press 2007), 15–16.
27. Lucy Moyse Ferreira, *Danger in the Path of Chic: Violence in Fashion between the Wars* (London: Bloomsbury Visual Arts, 2022), 1, 77–9.
28. Rachel Alpha Johnston Hurst, "The Skin-Textile in Cosmetic Surgery," in *Skin, Culture and Psychoanalysis*, ed. Sheila L. Cavanagh et al. (New York: Palgrave Macmillan, 2013), 145–6.
29. Jacques Lacan, "Aggressiveness in Psychoanalysis," in Lacan, *Écrits*, 85.
30. Lacan, "Aggressiveness in Psychoanalysis," 85.
31. Diana Tietjens Meyers, *Gender in the Mirror: Cultural Imagery and Women's Agency* (Oxford: Oxford University Press, 2002), 115.
32. Simone de Beauvoir, *The Second Sex* (New York: Vintage, [1949] 1974), 340, 757–8.
33. Lemma, *Under the Skin*, 58–9.
34. Anouchka Grose, *From Anxiety to Zoolander: Notes on Psychoanalysis* (London: Karnac Books, 2018), 90, 97–8.
35. Lemma, *Under the Skin*, 61.
36. Shiaparelli, *Shocking Life*, 245, 255.
37. Caroline Evans, "Fashion," in *Feminism and Psychoanalysis: A Critical Dictionary*, ed. Elizabeth Wright (Oxford: Blackwell, 1992), 89. See also "Image" and "Representation."
38. Dilys Blum, *Shocking! The Art and Fashion of Elsa Schiaparelli* (New Haven: Yale University Press and the Philadelphia Museum of Art, 2004), 191.
39. Caroline Evans and Minna Thornton, *Women and Fashion: A New Look* (New York: Quartet, 1989), 143.
40. Elizabeth Wilson, *Adorned in Dreams: Fashion and Modernity* (Berkeley: University of California Press, 1985), 11.

41 Elisabeth Roudinesco, *Lacan: In Spite of Everything* (New York: Verso, 2014), 11–12.
42 Grose, *From Anxiety to Zoolander*, 41.
43 Roudinesco, *Jacques Lacan*, 79, 170.
44 Lacan, "The Signification of the Phallus," *Écrits*, 583–4.
45 Jean-Michel Rabaté, "Lacan's Turn to Freud," in *The Cambridge Companion to Lacan*, ed. Jean-Michel Rabaté (Cambridge: Cambridge University Press, 2003), 2.
46 Roudinesco, *Jacques Lacan*, 344, 352.
47 Roudinesco, *Jacques Lacan*, 242.
48 Sherry Turkle, *The Empathy Diaries: A Memoir* (New York: Penguin, 2021), 209.
49 Anouchka Grose, "Shrinking Clothes," *Fashion Theory* 24, no. 1 (2020): 85–91.
50 Email from Montserrat Albores Gleason to Valerie Steele, May 31, 2024.

Chapter 5

1 Adrienne Harris, "Foreword," in *Disorienting Sexuality: Psychoanalytic Reappraisals of Sexual Identities*, ed. Thomas Domenici and Ronnie C. Lesser (New York: Routledge, 1995), xi.
2 Dagmar Herzog, *Cold War Freud: Psychoanalysis in an Age of Catastrophes* (Cambridge: Cambridge University Press, 2017), 1.
3 Edmund Bergler, *Fashion and the Unconscious* (New York: Robert Brunner, 1953), 3, vi–viii.
4 Robert Radford, "'Women's Bitterest Enemy': The Uses of the Psychology of Fashion," *Journal of Design History* 6, no. 2 (1993): 115–20.
5 Bergler, *Fashion and the Unconscious*, 3–5.
6 The phrase "spectacular femininity and invisible gay men" is from Annamari Vänskä, "Gender and Sexuality," in *A Cultural History of Dress and Fashion in the Modern Age*, ed. Alexandra Palmer (London: Bloomsbury, 2017).
7 Bergler, 7–9.
8 Christopher Breward, "Couture as Queer Auto/Biography," in *A Queer History of Fashion: From the Closet to the Catwalk*, ed. Valerie Steele (New Haven: Yale University Press, 2013), 129.
9 Franco Zeffirelli, *Zeffirelli, An Autobiography* (New York: Weidenfeld and Nicolson, 1986), 100.
10 Cecil Beaton, *Self-Portrait with Friends* (New York: New York Times Book Company, 1982), 307.
11 Paul Morand, *L'Allure de Chane'* (Paris: Hermann, 1976), 110–12.
12 Gregory Woods, *Homintern: How Gay Culture Liberated the Modern World* (New Haven: Yale University Press, 2016), 26.
13 Hope Johnson, "Are Men Best Dress Designers?," *New York-World Telegram and The Sun* (January 18, 1954), in the designer file, Library of The Costume Institute, The Metropolitan Museum of Art.
14 Bergler, *Fashion and the Unconscious*, 5–6, 19, 28, 95. Emphasis added.
15 Bergler, 117–25.
16 Bergler, vii, 195–6. Emphasis added.
17 Ferdinand Lundberg and Marynia F. Farnham, *Modern Woman: The Lost Sex* (New York: Harper & Brothers Publishers, 1947), v, 16–17, 23, 48, 123, 159, 210, 304, 318–19.
18 Doris Langley Moore, *The Woman in Fashion* (London: B.T. Batsford, 1949), 2–11.
19 James Laver, *Dress: How and Why Fashions in Men's and Women's Clothes Have Changed during the Past Two Hundred Years* (London: John Murray, 1950), 47; James Laver, *Modesty in Dress* (Boston: Houghton Mifflin, 1969), 14, 37, 96–7.
20 *Psychoanalysis* (New York: Tiny Tots Comics, 1955), 1, nos 1 & 2, unpaginated.
21 Edmund Bergler, *Homosexuality: Disease or Way of Life?* (New York: Hill and Wang, 1956), 28–9.
22 Richard C. Friedman and Jennifer I. Downey, "Psychoanalysis and the Model of Homosexuality as Psychopathology: A Historical Overview," *American Journal of Psychoanalysis* 58, no. 3 (1998): 263, 251.
23 Herzog, *Cold War Freud*, 56–69.
24 Martin Duberman, *Cures: A Gay Man's Odyssey* (New York: Simon and Schuster, 1991), 54.
25 See Myron Sharaf, *Fury on Earth: A Biography of Wilhelm Reich* (New York: St. Martin's Press, 1983).
26 Herbert Marcuse, *Eros and Civilization: A Philosophical Inquiry into Freud* (Boston: Beacon Press, [1955] 1966), vii, viii, xvi, xxi.
27 Frantz Fanon, *Black Skin, White Masks*, translated by Charles Lam Markmann (New York: Grove Press, 1967), 10–11, 25, 101, 167. See also Adam Shatz, *The Rebel's Clinic: The Revolutionary Life of Frantz Fanon* (New York: Farrar, Straus, and Giroux, 2024).

28. See Gabriele N. Mendes, *Under the Strain of Color: The Lafargue Clinic and the Promise of an Antiracist Psychiatry* (Ithaca: Cornell University Press, 2021).

29. See William Grier and Price Cobbs, *Black Rage* (New York: Basic Books, 1968) and Beverly J. Stoute, "Black Rage: The Psychic Adaptation to the Trauma of Oppression," *Journal of the American Psychoanalytic Association* 69, no. 2 (2021).

30. Anne Fogarty, *Wife Dressing: The Fine Art of Being a Well-Dressed Wife* (New York: Julian Messer, 1959), 144–5.

31. Renata Strauss, "Passing as Fashionable, Feminine and Sane: 'Therapy of Fashion' and the Normalization of Psychiatric Patients in 1960s US," *Fashion Theory: The Journal of Dress, Body and Culture* 24, no. 4 (2020).

32. Betty Friedan, *The Feminine Mystique* (Hammondsworth: Penguin, 1963), 18.

33. Sigmund Freud, "The Psychogenesis of a Case of Female Homosexuality," *International Journal of Psycho-Analysis* 1, no. 2 (1920).

34. Evelyn Toron Beck and Susan (Shanee) Stepakoff, "Review: Lesbians in Psychoanalytic Theory and Practice," *Feminist Studies* 26, no. 2 (2000).

35. Maria Remedios Varos, *On Homorodans and Other Writings*, edited and translated by Margaret Carson (Cambridge: Wakefield Press, 2024), 147. See also Caitlin Haskell and Tere Arcq, *Remedios Varo: Science Fictions* (Chicago: Art Institute of Chicago, 2023).

36. Remedios Varo, *On Homorodans*, 60–1.

37. Ellen Berry, "He Spurred a Revolution in Psychiatry. Then He 'Disappeared'," *The New York Times* (June 22, 2023), www.nytimes.com/2022/05/02/health/john-fryer-psychiatry.html.

38. Herzog, *Cold War Freud*, 72.

39. Ellen Berry, "He Spurred a Revolution in Psychiatry."

40. David Goldenberg and Patrick Vierson Brown, "Fashioning Hate: Driving the Runway of Desire," *International Journal of Applied Psychoanalytic Studies* 20, no. 3 (2023).

41. Lewes, quoted in Herzog, *Cold War Freud*, 85–6.

42. Juliet Mitchell, *Psychoanalysis and Feminism: An American Humanist's View* (New York: Random House, [1974] 1975), xiii.

43. Jacques Lacan, "The Signification of the Phallus," *Écrits*, translated by Bruce Fink (New York: W.W. Norton, 2006), 582.

44. Jacqueline Rose, "Introduction," in *Feminine Sexuality: Jacques Lacan and the Ecole Freudienne*, ed. Juliet Mitchell and Jacqueline Rose (New York: W.W. Norton, 1985), 40.

45. Mitchell, *Psychoanalysis and Feminism*, xiv; see also Lisa Appignanesi and John Forrester, *Freud's Women* (New York: Basic Books, 1993), 460.

46. Heinz Kohut, in Elizabeth Lunbeck, *The Americanization of Narcissism* (Cambridge: Harvard University Press, 2014), 162–3.

47. Luce Irigaray, "This sex which is not one," in *New French Feminisms*, ed. Elaine Marks and Isabelle de Courtivron (New York: Schocken Books, 1981), 99–100.

48. Marks and de Courtivron, *New French Feminisms*, xii, 332.

49. Hélène Cixous, "The Laugh of the Medusa," in *New French Feminisms*, 255.

50. Hélène Cixous, "Sonia Rykiel in Translation," translated by Deborah Jenson, in *On Fashion*, ed. Shri Benstock and Suzanne Ferriss (New Brunswick: Rutgers University Press, 1994), 96.

51. Cixous, "Sonia Rykiel in Translation," 97.

52. Laura Mulvey, "Visual Pleasure and Narrative Cinema," *Screen* (1975). See also Gillian Rose, *Visual Methodologies: An Introduction to the Interpretation of Visual Materials* (London: Sage, 2001).

53. Dick Hebdidge, *Subculture: The Meaning of Style* (London: Routledge, 1993), 107–8.

54. Julia Kristeva, "Feminism and Psychoanalysis," in *Julia Kristeva Interviews*, ed. Ross Mitchell Guberman (New York: Columbia University Press, 1996), 114–18.

55. Jane Mulvagh, *Vivienne Westwood: An Unfashionable Life* (London: HarperCollins, 1998), 100, 103.

Chapter 6

1. Susie Orbach, *Bodies* (New York: Picador, 2009), 12.

2. Versace, quoted in Hal Rubinstein, *100 Unforgettable Dresses* (New York: Harper Design, 2011), 15.

3. Quotes from Valerie Steele, *Fetish: Fashion, Sex, and Power* (New York: Oxford University Press, 1996), 164, 166.

4. Richard Martin, "Gianni Versace's Anti-Bourgeois Little Black Dress," *Fashion Theory: The Journal of Dress, Body and Culture* 2, no. 1 (1996): 95–100.

5. John Harvey, "Showing and Hiding: Equivocation in the Relations of Body and Dress," *Fashion Theory: The Journal of Dress, Body and Culture* 11, no. 1 (2007): 65, 73.

6. Robert C. Bak, M.D., "The Phallic Woman: The Ubiquitous Fantasy in Perversions," *The Psychoanalytic Study of the Child* 23, no. 1 (1968).

7. Caroline Evans and Minna Thornton, *Women and Fashion: A New Look* (London: Quartet Books, 1989), 92–5.

8. Otto Fenichel, "The Symbolic Equation: Girl = Phallus" (1936), in *The Collected Papers of Otto Fenichel* (New York: Norton, 1954), 2.

9. Bak, "The Phallic Woman," 18–19. Emphasis added.

10. Geneviève Morel, *Sexual Ambiguities: Sexuation and Psychosis*, translated by Lindsay Warren (London: Karnac Books, 2011), 101.

11. Jacques Lacan, "The Subversion of the Subject and the Dialectic of Desire in the Freudian Unconscious" (1960), in *Écrits: The First Complete Edition in English*, translated by Bruce Fink (New York: W. W. Norton & Company, [2002] 2006), 699. Emphasis added.

12. Eugenie Lemoine-Luccioni, *La robe: Essai psychanalytique sur le vetement* (Paris: Editions du Seuil, 1983), 33–4. Emphasis added.

13. Anouchka Grose, *From Anxiety to Zoolander: Notes on Psychoanalysis* (London: Karnac Books, 2018), 72.

14. Nina Hyde, "Jean Paul Gaultier: Giving New Twists to Old Fashion Notions & Clowning with the Classics," *The Washington Post* (October 20, 1984), www.washingtonpost.com/archive/lifestyle/1984/10/21/jean-paul-gaultier/32cd3698-12ad-472b-81da-829a2e6347a4/.

15. Gaby Wood, "Rebel with a Corset," *The Guardian* (August 27, 2005), www.theguardian.com/lifeandstyle/2005/aug/28/fashion.shopping3.

16. Wood, "Rebel with a Corset."

17. Wood, "Rebel with a Corset," emphasis added.

18. Arthur Dreyfus, "'I Have Always Worked to Make Women Feel Powerful': Thiery Mugler on his Career," French *Vogue* (January 26, 2022), www.vogue.fr/fashion-culture/article/thierry-mugler-interview-exposition-paris.

19. Holly Brubach, "[Encounter]: Whose Vision is it, Anyway?" *The New York Times Magazine* (July 12, 1994), www.nytimes.com/1994/07/17/magazine/encounter-whose-vision-is-it-anyway.html.

20. Brubach, "Whose Vision is it, Anyway?"

21. Alison Bancroft, *Fashion and Psychoanalysis: Styling the Self* (New York: I.B. Tauris, 2012), 89–94, 59. See also Alison Bancroft, "Inspiring Desire: Lacan, Couture, and the Avant-Garde. *Fashion Theory* 15, no. 1 (2011).

22. Google Arts & Culture, E.V. Day, *Transporter*.

23. Néstor Braunstein "Desire and Jouissance in the Teachings of Lacan," in *The Cambridge Companion to Lacan*, ed. Jean-Michel Rabaté (Cambridge: Cambridge University Press, 2003), 102–15.

24. Bancroft, *Fashion and Psychoanalysis*, 96–101.

25. Bancroft, *Fashion and Psychoanalysis*, 96–101.

26. Bancroft, *Fashion and Psychoanalysis*, 89–90.

27. McQueen, quoted in Andrew Bolton, *Alexander McQueen: Savage Beauty* (New Haven: Yale University Press for The Metropolitan Museum of Art, 2011), 16.

28. McQueen, quoted in Tony Marcus, "I am the Resurrection," *i-D Magazine* (September, 1998), 148.

29. Alison Bancroft, "Masculinity, Masquerade and Display: Some Thoughts on Rick Owens's Sphinx Collection and Men in Fashion," *Critical Studies in Fashion & Beauty* 7, no. 1 (2016): 19–29.

30. Hilary Alexander, "Galliano Reveals a Fashion for Fetish," *The Telegraph* (July 8, 2000), www.telegraph.co.uk/news/worldnews/1347763/Galliano-reveals-a-fashion-for-fetish.html.

31. Robert Stroller, quoted in Valerie Steele, *Fetish: Fashion, Sex & Power* (Oxford: Oxford University Press, 1996), 12.

32. Christian Dior show program, Autumn/Winter 2000 haute couture collection.

33. Galliano, quoted in *Dior Catwalk: The Complete Collections*, ed. Alexander Fury (London: Thames & Hudson, 2018), 328.

34. Jacques Lacan, *The Seminar of Jacques Lacan, Book XVII, The Other Side of Psychoanalysis (1969–1970)* (Cambridge: Polity, 1993), 129.

35 Suzy Menkes, "Paris Fashion: Fetishism on the Runway: Chic or Sick?," *International Herald Tribune* (July 10, 2000), www.nytimes.com/2000/07/10/style/IHT-paris-fashion-fetishism-on-the-runway-chic-or-sick.html.

36 Caroline Evans, *Fashion at the Edge: Spectacle, Modernity, and Deathliness* (New Haven: Yale University Press, 2003), 54.

37 Geneviève Morel, "Filles fétiches, femmes fétichistes," *Savoirs et Cliniques* 1, no. 1 (2009): 1, 2.

38 Morel, "Filles fétiches, femmes fétichistes," 13–17.

39 Lorraine Gamman, "Self-Fashioning, Gender Display, and Sexy Girl Shoes: What's at Stake – Female Fetishism or Narcissism?," in *Footnotes on Shoes*, ed. Shari Benstock and Suzanne Ferriss (New Brunswick: Rutgers University Press, 2001), 101, 108–12.

Chapter 7

1 Carla Bruni, "Karl Lagerfeld par Carla Bruni," *Le Figaro* (October 6, 2007), 141–6. Accessed on *Le Figaro* Archives online, May 30, 2021.

2 Pascal Navarri, *Trendy, sexy et inconscient: Regards d'une psychoanalyst sur la mode* (Paris: Presses Universitaire de France, 2008), 9.

3 J.G. Ballard, *A User's Guide to the Millennium: Essays and Reviews* (London: HarperCollins, 1996), 278. Emphasis added.

4 Navarri, *Trendy, sexy et inconscient*, 9–13.

5 Roland Barthes, *A Lover's Discourse*, translated by Richard Howard (London: Penguin, 1990), 41, 43. Emphasis added.

6 Alessandra Lemma, *Under the Skin: A Psychoanalytic Study of Body Modification* (New York: Routledge, 2010), 60–1.

7 Navarri, *Trendy, sexy et inconscient*, 9–13.

8 Ovid, *Metamorphoses*, translated by C. Martin (New York: W.W. Norton & Company, 2004), book III, lines 621–2.

9 Doris Bernstein, "The Female Superego: A Different Perspective," *International Journal of Psychoanalysis* 64 (1983): 194. Emphasis added.

10 Arlene Kramer Richards, "Ladies of Fashion: Pleasure, Perversion or Paraphilia," *International Journal of Psychoanalysis* 77, no. 337 (1996): 340.

11 Ernest Becker and O. Kernberg, quoted in Philip M. Bromberg, "The Mirror and the Mask: On Narcissism and Psychoanalytic Growth," *Contemporary Psychoanalysis* 19 (1983): 359, 360.

12 Bromberg, "The Mirror and the Mask," 359–60.

13 Simine Vazire, Laura P. Naumann, Peter J. Renfrow, and Samuel D. Gosling, "Portrait of a Narcissist: Manifestations of Narcissism in Physical Appearance," *Journal of Research in Personality* 42 (2008): 1439–47.

14 Eve Golden, "Clothes, Inside Out," in *I Shop, Therefore I Am*, ed. April Lane Benson (Norvale: Jason Aronson, 2000), 146.

15 Sigmund Freud, "Medusa's Head", S.E. vol. 18.

16 Claudia Benthian, *Skin: On the Cultural Border between the Self and the World* (New York: Columbia University Press, 2002), 99.

17 Benthien, *Skin*, 99.

18 Paul-Laurent Assoun, "L'impossible mise à nu: Psychoanalyse du vêtement," *Modes Pratiques: Revue d'histoire du vêtement et de la mode* no. 4 (2019): 241–5.

19 Françoise Frontisi-Ducroux, "In the Mirror of the Mask," in *A City of Images: Iconography and Society in Ancient Greece*, ed. Claude Bérard et al. (Princeton: Princeton University Press, 1989), 159.

20 Sigmund Freud, *The Ego and the Id*, S.E. vol. 19, 26.

21 Didier Anzieu, *A Skin for Thought: Interviews with Gilbert Tarrab on Psychology and Psychoanalysis* (New York: Routledge, [1990] 2018), 3.

22 Naomi Segal, "The Other French Freud: Didier Anzieu – The Story of a Skin," paper given at the University of Sussex, May 10, 2006.

23 Email from Christine Anzieu-Premmereur, April 3, 2024.

24 Didier Anzieu, *The Skin Ego*, translated by C. Turner (New Haven: Yale University Press, 1989), 4, 38, 40, 42.

25 Esther Bick, "The Experience of the Skin in Early Object Relations," *International Journal of Psychoanalysis* 49 (1968): 484–6; Esther Bick, "Further Considerations on the Function of the Skin in Early Object Relations: Findings from Infant Observation Integrated into Child and Adult Analysis," *British Journal of Psychotherapy* 2, no. 4 (1986): 296, 293.

26 Christine Anzieu-Premmereur, "Perspectives on the Body Ego and Mother-Infant Interaction: I've Got You Under My Skin," in *A Psychoanalytic Exploration of the Body in Today's World*, ed. Vaia Tsolas and Christine Anzieu-Premmereur (New York: Routledge, 2018), 89. See also Christine Anzieu-Premmereur, "The Skin Ego Theory: Dyadic Sensuality, Trauma in Infancy and Adult Narcissistic Issues," paper given in San Francisco, PINC, November 2019.
27 Anzieu, *The Skin Ego*, 98, 40.
28 Quotes from Instagram.
29 Alice Channer, quoted in Louisa Buck, "Exhibitions: Interview with Alice Channer," *The Art Newspaper* no. 333 (April 2021), 46. Emphasis added.
30 Anzieu, *The Skin Ego*, 124.
31 Lemma, *Under the Skin*, 94, 114, 21, 61.
32 Lucia Ruggerone and Renate Strauss, "The Deceptive Mirror: The Dressed Body beyond Reflection," *Fashion Theory* 26, no. 2 (2020): 211–35.
33 Author interview with Veronica Webb, May 6, 2024.
34 Lisa Armstrong, quoted in Caroline Evans, *Fashion at the Edge: Spectacle, Modernity, and Deathliness* (New Haven: Yale University Press, 2007), 115.
35 Leah Dolan, "Remember when Jennifer Lopez's Grammy Awards dress helped invent Google Image Search?," *CNN Style* (February 3, 2023), www.edition.cnn.com/style/article/jlo-green-dress-grammys-remember-when/index.html.
36 Roland Barthes, *The Pleasure of the Text*, translated by Richard Miller (New York: Hill and Wang, 1975), 9–10.
37 Anzieu-Premmereur, "The Skin Ego Theory," 14.
38 Saman Javed, "Olivier Rousteig Shares Details of Fireplace Explosion, Says it Inspired his Work at Balmain," *Independent* (February 27, 2022), www.independent.co.uk/life-syle/fashion/Olivier-rousteing-explosion-burns-balmain-b2024328.html.
39 *Le Monde,* quoted in Alexandre Samson, *Martin Margiela: Collections Femme 1989-2009* (Paris: Palais Galliera, Paris Musées, 2018).
40 Patrick Avrane, *Quand les vêtements nous déshabillent* (Paris: Presses Universitaires de France, 2024), 59.
41 Marc Lafrance, "From the Skin Ego to the Psychic Envelope: An Introduction to the Work of Didier Anzieu," in *Skin, Culture, and Psychoanalysis*, ed. Sheila Cavanagh, Angela Failler, and Alpha Johnston Hurst (New York: Palgrave Macmillan, 2013), 19.
42 Naomi Segal, *Consensuality: Didier Anzieu, Gender and the Sense of Touch* (Amsterdam: Rodopi, 2009), 72–3.
43 Stella North, "The Surfacing of the Self: The Clothing Ego," in *Skin, Culture and Psychoanalysis*, ed. Sheila Cavanagh et al., 66, 68, 71.
44 North, "The Surfacing of the Self," 66, 82, 83.
45 Kate Barrows, *Ideas in Psychoanalysis: Envy* (Cambridge: Icon Books, 2002), 42, 54–6.
46 Steven Conner, "Mortification," in *Thinking Through the Skin*, ed. Sara Ahmed and Jackie Stacey (London: Routledge, 2001), 36.
47 Agnès Rocamora, "Personal Fashion Blogs: Screens and Mirrors in Digital Self-Portraits," *Fashion Theory: The Journal of Dress, Body and Culture* 15, no. 4 (2011): 417–18.

Chapter 8

1 Katie Steinmetz, "The Transgender Tipping Point," *Time* magazine, May 29, 2014. https://time.com/135480/transgender-tipping-point.
2 Moses Mendez III, "Laverne Cox on What's Changed Since the 'Transgender Tipping Point'", *Time* magazine (February 28, 2023), https://time.com/6258454/laverne-cox-interview-transgender-tipping-point-cover/.
3 Patricia Gherovici, *Transgender Psychoanalysis: A Lacanian Perspective on Sexual Difference* (New York: Routledge, 2017), 58.
4 Robert Stoller, quoted in Laure Laufer, "Ce que le genre fait à la psychanalyse," in *Qu'este-ce que le genre?*, Laurie Laufer and Florence Rochefort (Paris: Payot & Rivages, 2014), 194.
5 Patricia Gherovici, *Please Select Your Gender: From the Invention of Hysteria to the Democratizing of Transgenderism* (New York: Routledge, 2010), 185.
6 Gherovici, *Please Select Your Gender*, 230.
7 Patricia Gherovici, "Bodies to Wear," lecture given on April 5, 2024 at The Fashion Institute of Technology.
8 Kate Bornstein, *Gender Outlaw: On Men, Women, and the Rest of Us* (New York: Vintage Books, 1994), 3.
9 Tim Blanks, "Gucci's Fall 2015 Menswear," *Vogue Runway* (January 19, 2015), www.vogue.com/fashion-shows/fall-2015-menswear/gucci.

10 Murray Healy, "The Radical Unisex Designs of JW Anderson," *The Guardian* (June 1, 2013), www.theguardian.com/fashion/2013/jun/01/radical-unisex-designs-jw-anderson.

11 Lynn Hirschberg, "Alessandro Michele Reflects on Making a Gucci Collection in One Week," *W* magazine (February 19, 2020), www.wmagazine.com/culture/gucci-alessandro-michele-interview.

12 Downing, and Greene, quoted in Ruth La Ferla, "In Fashion, Gender Lines are Blurring," *The New York Times* (August 19, 2015), www.nytimes.com/2015/08/20/fashion/in-fashion-gender-lines-are-blurring.html.

13 Author interview with Bella Freud on August 23, 2023 in London.

14 Guy Trebay, "She's Only Playing a Therapist but the Revelations are Real," *The New York Times* (October 10, 2024), www.nytimes.com/2024/10/10/style/bella-freud-fashion-neurosis-podcast.html.

15 "The Year Ahead: Gender-Fluid Fashion Hits the High Street," *The Business of Fashion* (December 16, 2022), from *The State of Fashion 2023*, co-published by BoF and McKinsey & Company.

16 Wren Saunders, "There's More at Stake with Fashion's Gender-Fluid Movement than You Realise," *British Vogue* (August 11, 2019), www.vogue.co.uk/article/the-meaning-of-gender-fluid-fashion.

17 Veronica G. Llamas, "Between Transgression and Tokenism: The Simultaneous Inclusion and Exclusion of Trans and Gender Non-Conforming Bodies in Fashion," *Fashion, Style & Popular Culture* 10, nos 1 & 2 (2023): 83–4.

18 Llamas, "Between Transgression and Tokenism," 89–92.

19 Erique Zhang, "'She is as Feminine as my Mother, as my Sister, as my Biologically Female Friends': On the Promise and Limits of Transgender Visibility in Fashion Media," *Communication, Culture and Critique* 16, no. 1 (2022): 25–32.

20 Zhang, "She is as Feminine," 25–8.

21 Pia Davis, as told to Liam Hess, "Let's Make Sure that Real Change is Happening—That It's Not Just Clickbait," *Vogue* (June 19, 2022), www.vogue.com/article/pia-davis-of-no-sesso-in-the-forefront-of-queer-representation-in-fashion.

22 Paul B. Preciado, *Je suis un monstre qui vous parle: Rapport pour une académie de psychanalystes* (Paris: Grasset, 2020), 11–12.

23 Preciado, *Je suis un monster qui vous parle*, 16–17.

24 Jacques-Alain Miller, *Lacan Quotidien*, 2021, quoted in Laurie Laufer, *Vers une psychanalyse emancipée: Renouer avec la subversion* (Paris: La Découverte, 2022), 8–11.

25 Avgi Saketopoulou, "Mourning the Body as Bedrock: Developmental Considerations in Treating Transsexual Patients Analytically," *Journal of the American Psychoanalytic Association* 62, no. 5 (2014): 776, and quote, 791.

26 Saketopoulou, "Mourning the Body," 773–4, 777–8, 798.

27 Rachel B. Blass, David Bell, and Avgi Saketopoulou, "Can We Think Psychoanalytically about Transgenderism? An expanded live Zoom debate with David Bell and Avgi Saketopoulou, moderated by Rachel Blass", *International Journal of Psychoanalysis* 102, no. 5 (2021): 968–1000.

28 Avgi Saketopoulou, "On Trying to Pass Off Transphobia as Psychoanalysis and Cruelty as 'Clinical Logic'," *The Psychoanalytic Quarterly* 91, no. 1 (2022): 177–90.

29 David Goldenberg and Patrick Viersen Brown, "Fashioning Hate: Driving the Runway of Desire," *International Journal of Applied Psychoanalytic Studies* 20, no. 3 (2023): 458–9.

30 Jan Morris, *Conundrum* (1974) and Diane Leslie Feinberg, *Journal of a Transsexual* (1980), both quoted in Patricia Gherovici, *Transgender Psychoanalysis: A Lacanian Perspective on Sexual Difference* (New York: Routledge, 2017), 106.

31 Gherovici, *Trangender Psychoanalysis*, 113, 109.

32 See Valerie Steele and Jennifer Park, *Gothic: Dark Glamour* (New Haven: Yale University Press, 2008), 65.

33 Barbara Vinken, "Fashion, Art of Dying, Art of Living," paper given at the Art of Fashion symposium at the Fashion Institute of Technology, November 9, 2007.

34 Emily Chan, "'It's Art': Inside Laverne Cox's Jaw-Dropping 500-Piece Vintage Mugler Collection," *British Vogue* (January 27, 2024), www.vogue.co.uk/article/laverne-cox-vintage-mugler-collection.

35 Lucia Ruggerone and Renate Stauss, "The Deceptive Mirror: The Dressed Body beyond Reflection," *Fashion Theory* 26, no. 2 (2020): 211–35.

BIBLIOGRAPHY

Abriat, Sophie. "L'habit fait le moi ou quand la mode deviant thérapeutique." *Madame Figaro*, December 9, 2018. https://madame.lefigaro.fr/style/la-mode-sur-le-divan-des-psys-karl-lagarfield-ami-simon-porte-jacquemus-301118-162375.

Adamson, Gleen and Victoria Kelley, eds. *Surface Tensions: Surface, Finish and the Meaning of Objects*. Manchester: Manchester University Press, 2013.

Albert, Nicole G. *Lesbian Decadence: Representations in Art and Literature of Fin-de-siècle France*. Translated by Nancy Erber and William Peniston. New York: Harrington Park Press, 2016.

Alexander, Hilary. "Galliano Reveals a Fashion for Fetish." *The Telegraph*. July 8, 2000. www.telegraph.co.uk/news/worldnews/134763/Galliano-reveals-a=fashion-for-fetish.html.

Allport, Gordon W. "The Psychology of Dress: An Analysis of Fashion and Its Motive." *The Annals of the American Academy of Political and Social Science*, 1930.

Anzieu, Didier. "Le Moi-Peau." *Nouvelle Revue de Psychoanalyse* 9 (1974): 195–203.

Anzieu, Didier. *Freud's Self-Analysis*. Translated by Peter Graham. London: The Hogarth Press, 1986.

Anzieu, Didier. *The Skin Ego*. Translated by C. Turner. New Haven: Yale University Press, 1989.

Anzieu, Didier. *A Skin for Thought: Interviews with Gilbert Tarrab on Psychology and Psychoanalysis*. Translated by G. Tarrab. London: Karnac, 1990.

Anzieu, Didier. *Le Moi-Peau*. Paris: Dunod, 1995.

Anzieu, Didier. "Apologie des trois manteaux." In *L'enveloppe psychique*, edited by Denis Mellier. Paris: Dunod, 2023.

Anzieu-Premmereur, Christine. "Perspectives on the Body Ego and Mother-Infant Interaction: I've Got You Under My Skin." In *A Psychoanalytic Exploration of the Body in Today's World*, edited by Vaia Tsolas and Christine Anzieu-Premmereur. New York: Routledge, 2018.

Anzieu-Premmereur, Christine. "The Skin Ego Theory: Dyadic Sensuality, Trauma in Infancy and Adult Narcissistic Issues." Paper presented in San Francisco, PINC, November 14, 2019.

Appignanesi, Lisa, and John Forrester. *Freud's Women*. New York: Basic Books, 1993.

Apter, Emily, and William Pietz. *Fetishism as Cultural Discourse*. Ithaca: Cornell University Press, 1993.

Arnold, Rebecca. *Fashion, Desire, and Anxiety*. New Brunswick: Rutgers University Press, 2001.

Assoun, Paul-Laurent. "L'impossible mise à nu: Psychoanalyse et vêtement." *Modes Pratiques: Revue d'histoire du vêtement et de la mode* 4 (December 2020): 241–52.

Atlas, Galit. *The Enigma of Desire: Sex, Longing, and Belonging in Psychoanalysis*. Abingdon: Routledge, 2016.

Avrane, Patrick. *Quand les vêtements nous déshabillent*. Paris: Presses Universitaires de France, 2024.

Bailly, Lionel. *Lacan: A Beginner's Guide*. Oxford: Oneworld Publications, 2012.

Bak, M.D., Robert C. "The Phallic Woman: The Ubiquitous Fantasy in Perversions." *The Psychoanalytic Study of the Child* 23, no. 1 (1968): 15–36.

Ballard, James Graham. *A User's Guide to the Millennium: Essays and Reviews*. London: HarperCollins, 1996.

Balsam, Rosemary H. "Women Showing Off: Notes on Female Exhibitionism." *Journal of the American Psychoanalytic Association* 56 (2008): 99–121.

Balsam, Rosemary H. *Women's Bodies and Psychoanalysis*. New York: Routledge, 2012.

Bancroft, Alison. *Fashion and Psychoanalysis: Styling the Self*. New York: I.B. Tauris, 2012.

Bancroft, Alison. "Masculinity, Masquerade and Display: Some Thoughts on Rick Owens's *Sphinx* Collection and Men in Fashion." *Critical Studies in Fashion & Beauty* 7, no. 1 (2016): 19–29.

Barcan, Ruth. *Nudity: A Cultural Anatomy*. Oxford: Berg, 2004.

Bard, Christine. *Les Garçonnes: Modes et fantomes des années folles*. Paris: Flammarion, 1998.

Barile, Nello. "The Essence of Fetishism." www.ocula.it/files/OCULA-8-BARILE-The-essence-of-fetishism.pdf.3.

Barky, Sandra Lee. "Narcissism, Femininity and Alienation." *Social Theory and Practice* 9, no. 2 (1982): 127–43.

Barnard, Suzanne, and Bruce Fink, eds. *Reading Seminar XX: Lacan's Major Work on Love, Knowledge, and Feminine Sexuality*. New York: State University of New York Press, 2002.

Barrows, Kate. *Ideas in Psychoanalysis: Envy*. Cambridge: Icon Books, 2002.

Barthes, Roland. *The Pleasure of the Text*. Translated by Richard Miller. New York: Hill and Wang, 1975.

Barthes, Roland. *A Lover's Discourse*. London: Penguin, 1990.

Bass-Krueger, Maude. "Fashion, Gender, and Anxiety." In *French Fashion, Women & the First World War*, edited by Maude Bass-Krueger and Sophie Kurkdjian. New Haven: Yale University Press and the Bard Graduate Center, 2019.

Beaton, Cecil. *Self Portrait with Friends: The Selected Diaries of Cecil Beaton 1922–1974*. New York: New York Times Book Company, 1982.

Beauvoir, Simone de. *The Second Sex*. New York: Random House, 1974.

Beck, Evelyn Torton, and Susan (Shanee) Stepakoff. "Lesbians in Psychoanalytic Theory and Practice." *Feminist Studies* 26, no. 2 (2000): 477–95.

Bendall, Sarah A. *Shaping Femininity: Foundation Garments, the Body and Women in Early Modern England*. London: Bloomsbury Visual Arts, 2022.

Benjamin, Jessica. "Father and Daughter: Identification with Difference." *Psychoanalytic Dialogues* 1, no. 3 (1991): 277–99.

Benson, April Lane, ed. *I Shop, Therefore I Am: Compulsive Buying and the Search for Self*. Northvale: Jason Aronson, 2000.

Benstock, Shari, and Suzanne Ferriss, eds. *On Fashion*. New Brunswick: Rutgers University Press, 1994.

Benstock, Shari, and Suzanne Ferriss, eds. *Footnotes on Shoes*. New Brunswick: Rutgers University Press, 2001.

Benthian, Claudia. *Skin: On the Cultural Border Between Self and the World*. New York: Columbia University Press, 2002.

Berger, John. *Ways of Seeing*. London: Penguin, 1972.

Bergler, Edmund. *Fashion and the Unconscious*. New York: Robert Brunner, 1953.

Bergler, Edmund. *Homosexuality: Disease or Way of Life?* New York: Hill and Wang, 1956.

Bernadac, Marie-Laure, and Bernard Marcardé. *Lacan l'exposition: Quand l'art rencontre la psychanalyse*. Paris: Gallimard, 2024.

Bernheimer, Charles. "'Castration' as Fetish." *Paragraph* 14, no. 1 (1991): 1–9.

Bernheimer, Charles. "A Question of Reference: Male Sexuality in Phallic Theory." In *Spectacles of Realism: Gender, Body, Genre*, edited by Margaret Cohen and Christopher Prendergast. Minneapolis: University of Minnesota Press, 1995.

Bernstein, Doris. "The Female Superego: A Different Perspective." *International Journal of Psychoanalysis* 64 (January 1, 1983): 194.

Berry, Ellen. "He Spurred A Revolution in Psychiatry. Then He 'Disappeared'." *The New York Times*, June 22, 2023. www.nytimes.com/2022/05/02/health/john-fryer-psychiatry.html.

Bick, Esther. "The Experience of the Skin in Early Object-Relations." *International Journal of Psychanalysis* 49 (1968): 484–6.

Bick, Esther. "Further Considerations on the Function of the Skin in Early Object Relations. Findings from Infant Observation Integrated into Child and Adult Analysis." *British Journal of Psychotherapy* 2, no. 4 (1986): 292–9.

Binet, Alfred. *Le fétichisme dans l'amour*. Paris: FV Editions, [1887] 2014.

Blanks, Tim. "Gucci Fall 2015 Menswear." *Vogue* Runway. January 19, 2015. www.vogue.com/fashion-shows/fall-2015-menswear/gucci.

Blass, Rachel, David Bell, and Avgi Saketopoulou. "Can We Think Psychoanalytically about Transgenderism?" An expanded live Zoom debate with David Bell and Avgi Saketopoulou, moderated by Rachel Blass." *International Journal of Psychoanalysis* 102, no. 5 (2021): 968–1000.

Bliss, Sylvia. "The Significance of Clothes." *American Journal of Psychology* 27 (1916): 217–26.

Blum, Dilys. *Shocking! The Art and Fashion of Elsa Schiaparelli*. New Haven: Yale University Press, 1989.

BOF Team, McKinsey & Company. "The Year Ahead: Gender-Fluid Fashion Hits the High Street." *Business of Fashion*. December 16, 2022.

Böhm, Steffan, and Aanka Batta. "Just Doing It: Enjoying Commodity Fetishism with Lacan." *Organization* 17, no. 3 (2010): 345–61.

Bollas, Christopher. *Being a Character: Psychoanalysis and Self Experience*. New York: Hill and Wang, 1992.

Bolton, Andrew. *Alexander McQueen: Savage Beauty*. New York: The Metropolitan Museum of Art, 2011.

Bornstein, Kate. *Gender Outlaw: On Men, Women, and the Rest of Us*. New York: Vintage Books, 1994.

Boudailliez, Sylvie. *Le corps à la mode ou les images du corps dans la psychanalyse*. Paris: Eres, 2009.

Boultwood, Anne, and Robert Jerrard. "Ambivalence, and its Relation to Fashion and the Body." *Fashion Theory* 4, no. 3 (2000): 301–22.

Bourdin, Dominique. *Janine Chasseguet-Smirgel*. Paris: Presses Universitaires de France, 1999.

Bower, Marion. *The Life and Work of Joan Riviere: Freud, Klein and Female Sexuality*. New York: Routledge, 2019.

Brand, Jan, Jose Teunissen, and Catelijne de Muijnck. *Fashion and Imagination: About Clothes and Art*. Arnhem: ArtEZ Press, 2009.

Braunstein, Néstor. "Desire and Jouissance in the Teachings of Lacan." In *The Cambridge Companion to Lacan*, edited by Jean-Michel Rabaté. Cambridge: Cambridge University Press, 2003.

Breward, Christopher. "Couture a Queer Auto/Biography." In *A Queer History of Fashion: From the Closet to the Catwalk*, edited by Valerie Steele. New Haven: Yale University Press, 2013.

Bromberg, Philip M. "The Mirror and the Mask: On Narcissism and Psychoanalytic Growth." *Contemporary Psychoanalysis* 19 (1983): 359–87.

Brombert, Beth Archer. *Edouard Manet: Rebel in a Frock Coat*. Boston: Little Brown, 1996.

Bronnimann, Catherine. *La Robe de Psyché: Essai de lien entre psychanalyse et vêtement*. Paris: L'Harmattan, 2015.

Brubach, Holly. "[Encounter]: Whose Vision Is it, Anyway?" *The New York Times Magazine*, July 12, 1994. www.nytimes.com/1994/07/17/magazine/encounter-whose-vision-is-it-anyway.html.

Bruni, Carla. "Karl Lagerfeld par Carla Bruni." *Le Figaro* (October 6, 2007): 141–6.

Buck, Louisa. "Exhibitions: Interview with Alice Channer." *The Art Newspaper* 333 (April 2021): 46.

Buhle, Mari Jo. *Feminism and Its Discontents*. Cambridge: Harvard University Press, 1998.

Buot, François. *Gay Paris*. Paris: Librairie Arthème Fayard, 2013.

Burke, Janine. *The Sphinx on the Table: Sigmund Freud's Art Collection and the Development of Psychoanalysis*. New York: Walker and Company, 2006.

Burman, Barbara. "Better and Brighter Clothes: The Men's Dress Reform Party, 1929–1940." *Journal of Design History* 9, no. 4 (1995): 275–90.

Campbell, Colin. "When the Meaning is not a Message." In *Fashion Theory: A Reader*, edited by Malcom Barnard. New York: Routledge, 2021.

Carter, Michael. "J.C. Flügel and the Nude Future." In *Fashion Classics from Carlyle to Barthes*. New York: Berg, 2003.

Casanova, Erynn Masi de. *Buttoned Up: Clothing, Conformity, and White-Collar Masculinity*. Ithaca: Cornell University Press, 2015.

Cavallaro, Dani, and Alexandra Warwick. *Fashioning the Frame: Boundaries, Dress and Body*. New York: Berg, 1998.

Cavanagh, Sheila L., Angela Failler, and Hurst Rachel Alpha Johnston. *Skin, Culture and Psychoanalysis*. New York: Palgrave Macmillan, 2013.

Cavanagh, Sheila L., Angela Failler, and Hurst Rachel Alpha Johnston. "Transsexuality as Sinthome: Bracha L. Ettinger and the Other (Feminine) Sexual Difference." *Studies in Gender and Sexuality* 17, no. 1 (2016): 27–44.

Cavanagh, Sheila L., Angela Failler, and Hurst Rachel Alpha Johnston. "Transgender Embodiment: A Lacanian Approach." *Psychoanalytic Review* 105, no. 3 (2018): 303–27.

Chabert, C. *Didier Anzieu*. Paris: Presses Universitaires de France, 1996.

Chadwick, Whitney, and Tirza True Latimer, eds. *The Modern Woman Revisited: Paris Between the Wars*. New Brunswick: Rutgers University Press, 2003.

Chaffee, Cathleen, ed. *Marisol: A Retrospective*. New York: DelMonico Books, 2023.

Chan, Emily. "It's Art": Inside Laverne Cox's Jaw-Dropping 500-Piece Vintage Mugler Collection." *Vogue UK*. January 27, 2024. www.vogue.co.uk/article/laverne-cox-vintage-mugler-collection.

Chapin, Chloe. "Masculine Renunciation or Rejection of the Feminine? Revisiting J.C. Flügel's Psychology of Clothes." *Fashion Theory* 25, no. 7 (2022): 983–1008.

Chaplin, Tamara. "'A Woman Dressed Like a Man': Gender Trouble at the Sapphic Cabaret, Paris, 1930–1960." *French Historical Studies* 44, no. 4 (2021): 711–48.

Chasseguet-Smirgel, Janine. *Creativity and Perversion*. New York: W.W. Norton & Company, 1984.

Chasseguet-Smirgel, Janine. *The Body as Mirror of the World*. Translated by Sophie Leighton. London: Free Association Books, 2003.

Christian Dior show program, Autumn/Winter Haute Couture 2000–2001.

Cixous, Hélène. "The Laugh of the Medusa." In *New French Feminisms*, edited by Elaine Marks and Isabelle de Courtivron. New York: Schocken Books, 1981.

Cixous, Hélène. "Sonia Rykiel in Translation," In *On Fashion*, edited by Shari Benstock and Suzanne Ferriss, translated by Deborah Jenson. New Brunswick: Rutgers University Press, 1994.

Clair, Jean. *Freud: Du regard à l'écoute*. Paris: Gallimard, 2018.

Clark, Judith, and Adam Phillips. *The Concise Dictionary of Dress*. London: Violette, 2010.

Clark, Kenneth. *The Nude*. New York: Doubleday, 1959.

Clarke, Alison, and Daniel Miller. "Fashion and Anxiety." *Fashion Theory* 6, no. 2 (2002): 191–213.

Clément, Catherine. *The Lives and Legends of Jacques Lacan*. Translated by Arthur Goldhammer. New York: Columbia University Press, 1983.

Clérambault, Gaëtan de. "Passion érotique des étoffes chez la femme." In *La passion des étoffes chez un neuro-psychiatre*, edited by Yolande Papetti. Paris: Solin, 1990.

Cohen, Lisa. *All We Know: Three Lives*. New York: Farrar, Straus and Giroux, 2012.

Cole, Shaun. *Gay Men's Style: Fashion, Dress and Sexuality in the 21st Century*. London: Bloomsbury Visual Arts, 2023.

Conner, Steven. "Mortification." In *Thinking Through the Skin*, edited by Sara Ahmed and Jackie Stacey. London: Routledge, 2001.

Conner, Steven. *The Book of Skin*. Ithaca: Cornell University Press, 2004.

Copjec, Joan. "The Sartorial Superego." In *Read my Desire: Lacan Against the Historicists*. London: Verso, 2015.

Corbett, Ken. *Boyhoods: Rethinking Masculinities*. New Haven: Yale University Press, 2009.

Corbett, Ken. "Gender Regulation." *Psychoanalysis Quarterly* 80, no. 2 (2011): 441–59.

Corrigan, Peter. "Interpreted, Circulating, Interpreting: The Three Dimensions of the Clothing Object." In *The Socialness of Things*, edited by Stephen Harold Riggins. New York: Mouton de Gruyter, 1994.

Crozier, Ivan. "(De-) Constructing Sexual Kings Since 1750." In *The Routledge History of Sex and the Body*, edited by Sarah Toulalan and Kate Fisher. New York: Routledge, 2013.

Csordas, Thomas J., ed. *Embodiment and Experience*. Cambridge: Cambridge University Press, 1994.

Cullum-Swan, Betsy, and Peter K. Manning. "What is a T-shirt? Codes, Chronotypes and Everyday Objects." In *The Socialness of Things*, edited by Stephen Harold Riggins. New York: Mouton de Gruyter, 1994.

Cupa, Dominique. "Une Topologie de la Sensualité: Le moi-peau." *Revue française de psychosomatique* 1, no. 29 (2006): 83–100. www.cairn.info/revue-francaise-de-psychosomatique-2006-1-page83.htm.

Dalí, Salvador. *The Secret Life of Salvador Dalí*. New York: Dial Press, 1942.

Dalí, Salvador. *The Unspeakable Confessions of Salvador Dalí*. New York: Quill, 1981.

Danet, Brenda, and Tamar Katriel. "Glorious Obsessions, Passionate Lovers, and Hidden Treasures: Collecting, Metaphor, and the Romantic Ethic." In *The Socialness *of Things*, edited by Stephen Harold Riggins. New York: Mouton de Gruyter, 1994.

Davis, Fred. *Fashion, Culture, and Identity*. Chicago: University of Chicago Press, 1992.

Davis, Pia, as told to Liam Hess. "Let's Make Sure that Real Change is Happening—That It's Not Just Clickbait." *Vogue* (June 19, 2022). www.vogue.com/article/pia-davis-of-no-sesso-on-the-forefront-of-queer-representation-in-fashion.

Davis, Whitney. *Queer Beauty*. New York: Columbia University Press, 2010.

Dean, Carolyn J. *The Self and Its Pleasures*. Ithaca: Cornell University Press, 1992.

Debo, Kaat, and Bart Marius, eds. *Mirror Mirror: Fashion & the Psyche*. Antwerp: Hannibal Books, 2022.

De Grazia, Victoria, and Ellen Furlough, eds. *The Sex of Things*. Berkeley: University of California Press, 1996.

Delebarre, Henri. "Fashion, Ego & Psyche: When Clothes Make the Mood." *Antidote* (June 24, 2022). https://magazineantidote.com/mode/fashion-ego-psyche/.

Deslandes, Paul R. "Exposing, Adorning, and Dressing the Body in the Modern Era." In *The Routledge History of Sex and the Body*, edited by Sarah Toulalan and Kate Fisher. New York: Routledge, 2013.

Didi-Huberman, Georges. *Invention of Hysteria: Charcot and the Photographic Iconography of the Salpêtrière*. Translated by Alisa Hartz. Cambridge: MIT Press, 2004.

Dimen, Muriel. "Perversion Is Us? Eight Notes." *Psychoanalytic Dialogues* 11, no. 6 (2001): 825–60.

Dittmar, Helga. "The Role of Self Image in Excessive Buying." In *I Shop, Therefore I Am: Compulsive Buying and The Search for Self*, edited by April Lane Benson. Northvale: Jason Aronson, 2000.

Dolan, Leah. "Remember when Jennifer Lopez's Grammy Awards Dress Helped Invent Google Image Search?" *CNN Style* (February 3, 2023). www.cnn.com/style/article/jlo-green-dress-grammys-remember-when/index.html.

Douglas, Mary. *Purity and Danger: An Analysis of Concept of Pollution and Taboo*. New York: Routledge, 1966.

Douglas, Mary. *Natural Symbols: Explorations in Cosmology*. New York: Routledge, 1970.

Drake, Alicia. *The Beautiful Fall: Fashion, Genius, and Glorious Excess in 1970s Paris*. New York: Back Bay Books, 2006.

Dreyfus, Arthur. "'I Have Always Worked to Make Women Feel Powerful': Thierry Mugler on his Career." *French Vogue* (January 26, 2022). www.vogue.fr/fashion-culture/article/thierry-mugler-interview-exposition-paris.

Duberman, Martin. *Cures: A Gay Man's Odyssey*. New York: Simon and Schuster, 1991.

Elise, Dianne. "Unlawful Entry: Male Fears of Psychic Penetration." *Psychoanalytic Dialogues* 11, no. 4 (2001): 499–531.

Ellenzweig, Allen, *George Platt Lynes. The Daring Eye*. Oxford: Oxford University Press, 2021.

Emanuel, Ricky. *Ideas in Psychoanalysis: Anxiety*. Cambridge: Icon Books, 2000.

Entwistle, Joanne. "The Dressed Body." In *Body Dressing*, edited by Joanne Entwistle and Elizabeth Wilson. Oxford: Berg, 2001.

Entwistle, Joanne. *The Fashioned Body: Fashion, Dress and Modern Social Theory*. Cambridge: Polity, 2015.

Erikson, Erik H., and Huey P. Newton. *In Search of Common Ground*. New York: W. W. Norton & Company, 1973.

Etcoff, Nancy. *Survival of the Prettiest. The Science of Beauty*. New York: Anchor/Doubleday, 1999.

Evans, Caroline. "Fashion." In *Feminism and Psychoanalysis*, edited by Elizabeth Wright. Malden: Wiley-Blackwell, 1992.

Evans, Caroline. "Masks, Mirrors and Mannequins: Elsa Schiaparelli and the Decentered Subject." *Fashion Theory* 3, no. 1 (1999): 3–31.

Evans, Caroline. *Fashion at the Edge: Spectacle, Modernity, and Deathliness*. New Haven: Yale University Press, 2007.

Evans, Caroline, and Minna Thornton. *Women & Fashion: A New Look*. New York: Quartet Books, 1989.

Fanon, Frantz. *Black Skin, White Masks*. Translated by Charles Lam Markmann. New York: Grove Press, 1967.

Fenichel M.D., Otto. *The Collected Papers of Otto Fenichel*. New York: Norton, 1954.

Fisher, Will. *Materializing Gender in Early Modern English Literature and Culture*. Cambridge: Cambridge University Press, 2006.

Fisher, Will. "'Had it a codpiece, 'twere a man indeed': The Codpiece as Constitutive Accessory in Early Modern English Culture." In *Ornamentalism:*

The Art of Renaissance Accessories, edited by Bella Mirabella. Ann Arbor: University of Michigan Press, 2016.

Flem, Lydia. "Les vêtements de l'âme." *Modes Patiques Revue d'histoire du vêtement et de la mode* 4 (December 2020): 235–7.

Flügel, J.C. "Clothes Symbolism and Clothes Ambivalence." *International Journal of Psycho-Analysis* 10 (January 1, 1929): 205–17.

Flügel, J.C. *The Psychology of Clothes*. London: Hogarth Press, 1930.

Fogel, Gerald, Frederick, M. Lane, and Robert S. Liebert, eds. *The Psychology of Men*. New Haven: Yale University Press, 1986.

Fogerty, Anne. *Wife Dressing: The Fine Art of Being a Well-Dressed Wife*. New York: Julian Messer, 1959.

Ford, Tanisha C. *Dressed in Dreams*. New York: St. Martin's Press, 2019.

Fraser, Mariam, and Monica Greco. *The Body: A Reader*. New York: Routledge, 2005.

Freud, Bella. Interview with Valerie Steele. August 25, 2023.

Freud, Ernst L. *The Letters of Sigmund Freud*. New York: Basic Books, 1975.

Freud, Martin. *Glory Reflected: Sigmund Freud, Man and Father*. London: Angus and Robertson, 1957.

Freud, Sigmund. *The Standard Edition of the Complete Psychological Works of Sigmund Freud*, 24 volumes. Translated by James Strachey. London: Hogarth Press and the Institute for Psychoanalysis, 1953–1975.

Freud, Sigmund. *The Interpretation of Dreams* (1900), S.E. vol. 4 and vol. 5.

Freud, Sigmund. *The Psychopathology of Everyday Life* (1901), S.E. vol. 6.

Freud, Sigmund. "A Case of Hysteria" (1901), S.E. vol. 7.

Freud, Sigmund. *Jokes and Their Relation to the Unconscious* (1905), S.E. vol. 8.

Freud, Sigmund. *"Civilized" Sexual Morality and Modern Nervous Illness* (1908), S.E. vol. 9.

Freud, Sigmund. "Creative Writers and Day-Dreaming" (1908), S.E. vol. 9.

Freud, Sigmund. "Hysterical Phantasies and their Relation to Bisexuality" (1908), S.E. vol. 9.

Freud, Sigmund. "On the Sexual Theories of Children" (1908), S.E. Vol. 9.

Freud, Sigmund. *Totem and Taboo* (1912), S.E. vol. 13.

Freud, Sigmund. "On Narcissism: An Introduction" (1914), S.E. vol. 14.

Freud, Sigmund. "On the History of the Psycho-Analytic Movement" (1914), S.E. vol. 14.

Freud, Sigmund. "Instincts and Their Vicissitudes" (1915), S.E. vol. 14.

Freud, Sigmund. *Introductory Lectures on Psychoanalysis* (1915–1916), S.E. vol. 15

Freud, Sigmund. "The Uncanny" (1919), S.E. vol. 17.

Freud, Sigmund. *Beyond the Pleasure Principle* (1920), S.E. Vol. 18.

Freud, Sigmund. "The Psychogenesis of a Case of Female Homosexuality." *The International Journal of Psycho-Analysis* 1, no. 2 (1920): 125–49.

Freud, Sigmund. "Medusa's Head" (1922), S.E. vol. 18.

Freud, Sigmund. *The Ego and the Id* (1923), S.E. vol. 19.

Freud, Sigmund. "Some Physical Consequences of the Anatomical Distinction between the Sexes" (1925), S.E. vol. 19.

Freud, Sigmund. "Fetishism" (1927), S.E. vol. 21.

Freud, Sigmund. *Civilization and Its Discontents* (1929), S.E. vol. 21.

Freud, Sigmund. "Female Sexuality" (1931), S.E. vol. 21.

Freud, Sigmund. *New Introductory Lectures on Psycho-Analysis* (1932), S.E. vol. 22.

Freud, Sigmund. "An Outline of Psychoanalysis" (1940), S.E. vol. 23.

Freud, Sigmund. *The Complete Letters of Sigmund Freud to Wilhelm Fliess 1887–1904*. Translated by Jeffrey Moussaieff Masson. Cambridge: Harvard University Press, 1985.

Freud, Sigmund. Previously unpublished minutes of the Vienna "Freud and Fetishism: Psychoanalytic Society," edited and translated by Louis Rose, *Psychoanalytic Quarterly* 57 (1988).

Freud, Sigmund. "Contribution à la thèorie du rêve." In *Les Premiers Psychanalystes*. Paris: Gallimard, 1979.

Freud, Sigmund. *Three Essays on the Theory of Sexuality: The 1905 Edition*. Translated by Ulrike Kistner. Edited and introduced by Philippe Van Haute and Herman Westerink. London: Verso, 2016.

Friedan, Betty. *The Feminine Mystique*. Hammondsworth: Penguin, 1963.

Friedman, Richard C., and Jennifer I. Downey. "Psychoanalysis and the Model of Homosexuality as

Psychopathology: A Historical Overview." *American Journal of Psychoanalysis* 58, no. 3 (1998): 249–70.

Frontisi-Ducroux, Françoise. "In the Mirror of the Mask." In *A City of Images: Iconography and Society in Ancient Greece*, edited by Claude Bérard, Christiane Bron, Jean Louis Durand, et al. Translated by Deborah Lyons. Princeton: Princeton University Press, 1989.

Fury, Alexander. *Dior Catwalk: The Complete Collections*. London: Thames & Hudson, 2018.

Fuss, Diana. "Interior Colonies: Frantz Fanon and the Politics of Identification." *Critical Crossings* 24, no. 2/3 (1994): 249–70.

Gallo, Rubén. *Freud's Mexico: Into the Wilds of Psychoanalysis*. Cambridge: The MIT Press, 2010.

Gallop, Jane. *The Daughter's Seduction: Feminism and Psychoanalysis*. Ithaca: Cornell University Press, 1982.

Gamman, Lorriane. "Self-Fashioning, Gender Display, and Sexy Girl Shoes: What's at Stake – Female Fetishism or Narcissism?" In *Footnotes on Shoes*, edited by Shari Benstock and Suzanne Ferriss. New Brunswick: Rutgers University Press, 2001.

Gamman, Lorraine, and Merja Makinen. *Female Fetishism*. New York: New York University Press, 1994.

Garber, Marjorie. "Fetish Envy." *October* 54 (Fall 1990): 45–6.

Gay, Peter. *Freud: A Life for Our Time*. New York: W.W. Norton & Company, 1988.

Gay, Peter. *The Freud Reader*. New York: W.W. Norton & Company, 1995.

Gherovici, Patricia. *Please Select Your Gender: From the Invention of Hysteria to the Democratizing of Transgenderism*. New York: Routledge, 2010.

Gherovici, Patricia. *Transgender Psychoanalysis: A Lacanian Perspective on Sexual Difference*. New York: Routledge, 2017.

Gherovici, Patricia. "Bodies to Wear." Lecture given at The Fashion Institute of Technology. April 5, 2024.

Gill-Peterson, Jules. *Histories of the Transgender Child*. Minneapolis: University of Minnesota Press, 2017.

Gilman, Sander L. *Freud, Race, and Gender*. Princeton: Princeton University Press, 1993.

Golden, Eve. "Clothes, Inside Out." In *I Shop, Therefore I Am: Compulsive Buying and the Search for Self*, edited by April Lane Benson. Northvale: Jason Aronson, 2000.

Goldenberg, David, and Patrick Viersen Brown. "Fashioning Hate: Driving the Runway of Desire." *International Journal of Applied Psychoanalytic Studies* 20, no. 3 (2023): 452–66.

Greenblatt, Stephen. *The Rise and Fall of Adam and Eve*. New York: W.W. Norton & Company, 2017.

Grier, William, and Price Cobbs. *Black Rage*. New York: Basic Books, 1968.

Grose, Anouchka. *Hysteria Today*. London: Routledge, 2016.

Grose, Anouchka. *From Anxiety to Zoolander: Notes on Psychoanalysis*. London: Karnac Books, 2018.

Grose, Anouchka. "Shrinking Clothes." *Fashion Theory* 24, no. 1 (2020): 85–91.

Grose, Anouchka. *Fashion: A Manifesto*. London: Notting Hill Editions, 2023.

Grosz, Elizabeth. *Jacques Lacan: A Feminist Introduction*. London: Routledge, 1990.

Grosz, Elizabeth. "The Body." In *Feminism and Psychoanalysis: A Critical Dictionary*, edited by Elizabeth Wright. Oxford: Blackwell, 1992.

Grosz, Elizabeth. *Volatile Bodies: Toward a Corporeal Feminism*. Indianapolis: Indiana University Press, 1994.

Guberman, Ross Mitchell. *Julia Kristeva: Interviews*. New York: Columbia University Press, 1996.

Handler Spitz, Ellen. *Art and Psyche*. New Haven: Yale University Press, 1985.

Harris. Adrienne. "Foreword." In *Disorienting Sexuality: Psychoanalytic Reappraisals of Sexual Identities*, edited by Thomas Domenici and Ronnie C. Lesser. New York: Routledge, 1995.

Harvey, John. "Showing and Hiding: Equivocation in the Relations of Body and Dress." *Fashion Theory* 11, no. 1 (2007): 65–94.

Haskell, Caitlin, and Tere Arcq. *Remedios Varo: Science Fictions*. Chicago: Art Institute of Chicago, 2023.

Healy, Murray. "The Radical Unisex Designs of JW Anderson." *The Guardian*. June 1, 2013. www.theguardian.com/fashion/2013/jun/01/radical-unisex-designs-jw-anderson.

Heath, Stephen. "Joan Riviere and the Masquerade." In *Formations of Fantasy*, edited by Victor Burgin, James Donald and Cora Kaplan. London: Methuen, 1986.

Hebdidge, Dick. *Subculture: The Meaning of Style*. London: Routledge, 1993.

Herzog, Dagmar. *Cold War Freud: Psychoanalysis in an Age of Catastrophes*. Cambridge: Cambridge University Press, 2017.

Heyam, Kit. *Before We Were Trans: A New History of Gender*. New York: Seal Press, 2022.

Hinshelwood, Robert, Susan Robinson, and Oscar Zarate. *Introducing Melanie Klein*. New York: Totem Books, 1998.

Hirschberg, Lynn. "Alessandro Michele Reflects on Making a Gucci Collection in One Week." *W magazine*. February 19, 2020. www.wmagazine.com/culture/gucci-alessandro-michele-interview.

Hoare, Sarah. "God Save McQueen," *Harper's Bazaar* 30, June, 1996.

Hollander, Anne. *Seeing Through Clothes*. Berkeley: University of California Press, 1993.

Hollander, Anne. *Sex and Suits*. New York: Knopf, 1994.

Holmes, Jeremy. *Ideas in Psychoanalysis: Narcissism*. Cambridge: Icon Books, 2001.

Holtzman, Deanna, and Nancy Kulish. "Female Exhibitionism: Identification, Competition, and Camaraderie." *International Journal of Psychoanalysis* 93, no. 2 (2012): 271–92.

Hughes, Athol. "Joan Riviere: Her Life and Work." In *The Inner World and Joan Riviere*. London: Karnac Books, 1991.

Hughes, Athol. "Personal Experiences—Professional Interests: Joan Riviere and Femininity." *The International Journal of Psychoanalysis* 78 (1997): 899–911.

Hughes, Athol. "Joan Riviere and the Masquerade." *Psychoanalysis and History* 6, no. 2 (2004): 161–75.

Hughes, Judith M. *Reshaping the Psychoanalytic Domain*. Berkeley: University of California Press, 1989.

Hunt, Lynn. "Psychology, Psychoanalysis, and Historical Thought." In *Companion to Western Historical Thought*, edited by Lloyd Kramer and Sara Maza. London: Blackwell Publishers, 2002.

Hurlock, Elizabeth. *The Psychology of Dress; An Analysis of Fashion and its Motive*. New York: Ronald Press Co., 1929.

Hurst, Rachel Alpha Johnston. "The Skin-Textile in Cosmetic Surgery." In *Skin, Culture and Psychoanalysis*, edited by Sheila L. Cavanagh, Angela Failler and Rachel Alpha Johnson Hurst. New York: Palgrave Macmillan, 2013.

Hustvedt, Asti. *Medical Muses: Hysteria in Nineteenth-Century Paris*. New York: W.W. Norton & Company, 2011.

Hyde, Nina. "Jean-Paul Gaultier: Giving New Twists to Old Fashion Notions & Clowning with the Classics." *The Washington Post*, October 20, 1984. www.washingtonpost.com/archive/lifestyle/1984/10/21/jean-paul-gaultier/32cd3698-12ad-472b-81da-829a2e6347a4.

Irigaray, Luce. "This Sex Which Is Not One." In *New French Feminisms*, edited by Elaine Marks and Isabelle de Courtivron. New York: Schocken Books, 1981.

Jastrow, Joseph. *Freud: His Dream and Sex Theories*. New York: Pocket Books, 1948.

Javed, Saman. "Oliver Rousteing Shares Details of Fireplaces Explosion, says it Inspired his Work at Balmain." *Independent*. February 27, 2022. www.independent.co.uk/life-style/fashion/olivier-rousteing-explosion-burns-balmain-b2024328.html.

Jay, Martin. *Downcast Eyes: The Denigration of Vision in Twentieth-Century French Thought*. Berkeley: University of California Press, 1993.

Johnson, Hope. "Are Men Best Dress Designers?" *New York World-Telegram and The Sun*. January 18, 1954.

Johnson, Kathryn, ed. *Surrealism and Design Now*. London: Design Museum Publishing, 2022.

Johnson, Kim, Susan J. Torntore, and Joanne Bubolz Eicher, eds. *Fashion Foundations: Early Writings on Fashion and Dress*. Oxford: Berg, 2003.

Jones, Amelia. *The Feminism and Visual Culture Reader*. New York: Routledge, 2010.

Jones, Ann Rosalind, and Peter Stallybrass. "Busks, Bodices, Bodies." In *Ornamentalism: The Art of Renaissance Accessories*, edited by Bella Mirabella. Ann Arbor: University of Michigan Press, 2011.

Joubert, Catherine, and Sarah Stern. *Déshabillez-moi: Psychanalyse des comportements vestimentaires*. Paris: Fayard, [2005] 2012.

Jung, Carl. *Memories, Dreams, Reflections*, edited by Aniela Jaffé. New York: Pantheon, 1963.

Jung, Carl. *Man and His Symbols*. New York: Dell, 1968.

Kahr, Brett. "Letter from London: Four Unknown Freud Anecdotes." *American Imago* 67, no. 2 (2010): 307–8.

Kaiser, Susan B. *The Social Psychology of Clothing: Symbolic Appearances in Context*. New York: Fairchild, 1997.

Kandel, Eric, *The Age of Insight: The Quest to Understand the Unconscious in Art, Mind, and Brain, from Vienna 1900 to the Present*. New York: Random House, 2012.

Kaplan, Jonathan C. "The Man in the Suit: Jewish Men and Fashion in Fin-de-siècle Vienna." *Fashion Theory* 25, no. 3 (2020): 339–66.

Kaplan, Jonathan C. *Jews in Suits Men's Dress in Vienna, 1890–1938*. London: Bloomsbury Visual Arts, 2023.

Kaplan, Louise J. *Female Perversions: The Temptations of Emma Bovary*. Northvale: Jason Aronson, 1997.

Keiser, Jess. "Brain Research Shows Freud Actually Got a Few Things Right," *The Washington Post*, February 28, 2021.

Kelley, Victoria. "A Superficial Guide to Deeper Meanings of Surface." In *Surface Tensions: Surface, Finish, and the Meaning of Objects*, edited by Glenn Adamson and Victoria Kelley. Manchester: Manchester University Press, 2013.

Kennedy, Roger. *Ideas in Psychoanalysis: Libido*. Cambridge: Icon Books, 2001.

Klein, Melanie. "Infantile Anxiety—Situations Reflected in a Work of Art and the Creative Impulse." In *Psychoanalysis and Art*, edited by Sandra Gosso. London: Routledge, 2004.

Kohler, Sheila. *Dreaming for Freud*. New York: Penguin Books, 2014.

Kraus, Karl. "The Eroticism of Clothes." In *The Rise of Fashion: A Reader*, edited by Daniel Leonhard Purdy. Minneapolis: University of Minnesota Press, 2004.

Kristeva, Julia. *Powers of Horror*. New York: Columbia University Press, 1982.

Kristeva, Julia. "Feminism and Psychoanalysis." In *Julia Kristeva: Interviews*, edited by Ross Mitchell Guberman. New York: Columbia University Press, 1996.

Kuchta, David. *The Three-Piece Suit and Modern Masculinity, England, 1550–1850*. Berkeley: University of California Press, 2002.

Kutahneci, Meltem. "La loi de la mère. Essai sur le sinthome sexuel, de Geneviève Morel." In *Le corps à la mode ou les images du corps dans la psychanalyse*. Paris: Eres, 2009.

Lacan, Jacques. *De la psychose paranoïaque dans ses rapports avec la personalité*. Paris: Éditions du Seuil, 1975.

Lacan, Jacques. *Feminine Sexuality: Jacques Lacan and the école freudienne*, edited by Juliet Mitchell and Jacqueline Rose. New York: W.W. Norton & Company, 1985.

Lacan, Jacques. *The Seminar of Jacques Lacan, Book XVII, The Other Side of Psychoanalysis*. Cambridge: Polity, 1993.

Lacan, Jacques. *The Four Fundamental Concepts of Psychoanalysis: The Seminar of Jacques Lacan Book XI*, edited by Jacques-Alain Miller. Translated by Alan Sheridan. New York: W.W. Norton & Company, 1998.

Lacan, Jacques. *Écrits: A Selection*. Translated by Alan Sheridan. New York: Routledge, 2001.

Lacan, Jacques. *Écrits*. Translated by Bruce Fink. New York: W.W. Norton, 2006.

La Ferla, Ruth. "In Fashion, Gender Lines are Blurring." *The New York Times*. August 19, 2015. www.nytimes.com/2015/08/20/fashion/in-fashion-gender-lines-are-blurring.html.

Lafrance, Marc. "From the Skin to the Psychic Envelope: An Introduction to the Work of Didier Anzieu." In *Skin, Culture and Psychoanalysis*, edited by Sheila L. Cavanagh, Angela Failler and Rachel Alpha Johnson Hurst. New York: Palgrave Macmillan, 2013.

Laing, Morna. "Sustainability and the Fashion Media: Micro-Utopia, Social Dreaming and Hope in the Margins." *Fashion Theory* 28, no. 3 (2024): 335–58.

Langley Moore, Doris. *The Woman in Fashion*. London: B.T. Batsford, 1949.

Laplanche, Jean. *Between Seduction and Inspiration: Man*. Translated by Jeffrey Mehlman. New York: The Unconscious in Translation, 2015.

Laplanche, Jean, and J.B. Pontalis. *The Language of Psycho-Analysis*. Translated by Donald Nicholson-Smith. New York: W.W. Norton & Company, 1973.

Larrett-Smith, Philip. *Louise Bourgeois: The Return of the Repressed: Psychoanalytic Writings*. London: Violette Editions, 2012.

Lauer, Robert H., and Jeannette C. Lauer. *Fashion Power: The Meaning of Fashion in American Society*. Englewood Cliffs: Prentice-Hall, 1981.

Laufer, Laurie. *Qu'est-ce que le genre?* Paris: Payot & Rivages, 2014.

Laufer, Laurie. *Vers un psychanalyse émancipée*. Paris: La Découverte, 2022.

Laver, James. *Taste and Fashion From the French Revolution Until Today*. London: George G. Harrap & Co. Ltd. 1937.

Laver, James. *Dress. How and Why Fashions in Men's and Women's Clothes Have Changed during the Past Two Hundred Years*. London: John Murray, 1950.

Laver, James. *Modesty in Dress*. Boston: Houghton Mifflin, 1969.

Laver, James. *A Concise History of Costume and Fashion*. New York: Scribner's, 1969.

Leader, Darian. *Jouissance: Sexuality, Suffering and Satisfaction*. Cambridge: Polity, 2021.

Lear, Jonathan. *Love and Its Place in Nature*. New Haven: Yale University Press, 1998.

Lear, Jonathan. *Open Minded: Working Out the Logic of the Soul*. Cambridge: Harvard University Press, 1998.

Lemma, Alessandra. "Being Seen or Being Watched? A Psychoanalytic Perspective on Body Dysmorphia." *Institute of Psychoanalysis* 90 (2009): 753–71.

Lemma, Alessandra. *Under the Skin: A Psychoanalytic Study of Body Modification*. New York: Routledge, 2010.

Lemma, Alessandra. *Minding the Body: The Body in Psychoanalysis and Beyond*. New York: Routledge, 2014.

Lemma, Alessandra. "Trans-itory Identities: Some Psychoanalytic Reflections on Transgender Identities." *International Journal of Psychoanalysis* 99, no. 5 (2018): 1089–106.

Lemoine-Luccioni, Eugenie. *La robe: Essai psychanalytique sur le vêtement*. Paris: Le champ freudien aux Editions du Seuil, 1983.

Levine, Philippa. "States of Undress: Nakedness and the Colonial Imagination." *Victorian Studies* 50, no. 2 (2008): 189–219.

Lewis, Reina. *Gendering Orientalism*. New York: Routledge, 1996.

Llamas, Veronica G. "Between Transgression and Tokensim: The Simulteaneous Inclusion and Exclusion of Trans and Gender Non-Conforming Bodies in Fashion." *Fashion, Style & Popular Culture* 10, no. 1/2 (2023): 83–102.

Loewenberg, Peter. "Psychoanalysis as a Hermenutic Science." In *Whose Freud? The Place of Psychoanalysis in Contemporary Culture*, edited by Peter Brooks and Alex Woloch. New Haven: Yale University Press, 2000.

Lomas, David. *The Haunted Self: Surrealism, Psychoanalysis, Subjectivity*. New Haven: Yale University Press, 2000.

Loos, Adolf. "Men's Fashion." In *The Rise of Fashion: A Reader*, edited by Daniel Leonhard Purdy. Minneapolis: University of Minnesota Press, 2004.

Lunbeck, Elizabeth. *The Americanization of Narcissism*. Cambridge: Harvard University Press, 2012.

Lundberg, Ferdinand, and Marynia F. Farnham. *Modern Woman: The Lost Sex*. New York: Harper & Brothers Publishers, 1947.

Lupton, Ellen. *Skin: Surface Substance and Design*. New York: Princeton Architectural Press, 2002.

Lyford, Amy. *Surrealist Masculinities: Gender Anxiety and the Aesthetics of Post-World War I Reconstruction in France*. Berkeley: University of California Press, 2007.

McColl, Pat. "Designers Look to Past for Inspiration," *Los Angeles Times*, July 29, 1982.

McNeil, Peter, and Vicki Karaminas. *The Men's Fashion Reader*. Oxford: Berg, 2009.

McRobbie, Angela. *The Aftermath of Feminism: Gender, Culture and Social Change*. London: Sage Publications, 2009.

Mair, Carolyn. *The Psychology of Fashion*. New York: Routledge, 2018.

Makari, George. *Revolution in Mind: The Creation of Psychoanalysis*. New York: Harper Perenial, 2009.

Marcus, Tony. "I am the Resurrection." *i-D Magazine*, September, 1998.

Marcuse, Herbert. *Eros and Civilization: A Philosophical Inquiry into Freud*. Boston: Beacon Press, [1955] 1966.

Margolis, Deborah P. *Freud and his Mother: Preoedipal Aspects of Freud's Personality*. Northvale: Jason Aronson, 1996.

Marinelli, Lydia. "Fort, Da: The Cap in the Museum." *Psychoanalysis & History* 11, no. 1 (2009): 117–20.

Marks, Elaine, and Isabelle de Courtivron. *New French Feminisms: An Anthology*. New York: Schocken Books, 1981.

Marneffe, Daphne de. "Looking and Listening: The Construction of Clinical Knowledge in Charcot and Freud." *Signs: Journal of Women in Culture and Society* 17, no. 1 (1991): 71–111.

Martin, Richard. *Fashion and Surrealism*. New York: Rizzoli, 1990.

Martin, Richard. "Gianni Versace's Anti-Bourgeois Little Black Dress." *Fashion Theory* 2, no. 1 (1996): 95–100.

Marx, Karl. *Economic and Philosophic Manuscripts of 1844.* In *Marx-Engels Collected Works.* Moscow: Progress, 1975.

Marx, Karl. *Capital*, vol 1. Translated by Ben Fowles. New York: Penguin, 1976.

Masquelier, Adeline. *Dirt, Undress, and Difference: Critical Perspectives on the Body's Surface.* Bloomington: Indiana University Press, 2005.

Mathews, Peter D. "The Symbolism of Clothing: The Naked Truth About Jacques Lacan." *CLCWeb: Comparative Literature and Culture* 23, no. 4 (2021): doi.org/10.7771/1481-4374.3740.

Matlock, Jann. "Masquerading Women, Pathologized Men: Cross-Dressing, Fetishism, and the Theory of Perversion, 1882–1935." In *Fetishism as Cultural Discourse*, edited by Emily Apter and William Pietz. Ithaca: Cornell University Press, 1993.

Mazurel, Hervé. *L'inconscient ou l'oubli de l'histoire. Profondeurs, metamorphoses et revolutions de la vie affective.* Paris: Éditions La Découverte, 2021.

Melchior-Bonnet, Sabine. *The Mirror: A History.* London: Routledge, 2001.

Mellier, Denis, Didier Houzel, René Kaës, et al. *L'enveloppe Psychique: Souffrance, psychopathologie, et associativité.* Paris: Dunod, 2023.

Mendes, Gabriel N. *Under the Strain of Color: Harlem's Lafargue Clinic and the Promise of an Antiracist Psychiatry.* Ithaca: Cornell University Press, 2015.

Mendez III, Moises. "Laverne Cox on What's Changed Since the 'Transgender Tipping Point.'" *Time* magazine. February 28, 2023. https://time.com/6258454/laverne-cox-interview-transgender-tipping-point-cover.

Menkes, Suzy. "Paris Fashion: Fetishism on the Runway: Chic or Sick?" *International Herald Tribune.* July 10, 2000. www.nytimes.com/2000/07/10/style/IHT-paris-fashion-fetishism-on-the-runwaychic-or-sick.html.

Menkes, Suzy. "The Freud of Fashion." *International Herald Tribune.* February 11–12, 2012.

Menninghaus, Winfried. "Caprices of Fashion in Culture and Biology: Charles Darwin's Aesthetics of Ornament." In *Philosophical Perspectives on Fashion*, edited by Giovanni Matteucci and Stefano Marino. London: Bloomsbury, 2017.

Merkin, Daphne. "Freud Rising." *The New Yorker Magazine.* November 1, 1998. www.newyorker.com/magazine/1998/11/09/freud-rising.

Mesch, Rachel. *Before Trans: Three Gender Stories from Nineteeth-Century France.* Stanford: Stanford University Press, 2020.

Micale, Mark S., and Roy Porter. *Discovering the History of Psychiatry.* Oxford: Oxford University Press, 1994.

Michaux, Henri. *Un barbare en Asie.* Paris: Gallimard, [1933] 1986.

Miller, Janice. "Sigmund Freud: More than a Fetish: Fashion and Psychoanalysis." In *Thinking Through Fashion: A Guy to Key Theorists*, edited by Agnès Rocamora and Anneke Smelik. London: I.B. Tauris, 2016.

Miller-Florsheim, Dvora. "Family Secrets as a Component of Disturbances in Gender Identity Formation." *Clinical Studies: International Journal of Psychoanalysis* 1, no. 2 (1995): 72.

Minsky, Rosalind. *Psychoanalysis and Culture: Contemporary States of Mind.* New Brunswick: Rutgers University Press, 1998.

Mitchell, Juliet. *Psychoanalysis and Feminism: An American Humanist's View.* New York: Vintage Books, 1975.

Mitchell, Juliet. *Feminine Sexuality.* Translated by Jacqueline Rose. New York: W.W. Norton & Company, 1985.

Mitchell, Juliet. *The Selected Melanie Klein.* New York: The Hogarth Press, 1986.

Moi, Toril. *What is a Woman?* New York: Oxford University Press, 1999.

Mollon, Phil. *Ideas in Psychoanalysis: The Unconscious.* Cambridge: Icon Books, 2000.

Monden, Masafumi. *Japanese Fashion Cultures.* London: Bloomsbury, 2015.

Montesquiou, Robert de. *La Divine Comtesse, Étude d'Apres Madame de Castiglione.* Paris: Goupil & Co. 1913.

Morand, Paul. *L'Allure de Chanel.* Paris: Hermann, 1976.

Morel, Geneviève. "Filles fétiches, femmes fétichistes." *Savoirs et Cliniques* 1, no. 10 (2009): 1–22.

Morel, Geneviève. *Sexual Ambiguities: Sexuation and Psychosis.* London: Karnac Books, 2011.

Morel, Geneviève, Parveen Adams, Sylvie Boudailliez, et al. *Le corps à la mode ou les images du corps dans la psychanalyse.* Paris: Eres and Savoirs et Clinique no. 10, 2009.

Morin, Catherine, and Stephane Thibierge. "Body Image in Neurology and Psychoanalysis: History and New Developments." *Journal of Mind and Behavior* 27, no. 3/4 (2006): 301–18.

Morris, Bernadine. "For Spring, Patches of Strategically Sited Bare Skin," *The New York Times*. November 21, 1989.

Morris, Rosalind C., and Daniel H. Leonard. *The Returns of Fetishism: Charles de Brosses and the Afterlives of an Idea*. Chicago: Chicago University Press, 2017.

Moss, Donald. "On Hating in the First-Person Plural: Thinking Psychoanalytically about Racism, Homophobia, and Misogyny." *Journal of the American Psychoanalytic Association* 49, no. 4 (2001): 1315–34.

Moss, Donald. *Hating in the First-Person Plural*. New York: Other Press, 2003.

Moyse Ferreira, Lucy. *Danger in the Path of Chic*. London: Bloomsbury Visual Arts, 2022.

Muensterberger, Werner. *Collecting: An Unruly Passion*. Princeton: Princeton University Press, 1994.

Mulvagh, Jane. *Vivenne Westwood: An Unfashionable Life*. London: HarperCollins, 1998.

Mulvey, Laura. "Visual Pleasure and Narrative Cinema." *Screen* 16, no. 3 (1975): 6–18.

Mulvey, Laura. "Some Thoughts on Theories of Fetishism in the Context of Contemporary Culture." *October* 65 (Summer, 1993): 3–20.

Mundy, Jennifer. *Surrealism Desire Unbound*. London: Tate Publishing, 2002.

Musil, Robert. *The Man Without Qualities*. Translated by Eithne Wilkins and Ernst Kaiser. London: Secker and Warburg, 1960.

Myers, Wayne A. "The Traumatic Element in the Typical Dream of Being Naked." *Journal of the American Psychoanalytic Association* 37, no. 1 (1989): 117–30.

Nasio, Juan D. *Art et psychanalyse*. Paris: Payot & Rivages, 2014.

Navarette, Susan J. *The Shape of Fear*. Kentucky: University Press of Kentucky, 1998.

Navarri, Pascale. *Trendy, sexy et inconscient: Regards d'une psychoanalyst sur la mode*. Paris: Presses Universitaires de France, 2008.

Nederman, Cary J., and Jacqui True. "The Third Sex: The Idea of the Hermaphrodite in the Twelfth-Century Europe." *Journal of the History of Sexuality* 6, no. 4 (1996): 497–517.

New Orleans Museum of Art. *A Queen Within: Adorned Archetypes*. Barrett Barrera Projects, 2018.

North, Stella. "The Surfacing of the Self: The Clothing-Ego." In *Skin, Culture and Psychoanalysis*, edited by Sheila L. Cavanagh, Angela Fuller and Rachel Alpha Johnson Hurst. New York: Palgrave Macmillan, 2013.

Nye, Robert A. "The Medical Origins of Sexual Fetishism." In *Fetishism as Cultural Discourse*, edited by Emily Apter and William Pietz. Ithaca: Cornell University Press, 1993.

Oberndorf, Clarence P. *A History of Psychoanalysis in America*. New York: Grune & Stratton, 1953.

Obeyesekere, Gananth. "Foreward." In *Hair: Its Power and Meaning in Asian Cultures*, edited by Alf Hiltebeitel and Barbara D. Miller. Albany: State University of New York Press, 1998.

Oldstone-Moore, Christopher. *Of Beards and Men: The Revealing History of Facial Hair*. Chicago: University of Chicago Press, 2016.

Oliner, Marion Michel. *Cultivating Freud's Garden in France*. Northvale: Jason Aronson, 1988.

O'Neill, John. "Psychoanalytic Jewels: The Domestic Drama of Dora and Freud." In *The Socialness of Things*, edited by Stephen Harold Riggins. Berlin: Mouton de Gruyter, 1994.

Orbach, Susie. *Bodies*. New York: Picador, 2009.

Orbach, Susie, and Frederick Crews. "How We Feel about Freud: Susie Orbach and Frederick Crews Debate his Legacy." *The Guardian*. August 20, 2017. www.theguardian.com/books/2017/aug/20/feel-about-freud-debate-frederick-crews-susie-orbach-making-of-an-illusion.

Otto von Busch, Lisa Rubin, Mitchell Abidor, et al. "Fashion, Emotion and the Depths of the Self." *Public Seminar*. February 10, 2020. https://publicseminar.org/essays/fashion-emotion-and-the-depths-of-the-self.

Ovid. *Metamorphoses*. Translated by Charles Martin. New York: W.W. Norton & Company, 2004.

Pacteau, Francette. *The Symptom of Beauty*. London: Reaktion Books, 2004.

Pajaczkowska, Claire. *Ideas in Psychoanalysis: Perversion*. Cambridge: Icon Books, 2000.

Pajaczkowska, Claire, and Ivan Ward. *Shame and Sexuality: Psychoanalysis and Visual Culture*. London: Routledge, 2008.

Parsons, Michael. "Sexuality and Perversion a Hundred Years On: Discovering What Freud Discovered." *International Journal of Psychoanalysis* 81 (2000): 37–51.

Pendergrast, Mark. *Mirror Mirror: A History of the Human Love Affair with Reflection*. New York: Basic Books, 2003.

Perchuk, Andrew, and Helaine Posner, eds. *The Masculine Masquerade*. Cambridge: The MIT Press, 1995.

Perniola, Mario. "Between Clothing and Nudity." In *Fashion: Critical and Primary Sources,* vol 1: *Late Medieval to Renaissance*, edited by Peter McNeil. Oxford: Berg, 2009.

Pick, Daniel, and Lyndal Roper. "Psychoanalysis, Dreams, History: An Interview with Hanna Segal." *History Workshop Journal*, no. 49 (Spring 1999): 165–6.

Phillips, Adam. *On Flirtation*. Cambridge: Harvard University Press, 1994.

Phillips, Adam. *The Beast in the Nursery*. New York: Pantheon Books, 1998.

Phillips, Adam. *Winnicott*. London: Penguin Books, 2007.

Phillips, Adam. *Becoming Freud*. New Haven: Yale University Press, 2014.

Preciado, Paul B. *Je suis un monstre qui vous parle: Rapport pour une Académie de Psychoanalystes*. Paris: Grasset, 2020.

Prosser, Jay. *Second Skins: The Body Narratives of Transsexuality*. New York: Columbia University Press, 1998.

Prum, Richard O. *The Evolution of Beauty*. New York: Anchor Books, 2017.

Psychoanalysis, 1, nos 1 & 2. New York: Tiny Tots Comics, 1955.

Pula, Jack. "Understanding Gender Through the Lens of Transgender Experience." *Psychoanalytic Inquiry* 35, no. 8 (2015): 809–22.

Rabaté, Jean-Michel. *The Cambridge Companion to Lacan*. Cambridge: Cambridge University Press, 2003.

Radford, Robert. "Women's Bitterest Enemy: The Uses of the Psychology of Fashion." *Journal of Design History* 6, no. 2 (1993): 115–20.

Rantala, Markus J. "Evolution of Nakedness in Homo sapiens." *Journal of Zoology* 273 (2007): 1–7.

Richards, Arlene Kramer. "Ladies of Fashion: Pleasure, Perversion or Paraphilia," *International Journal of Psychoanalysis* 77, no. 337 (1996): 337–51.

Richards, Barry. *Disciplines of Delight: The Psychoanalysis of Popular Culture*. London: Free Association Books, 1994.

Riggins, Stephen Harold. *The Socialness of Things*. Berlin: Mouton de Gruyter, 1994.

Riviere, Joanne. "Womanliness as a Masquerade." In *Formations of Fantasy*, edited by Victor Burgin, James Donald and Cora Kaplan. London: Methuen, 1986.

Roach-Higgens, Mary Ellen, and Joanne B. Eicher. *Dress and Identity*. New York: Fairchild Publications, 1995.

Robcis, Camile. *The Law of Kinship: Anthropology, Psychoanalysis, and the Family in France*. Ithaca: Cornell University Press, 2013.

Roberts, Mary Louise. *Civilization Without Sexes: Reconstructing Gender in Postwar France, 1917–1927*. Chicago: University of Chicago Press, 1994.

Rocamora, Agnès. "Personal Fashion Blogs: Screens and Mirrors in Digital Self-Portraits.' *Fashion Theory: The Journal of Dress, Body and Culture* 15, no. 4 (2011): 407–24.

Rose, Gillian. *Visual Methodologies: An Introduction to the Interpretation of Visual Materials*. London: Sage Publications, 2007.

Rose, Jacqueline. "Introduction." In *Feminine Sexuality: Jacques Lacan and the Ecole Freudienne*, edited by Juliet Mitchell and Jacqueline Rose. New York: W.W. Norton, 1985.

Rose, Jacqueline. "The Analyst." *The New York Review*, September 21, 2023.

Roudinesco, Elizabeth. *Jacques Lacan: An Outline of a Life and a History of a System of Thought*. Translated by Barbara Bray. Cambridge: Polity 1997.

Roudinesco, Elizabeth. *Lacan: In Spite of Everything*. New York: Verso, 2014.

Rubenstein, Hal. *100 Unforgettable Dresses*. New York: Harper Design, 2011.

Ruggerone, Lucia, and Renate Stauss. "The Deceptive Mirror: The Dressed Body beyond Reflection." *Fashion Theory* 26, no. 2 (2020): 211–35.

Saketopoulou, Avgi. "Minding the Gap: Race and Class in Clinical Work with Gender Variant Children." *Psychoanalytic Dialogues* 21, no. 2 (2011): 192–209.

Saketopoulou, Avgi. "Mourning the Body as Bedrock: Development Considerations in Treating Transsexual Patients Analytically." *Journal of the American Psychoanalytic Association* 62, no. 5 (2014): 773–805.

Saketopoulou, Avgi. "On Trying to Pass off Transphobia as Psychoanalysis and Cruelty as 'Clinical Logic'." *Psychoanalytic Quarterly* 91, no. 1 (2022): 177–90.

Saketopoulou, Avgi. *Sexuality Beyond Consent: Risk, Race, Traumatophilia*. New York: New York University Press, 2023.

Saketopoulou, Avgi, and Ann Pellegrini. *Gender Without Identity*. New York: The Unconscious in Translation, 2023.

Samson, Alexandre. *Martin Margiela: Collections Femme 1989–2009*. Paris: Palais Galliera, Paris Musées, 2018.

Samuel, Lawrence. *Shrink: A Cultural History of Psychoanalysis in America*. Lincoln: University of Nebraska Press, 2013.

Saunders, Wren. "There's More at Stake with Fashion's Gender-Fluid Movement than You Realise." *British Vogue*. August 11, 2019. www.vogue.co.uk/article/the-meaning-of-gender-fluid-fashion.

Schiaparelli, Elsa. *Shocking Life*. London: J.M. Dent, 1954.

Schilder, Paul. *The Image and Appearance of the Human Body*. London: Routledge, [1935] 1999.

Schmidt, Jessica. "Subversion in Style: Clothing, Identity, and Social Change in 1920s Paris." *Footnotes* 2 (2009): 25–35.

Segal, Hanna. *Dream, Phantasy and Art*. New York: Tavistock/Routledge, 1991.

Segal, Julia. *Ideas in Psychoanalysis: Phantasy*. Cambridge: Icon Books, 2000.

Segal, Naomi. "The Other French Freud: Didier Anzieu – The Story of a Skin." Paper given at the University of Sussex, May 10, 2006.

Segal, Naomi. *Consensuality: Didier Anzieu, Gender and the Sense of Touch*. Amsterdam: Rodopi, 2009.

Semerene, Diego. "Tailoring the Impenetrable Body All over Again: Digitality, Muscle, and the Men's Suit." *The Routledge Companion to Fashion Studies*. New York: Routledge, 2022.

Shapiro, Elana. "Adolf Loos and the Fashion of 'the Other': Memory, Fashion and Interiors." *Interiors* 2, no. 2 (2011): 213–37.

Sharaf, Myron. *Fury on Earth*. New York: St. Martin's Press, 1983.

Shatz, Adam. *The Rebel's Clinic*. New York: Farrar, Straus and Giroux, 2024.

Shelton, Anthony. "The Chameleon Body: Power, Mutilation and Sexuality." In *Fetishism: Visualising Power and Desire*. London: Lund Humphries Publishers, 1995.

Silverman, Deborah. *Art Nouveau in Fin-de-Siècle France: Politics, Psychology and Style*. Berkeley: University of California Press, 1989.

Silverman, Kaja. "Fragments of a Fashionable Discourse." In *Studies in Entertainment: Critical Approaches to Mass Culture*, edited by Tania Modleski. Bloomington: Indiana University Press, 1986.

Simmel, Georg. "Fashion." In *The Rise of Fashion: A Reader*, edited by Daniel Leonard Purdy. Minneapolis: University of Minnesota Press, 2004.

Soler, Colette. "What Does the Unconscious Know about Women?" In *Reading Seminar XX: Lacan's Major Work on Love, Knowledge, and Feminine Sexuality*, edited by Suzanne Barnard and Bruce Fink. New York: State University of New York Press, 2002.

Solms, Mark. *The Hidden Spring: A Journey to the Source of Consciousness*. New York: W.W. Norton, 2021.

Springer, Anne. "Female Perversion: Scenes and Strategies Analysis and Culture." *Journal of Analytical Psychology* 41 (1996): 325–38.

Squire, Michael. *The Art of the Body: Antiquity and Its Legacy*. New York: Oxford University Press, 2011.

Steakley, James. "Cinema and Censorship in the Weimar Republic: The Case of Anders an Die Andern." *Film History* 11, no. 2 (1999): 181–203.

Steele, Valerie. *Fashion and Eroticism: Ideals of Feminine Beauty from the Victorian Era Through the Jazz Age*. Oxford: Oxford University Press, 1985.

Steele, Valerie. *Women of Fashion*. New York: Rizzoli, 1991.

Steele, Valerie. "The F Word." *Lingua Franca: The Review of Academic Life* (April 1991): 17–20.

Steele, Valerie. *Fetish: Fashion, Sex and Power*. Oxford: Oxford University Press, 1996.

Steele, Valerie. *The Corset: A Cultural History*. New Haven: Yale University Press, 2003.

Steele, Valerie, and Jennifer Park. *Gothic: Dark Glamour*. New Haven: Yale University Press, 2008.

Steinmetz, Katie. "The Transgender Tipping Point." *Time* magazine. May 29, 2014. https://time.com/135480/transgender-tipping-point.

Stewart, Janet. *Fashioning Vienna: Adolf Loos's Cultural Criticism*. New York: Routledge, 2000.

Stoute, Beverly. "Black Rage: The Psychic Adaptation to the Trauma of Oppression." *Journal of the American Psychoanalytic Association* 69, no. 2 (2021): 259–90.

Strathern, Andrew. "Why is Shame on Skin?" *Ethnology* 14, no. 4 (1975): 347–56.

Strauss, Renata. "Passing as Fashionable, Feminine and Sane: 'Therapy of Fashion' and the Normalization of Psychiatric Patients in 1960s US." *Fashion Theory* 24, no. 4 (2020): 601–37.

Svendsen, Lars. *Fashion: A Philosophy*. Translated by John Irons. London: Reaktion Books, 2006.

Sweeney, Megan. *Mendings*. Durham: Duke University Press, 2023.

Sweeny-Risko, Jennifer. "The New Woman and Surrealist Politics." *Interdisciplinary Literary Studies* 17, no. 3 (2015): 309–29.

Tate, Shirley Anne. *Black Skins, Black Masks*. Aldershot: Ashgate, 2005.

Tietjens Meyers, Diana. *Gender in the Mirror: Cultural Imagery and Women's Agency*. Oxford: Oxford University Press, 2002.

Toron Beck, Evelyn, and Susan (Shanee) Stepakoff. "Review: Lesbians in Psychoanalytic Theory and Practice." *Feminist Studies* 26, no. 2 (2000): 477–95.

Toulalan, Sarah, and Kate Fisher, eds. *The Routledge History of Sex and the Body 1500 to the Present*. New York: Routledge, 2013.

Townsend, Patricia. *Creative States of Mind: Psychoanalysis and the Artist's Process*. New York: Routledge, 2019.

Trebay, Guy. "She's Only Playing a Therapist, but the Revelations Are Real." *The New York Times*. October 10, 2024. www.nytimes.com/2024/10/10/style/bella-freud-fashion-neurosis-podcast.html.

Tsolas, Vaia, and Christine Anzieu-Premmereur, eds. *A Psychoanalytic Exploration of the Body in Today's World*. New York: Routledge, 2018.

Turkle, Sherry. *Psychoanalytic Politics: Jacques Lacan and Freud's French Revolution*. London: Free Association Books, 1992.

Turkle, Sherry. *The Empathy Diaries: A Memoir*. New York: Penguin, 2021.

Ucko, Peter J. "Penis Sheaths: A Comparative Study." *Proceedings of the Royal Anthropological Institute of Great Britain and Ireland* (1969): 24A–67.

Ulbrich, Claudia, and Richard Wittman, eds. *Fashioning the Self in Transcultural Settings: The Uses and Significance of Dress in Self-Narratives*. Würzburg: Ergon Verlag, 2015.

Vänskä, Annamari. "Gender and Sexuality." In *A Cultural Dress and Fashion in Modern Age*, edited by Alexandra Palmer. London: Bloomsbury, 2017.

Vänskä, Annamari. "From Gay to Queer or, Wasn't Fashion Always Already a Very Queer Thing?" In *Fashion Theory: A Reader*, edited by Malcolm Barnard. New York: Routledge, 2021.

Varo Remedios, Maria. *On Homoradars and Other Writings*, edited and translated by Margaret Carson. Cambridge: Wakefield Press, 2024.

Vazire, Simine, Laura Naumann, Peter Rentfrow, and Samuel Gosling. "Portrait of a Narcissist: Manifestations of Narcissism in Physical Appearance." *Journal of Research in Personality* 42 (December 2008): 1439–47.

Vicary, Grace Q. "Visual Art as Social Data: The Renaissance Codpiece." *Cultural Anthropology* 4, no. 1 (1989): 3–25.

Vincent, Susan J. *The Anatomy of Fashion: Dressing the Body from the Renaissance to Today*. Oxford: Berg, 2009.

Vinken, Barbara. "Fashion, Art of Dying, Art of Living." Paper given at the Art of Fashion Symposium at the Fashion Institute of Technology. November 9, 2007.

Vischer, Friedrich T. "Fashion and Cynicism." In *The Rise of Fashion: A Reader*, edited by Daniel Leonard Purdy. Minneapolis: University of Minnesota Press, 2004.

Von Krafft-Ebing, Richard. *Psychopathia Sexualis*. Translated by F.J. Rebman. New York: Physicians and Surgeons Book Company, [1906] 1934.

Wahrman, Dror. *The Making of the Modern Self*. New Haven: Yale University Press, 2006

Wallace, Edwin R., and John Gach. *History of Psychiatry and Medical Psychology*. New York: Springer Science, 2008.

Wallenberg, Louise, and Andrea Kollnitz, eds. *Fashion Aesthetics and Ethics Past and Present*. London: Bloomsbury Visual Arts, 2023.

Ward, Ivan. *Ideas in Psychoanalysis: Castration*. Cambridge: Icon Books, 2003.

Webb, Veronica. Interview with Valerie Steele, May 6, 2024.

Weissberg, Liliane. "Adriadne's Thread." *MLN* 125 (April 2010): 661–81.

Wendel, Frederich. *Weib und Mode*. Dresdin: Paul Aretz Verlag, 1928.

White, Kathleen Pogue. "Surviving Hating and Being Hated." *Contemporary Psychoanalysis* 38, no. 3 (2002): 401–22.

Winnicott, Donald. *Playing and Reality*. London: Tavistock Publications, 1971.

Wilson, Cintra. *Fear and Clothing*. New York: W.W. Norton & Company, 2015.

Wilson, Elizabeth. *Adorned in Dreams: Fashion and Modernity*. Berkeley: University of California Press, 1985.

Wood, Gaby. "Rebel with a Corset." *The Guardian*. August 27, 2005. www.theguardian.com/lifeandstyle/2005/aug/28/fashion.shopping3.

Wood, Ghislaine. *The Surreal Body: Fetish and Fashion*. London: V & A, 2007.

Woods, Gregory. *Homintern: How Gay Culture Liberated the Modern World*. New Haven: Yale University Press, 2016.

Wright, Elizabeth. *Feminism and Psychoanalysis*. Oxford: Blackwell Publishers, 1992.

Wright, Lee. "Objectifying Gender: The Stiletto Heel." In *Fashion Theory: A Reader*, edited by Malcom Barnard. New York: Routledge, 2021.

Young, Kimball. "The Psychology of Dress: An Analysis of Fashion and its Motive. Elizabeth B. Hurlock." *American Journal of Sociology* 36, no. 2 (1930).

Young-Bruehl, Elisabeth. *Anna Freud: A Biography*. New Haven: Yale University Press, 2008.

Zaretsky, Eli. *Secrets of the Soul: A Social and Cultural History of Psychoanalysis*. New York: Alfred A. Knopf, 2004.

Zeffirelli, Franco. *Zeffirelli, An Autobiography*. New York: Weidenfeld and Nicolson, 1986.

Zhang, Erique. "'She is as Feminine as my Mother, as my Sister, as my Biologically Female Friends': On the Promise and Limits of Transgender Visibility in Fashion Media." *Communication, Culture and Critique* 16, no. 1 (2022): 25–32.

IMAGE CREDITS

0.0 Artist Alisa Gorshenina wearing artificial eyes and a jeweled mouth. Photo by Elizaveta Porodina (@elizavetaporodina) ii

I.1 John Galliano for Dior Haute Couture Autumn/Winter 2000, two figures. © Robert Fairer x

I.2 Screen grab from Prada's short film *A Therapy* (2012). Directed by Roman Polanski, starring Helena Bonham Carter and Ben Kingsley. Cinematography by Eduardo Serra. Prada/YouTube 2

I.3 *Machine Worker in Summer* (*Joan Richards*) by Yevonde, tri-colour separation negative, 1937. Purchased with support from the Portrait Fund, 2021. Photographs Collection. NPG x220579 © National Portrait Gallery, London 5

I.4 Mademoiselle de Beaumont or The Chevalier D'Éon, 1777. British Cartoon Prints Collection. Library of Congress Prints and Photographs Division, Washington, D.C. 20540 6

I.5 Ramon Casas, *Decadent Young Woman. After the Dance,* 1899. Oil on canvas. Museu de Montserrat, Abadia de Montserrat, SpainIndex Fototeca/Bridgeman Images 8

1.1 Sigmund Freud, c. 1906. Photo by Imagno/Getty Images 12

1.2 Sigmund Freud next to his father Jakob Freud. Austria, 1864. Mondadori Portfolio via Getty Images 14

1.3 Sigmund Freud and Mutter Amalie, 1872. Photo by Sigmund Freud. Copyrights/ullstein bild via Getty Images 16

1.4 Sigmund Freud with his wife Martha (Bernays), 1885. Library of Congress Prints and Photographs Division, Washington, D.C. 20540 USA 17

1.5 Alfred (seated) and Stefan Zweig, 1898. Photographed by Kunst Salon Pietzner, Vienna. The Stefan Zweig Collection, Daniel A. Reed. Library Archives & Special Collections, State University of New York at Fredonia 18

1.6 André Brouillet, *A Clinical Lesson at the Salpêtrière,* 1887. Image source: Wikimedia Commons (public domain) 22

1.7 Gustave Moreau, *Oedipus and the Sphinx,* 1864. Oil on canvas. The Metropolitan Museum of Art, New York. Bequest of William H. Herriman, 1920 23

1.8 Octave Uzanne, *La Femme à Paris* Cover illustration of La Parisienne as a sphinx by Leon Rudnicki. Photo by: Universal History Archive/Universal Images Group via Getty Images 24

1.9 Emile Pasquier, ballgown, 1889–1890, France. Photo © The Museum at FIT 25

1.10 Edouard Manet, *Nana,* 1877. Oil on canvas. Hamburger Kunsthalle, Hamburg, Germany/Bridgeman Images 27

2.1 *Cupid and Psyche*, 1589, by Jacopo Zucchi (1540–1589-90), oil on canvas. Villa and Galleria Borghese, Rome, Lazio, Italy. © NPL – DeA Picture Library/G. Nimatallah/Bridgeman Images 30

2.2 Portrait of Adele Bloch-Bauer I, 1907, by Gustav Klimt, oil, silver, and gold on canvas. Photo by Imagno/Getty Images 32

2.3 Félix Vallotton, *Intérieur avec femme en rouge de dos*, 1903, Kunsthaus, Zurich. Photo: Peter Barritt/Alamy Stock Photo 33

2.4 Jack Jacobus, Ltd. side-button boots of leather and silk. 1895–1900, England. The Museum at FIT, Gift of Victoria and Albert Museum. Photo © The Museum at FIT 34

2.5 Bag, c. 1907. Photo © The Museum at FIT 35

2.6 Karl Lagerfeld for Chanel, shoes, cruise 2009. Photo © The Museum at FIT 36

2.7 Masaccio, *The Expulsion from the Garden of Eden*, 1426–27. Wilkipedia Commons 37

2.8 Cover of *From Nudity to Raiment*, by Hilaire Hiler, featuring a photograph by Charles Martin of Bontoc Igorot women wearing skirts of leaves. Courtesy of the author 39

2.9 Lanvin, "naked torso" dress, Summer 2013. Photo © The Museum at FIT 42

2.10 Jean Paul Gaultier, Femme trompe l'oeil cyber muscle suit, Spring 1996. Photo © The Museum at FIT 42

2.11 Jeremy Scott for Moschino, Chocolate bar dress, Fall 2014. Photo by Jacopo Raule/Getty Images 43

2.12 René Magritte, *Les Jours gigantesques* (*The Titanic Days*), Paris, 1928. Private Collection. Photo © Christie's Images/Bridgeman Images. © 2024 C. Herscovici/Artists Rights Society (ARS), New York 45

2.13 Rick Owens, ensemble, Spring 2009. Gift of Rick Owens. Photo © The Museum at FIT 47

2.14 Grandville (Jean-Ignace-Isidore Gerard), *Venus at the Opera*, 1844. INTERFOTO/Alamy Stock Photo 49

2.15 Countess Greffulhe, 1896. Photograph by Paul Nadar. Palais Galleria, Musée de la Mode de la Ville de Paris. © Eric Emo/Galliera/Roger-Viollet 50

2.16 Barbara Kruger, *Untitled (You are seduced by the sex appeal of the inorganic)*, 1981. Gelatin silver print, 96.2 × 127.6 cm, 37 7/8 × 50 1/4 inches. Courtesy of the artist and Sprüth Magers 51

2.17 Eva Gonzàles, *A Box at the Théâtre des Italiens*, 1874, oil on canvas. Musée d'Orsay, Paris, France/Bridgeman Images 52

2.18 Pair of fetish buttoned boots, European, c. 1895. Francesca Galloway, London. Image © Francesca Galloway (Photograph Katrina Lawson Johnston) 54

2.19 G. de Clérambault, *Femme Marocaine Voilée*, 1917–1920. © Musée du quai Branly – Jacques Chirac, Dist. RMN-Grand Palais/Art Resource, NY 55

2.20 Hans Memling, *Vanity*, central panel from the *Triptych of Earthly Vanity and Divine Salvation*, c. 1485. Musee des Beaux-Arts, Strasbourg, France. Art Heritage/Alamy Stock Photo 57

3.1 *Les Garçonnes*, 1928. Photograph by Jacques Henri Lartigue. © Ministère de la Culture (France), MPP-AAJHL 60

3.2 American actress Colleen Moore with Neil Hamilton in the 1929 film *Why Be Good?* Photo by First National Pictures/Michael Ochs Archives/Getty Images 62

3.3 Two women smoking. Photo by Henry Guttmann Collection/Hulton Archive/Getty Images 64

3.4 Man Ray, *Barbette Dressing*, c. 1926. Gelatin silver print. Ford Motor Company Collection, Gift of Ford Motor Company and John C. Waddell, 1987. Image copyright © The Metropolitan Museum of Art. Image source: Art Resource, NY. © Man Ray 2015 Trust/Artists Rights Society (ARS), NY/ADAGP, Paris 2024 65

3.5 Jeanne Mammen, *She Represents*. Illustration from the *Führer durch das 'lasterhafte' Berlin* (*Guide to Immoral Berlin*). Author: Konrad Haemmling, Leipzig, 1931. Inv. Tc 10226/9. Historical Prints Division. Location: Staatsbibliothek zu Berlin/Stiftung Preussischer Kulturbesitz/Berlin/Germany. Credit: bpk Bildagentur/Staatsbibliothek zu Berlin/Stiftung Preussischer Kulturbesitz/Berlin/Germany/Art Resource, NY. © 2024 Artists Rights Society (ARS), New York/VG Bild-Kunst, Bonn 65

3.6 Photograph of a costume party held at the Institute for Sexual Research (Institut für Sexualwissenschaft) in Berlin, c. 1920s. Magnus-Hirschfeld-Gesellschaft e.V., Berlin 66

3.7 Manuel Rodríguez Lozano, *Retrato de Salvador Novo*, 1924. Oil on cardboard. Courtesy of Museo Nacional de Arte INBAL 67

3.8 Gabrielle "Coco" Chanel, c. 1929–30. Courtesy of the author 68

3.9 Irving Penn, *Chanel Sequined Suit* (1926), New York, 1974. Photograph by Irving Penn. © The Irving Penn Foundation 71

3.10 Joan Riviere, c. 1931. Joan Riviere collection, the British Psychoanalytical Society Archive, P02-D-12. Reproduced by kind permission 73

3.11 Maison Roger, dress, c. 1877. Photo © The Museum at FIT 76

3.12 Callot Soeurs, evening dress, c. 1924. Photo © The Museum at FIT 77

3.13 Augusta Bernard, evening dress, 1933. Photo © The Museum at FIT 78

3.14 J.C. Flügel wearing hat and shorts with other members at the first Men's Dress Reform Party rally, 1929. British Library/Granger. © The Granger Collection Ltd d/b/a GRANGER Historical Picture Archive 80

3.15 Agnolo Bronzino, *Portrait of Guidobaldo II della Rovere, Duke of Urbino*, 1531–32. Galleria Palatina, Palazzo Pitti, Florence, Italy. Luisa Ricciarini/Bridgeman Images 82

4.1 Portrait of Elsa Schiaparelli, September 1, 1937. Horst P. Horst, *Vogue*, © Condé Nast 84

4.2 Model wearing suit and shoe hat by Elsa Schiaparelli, 1937. Photo by ullstein bild/ullstein bild/Getty Images 87

4.3 André Kertész, *Muguet Seller on the Champs-Élysées*, 1928. © The Estate of André Kertész/courtesy Stephen Bulger Gallery 91

4.4 March 4, 1938 cover of *Harper's Bazaar*. Courtesy of *Harper's Bazaar*, Hearst Magazine Media, Inc. © 2024 – Approval A.M. Cassandre/Artists Rights Society (ARS), New York 92

4.5 Elsa Schiaparelli, Tears dress from the "Circus Collection," fabric designed by Salvador Dalí. Paris, France, 1938. © Victoria and Albert Museum, London 93

4.6 The wicked stepmother in the Disney film *Snow White and the Seven Dwarfs*, 1937. Directed by William Cottrell, David Hand, Wilfred Jackson, Larry Morey, Perce Pearce, Ben Sharpsteen. Produced by Walt Disney Productions. Disney Enterprises, Inc.. Screen grab 95

4.7 Dress by Madeleine Vionnet, 1931. Paris, Musée des Arts Décoratifs. © Les Arts Décoratifs 96

4.8 Elsa Schiaparelli, evening jacket, Spring 1939. Francesca Galloway, London. Image © Francesca Galloway (Photograph Katrina Lawson Johnston) 98

4.9 Portrait of Jacques Lacan, October 1967. Photo by Giancarlo BOTTI/Gamma-Rapho via Getty Images 101

4.10 Larry Shox, "Celestial Eye" suit, 1985. © The Museum at FIT 102

4.11 Daniel Roseberry for Schiaparelli, Autumn/Winter 2023/2024 haute couture collection. Photo by Peter White/Getty Images 103

4.12 PTRA, "Walking lip" dress, 004 Collection, 2019. Photograph Victor Trani, courtesy PTRA 105

5.1 Christian Dior, 1955. Photo by Willy Maywald. © 2024 Association Willy Maywald/Artists Rights Society (ARS), New York/ADAGP, Paris, 2024 106

5.2 Marlene Dietrich in Dior by Horst P. Horst, 1947. Horst P. Horst, *Vogue*, © Condé Nast 109

5.3 Jacques Fath with model Bettina, 1950. Photograph by Louise Dahl-Wolfe. Collection Center for Creative Photography. © Center for Creative Photography, Arizona Board of Regents 110

5.4 "Dress Right" advertisement. American Institute of Men's and Boys' Wear 113

5.5 *Spellbound*, 1945, USA. Set design by Salvador Dalí. Directed by Alfred Hitchcock. Courtesy The Museum of Modern Art. © 2024 Salvador Dalí, Fundació Gala-Salvador Dalí, Artists Rights Society. Digital Image © The Museum of Modern Art/Licensed by SCALA/Art Resource, NY 114

5.6 Actress Ava Gardner on the set of *The Killers*, directed by Robert Siodmak. Photo by Sunset Boulevard/Corbis via Getty Images 115

5.7 *Psychoanalysis* comic books, issues 1 and 2, 1955. EC Comics. Writers: Daniel Keyes, Robert Bernstein. Artists: Jack Kamen, Marie Severin. Photo courtesy © The Museum at FIT 115

5.8 Vietnam War protests, 1966. Photo by Fairfax Media via Getty Images/Fairfax Media via Getty Images via Getty Images 117

5.9 Stokely Carmichael reading Fanon, 1967. © John Haynes. All rights reserved 2024/Bridgeman Images 120

5.10 Panther Party members, 1969. Photo by David Fenton/Getty Images 120

5.11 Willi Posey, ensemble, c. 1970. Photo © The Museum at FIT 121

5.12 Anne Fogarty, August 1951. Nina Leen/The LIFE Picture Collection/Shutterstock 121

5.13 Remedios Varo, *Woman Leaving the Psychoanalyst*, 1960. Museo de Arte Moderno, Mexico City. © 2024 Remedios Varo, Artists Rights Society (ARS), New York/VEGAP, Madrid 123

5.14 Kay Tobin Lahusen, Barbara Gittings protesting at Independence Hall, Philadelphia, PA, July 4, 1966. Photo by Kay Tobin © Manuscripts and Archives Division, The New York Public Library 124

5.15 Peter Hujar, *COME OUT!*, 1970. Black and white poster. © 2024 The Peter Hujar Archive/Artists Rights Society (ARS), New York 125

5.16 Barbara Gittings, Frank Kameny, and Dr. John Fryer as Dr. H. Anonymous at the American Psychiatric Association's 1972 convention. Photo by Kay Tobin © Manuscripts and Archives Division, The New York Public Library 126

5.17 Sonia Rykiel, striped wool pant set, c. 1975. Photo © The Museum at FIT 129

5.18 A pinstriped trouser suit by Yves Saint Laurent, 1967. Photo by Reg Lancaster/Daily Express/Hulton Archive/Getty Images 131

5.19 Publicity still from the 1966 film *Blow-Up*. MGM/Photofest 132

5.20 Johnny Rotten, dressed in the prototype black sateen bondage suit. Heathrow, 1976. Photograph © Ray Stevenson 133

6.1 Elizabeth Hurley in Versace's safety pin dress with Hugh Grant, 1994. Photo by Gareth Davies/Mission Pictures/Getty Images 134

6.2 1992 Versace collection. Photograph by Irving Penn. © The Irving Penn Foundation. Image courtesy of Versace 136

6.3 Peter Lindbergh for *Vogue Paris*, August 1985. © Condé Nast 139

6.4 Vivienne Westwood, brassiere as outerwear, *Nostalgia of Mud* collection, Fall/Winter 1983. Photograph by Niall McInerney, © Bloomsbury Publishing Plc 141

6.5 Jean Paul Gaultier showing a bra from his 1984 *Barbès* collection. Photo by: Photo12/Universal Images Group via Getty Images 141

6.6 Jean Paul Gaultier, cone bra dress, also described as a corset dress with a torpedo brassiere, Fall 1984. Photo by Daniel SIMON/Gamma-Rapho via Getty Images 142

6.7 Jean Paul Gaultier Homme, jacket, 1988. Photo © The Museum at FIT 144

6.8 Richard Gere, on the set of the film *American Gigolo*, Paramount Pictures, 1980. Glasshouse Images/Alamy Stock Photo 145

6.9 Timothée Chalamet wearing Haider Ackermann at the 2022 Venice Film Festival. Photo by Maria Moratti/Getty Images 146

6.10 Jean Paul Gaultier, pink halter-top jumpsuit, Spring 1998 collection. Photo by Giovanni Giannoni/Fairchild Archive/Penske Media via Getty Images 146

6.11 Jean Paul Gaultier, man's jumpsuit, Spring 1998. Photo © The Museum at FIT 147

6.12 Madonna wearing Jean Paul Gaultier conical bra corset, *Blonde Ambition* world tour, Feyenoord Stadion, De Kuip, Rotterdam, Holland, July 24, 1990. Photo by Gie Knaeps/Getty Images 148

6.13 Jerry Hall modeling in Thierry Mugler, 1980. Photo by Allan Tannenbaum/Getty Images 149

6.14 Thierry Mugler, evening set, *Les Atlantes* collection, Spring 1989. Photo © The Museum at FIT 150

6.15 Connie Girl modeling at the Thierry Mugler Spring/Summer 1992 fashion show. Photo by Pierre Vauthey/Sygma/Sygma via Getty Images 151

6.16 Thierry Mugler, Spring 1985 ready-to-wear collection. Photograph by Niall McInerney, © Bloomsbury Publishing Plc 151

6.17 John Galliano, *Suzy Sphinx* collection, Autumn/Winter 1997. Photo by Niall McInerney, © Bloomsbury Publishing Plc 152

6.18 E.V. Day, *Transporter*, 2000, from the "Exploding Couture" series. Photo courtesy E.V. Day Studio 153

6.19 Alexander McQueen, *La Poupée* collection, Spring/Summer 1997. Photo by Niall McInerney, © Bloomsbury Publishing Plc 155

6.20 Alexander McQueen, *The Hunger* collection, Spring/Summer 1996. Photo by Niall McInerney, © Bloomsbury Publishing Plc 156

6.21 Alexander McQueen, *Joan* collection, Autumn/Winter 1998. Photo by Niall McInerney, © Bloomsbury Publishing Plc 157

6.22 Alexander McQueen, *Joan*, Autumn/Winter 1998 collection. Photo: firstVIEW 157

6.23 Model wearing Christian Dior ballgown, Spring-Summer 1950. Photograph by Louise Dahl-Wolfe. Collection Center for Creative Photography. © Center for Creative Photography, Arizona Board of Regents 159

6.24 Chauffeur, John Galliano for Dior Haute Couture Autumn/Winter 2000. Photo by Victor VIRGILE/Gamma-Rapho via Getty Images 161

6.25 John Galliano for Dior Haute Couture Autumn/Winter 2000–2001, crocodile woman. Photo by Victor VIRGILE/Gamma-Rapho via Getty Images 162

6.26 Sylvie Fleury, *Untitled*, 1994, from the exhibition *Spring* at Galerie Philomene Magers in Cologne (March 21–April 19, 1997). Art & Public Geneva. © Sylvie Fleury, Courtesy the artist and Sprüth Magers 163

6.27 VVB35 Vanessa Beecroft Performance, 1998. Solomon R. Guggenheim Museum, New York © 2024 Vanessa Beecroft 164

7.1 Karl Lagerfeld wearing sunglasses. Photo by Bertrand Rindoff Petroff/Getty Images 166

7.2 Caravaggio, *Narcissus*, c. 1600. Galleria Nazionale d'Arte Antica. Wikimedia Commons 169

7.3 Caravaggio, *Medusa*, 1595–98. Galleria degli Uffizi, Florence. Photo by Fine Art Images/Heritage Images/Getty Images 171

7.4 Versace, purse, c. 1992. Photo © The Museum at FIT 172

7.5 Didier Anzieu and his wife Annie Péghaire Anzieu, 1976. Photo courtesy Christine Anzieu-Premmereur 174

7.6 Romeo Gigli, cocoon coat, Fall 1991. © The Museum at FIT 176

7.7 Comme des Garçons, hooded dress, Spring 2017. Photo: firstVIEW 178

7.8 Azzedine Alaïa, hooded evening dress, Winter 1986. Photo © The Museum at FIT 179

7.9 Supermodel Veronica Webb, wearing an Azzedine Alaïa snakeskin bustier and skirt at El Teddy's restaurant, NYC, 1995. DMI/The LIFE Picture Collection/Shutterstock 181

7.10 Jennifer Lopez wearing Donatella Versace at the 42nd Grammy Awards, 2000. Photo by Jeff Vespa/WireImage 182

7.11 Bach Mai, Look 16, Spring 2023. Photo by Amber Gray, © Bach Mai 183

7.12 Helmut Lang, evening dress, Fall 2004. Photo © The Museum at FIT 184

7.13 Viktor & Rolf, "I'm Not Shy I Just Don't Like You" dress, Spring/Summer 2019 haute couture. Photo by Thierry Chesnot/Getty Images 185

7.14 Balmain, Spring 2022 collection. Photo by Dominique Charriau/Getty Images 186

7.15 Maison Martin Margiela, Linen dress form tunic, Spring 1997. Photo © The Museum at FIT 187

7.16 Rei Kawakubo of Comme des Garçons, dress, *Body Meets Dress, Dress Meets Body* collection, Spring 1997. Photo © The Museum at FIT 188

7.17 Viktor & Rolf, Autumn/Winter 2020 haute couture. Photo by Casper Kofi, courtesy Viktor & Rolf 190

7.18 Viktor & Rolf, Autumn/Winter 2020 haute couture. Photo by Casper Kofi, courtesy Viktor & Rolf 191

7.19 Spider Dress 2.0, dress created by Anouk Wipprecht for INTEL (2015) collaboration with Philip H. Wilck. Photography by Jason Perry 192

7.20 Noir Kei Ninomiya, dress, Fall 2021. Photograph courtesy Comme des Garçons 193

7.21 Issey Miyake, bustier, 1983. Photo © The Museum at FIT 195

8.1 Laverne Cox wearing a vintage Thierry Mugler jacket from the A/W 1990 collection. Photography by Sequoia Emmanuelle @sequoiaemmanuelle. Photo assistant: @mariaqphotography. Makeup: @theladydeja. Hair: @kiyahwright1. Styled by: @christinajpacelli 196

8.2 Alessandro Michele for Gucci, man's ensemble, Spring 2017. Photo © The Museum at FIT 199

8.3 David Bowie wearing a dress designed by Michael Fish at his home, Haddon Hall, Beckenham, Kent, 1971. Trinity Mirror/Mirrorpix/Alamy Stock Photo 200

8.4 Grace Wales Bonner, man's suit, Spring 2017. Photo © The Museum at FIT 201

8.5 *Mamado* pantsuit by Bárbara Sánchez-Kane as featured in "Amantes Encontrados" for *Vogue Italia*, 2019. Photo by Paola Vivas. Styling by Chino Castilla. Models: Emiliano and Samuel for GUERXS AGENCY MX 202

8.6 Undercover, dress, Fall 2020, Japan. Photo © The Museum at FIT 207

8.7 Noir Kei Ninomiya, Spring/Summer 2023 collection. Photo courtesy Comme des Garçons 208

INDEX

abjection 130
Ackermann, Haider 137, 146
African styles 119
aggression 88, 94, 99, 112, 130, 177
"Aimée" 89, 173
Alexander, Hilary 158
ambiguity 3, 70, 143, 144–5, 160, 173
American Gigolo (film) 144, 145
American Psychiatric Association 125
American Tobacco Company 28
American Vogue 203
Amies, Hardie 108, 109
Anders als die Andern (*Different from the Others*) (film) 64
Anderson, Jonathan W. 198
Andreas-Salomé, Lou 58
androgyny 7, 63, 64, 70, 71, 110, 145, 148, 203
anger 70, 112, 116
anima/animus 46
anorexia 177, 180
antisemitism 15, 20, 40, 118
anxiety 20, 28–9, 32, 74, 189, 192
    castration 171
    gender 91
    parental 174
Anzieu, Didier 9, 10, 41, 173–5, 185, 189, 194
Anzieu, René 173
Anzieu-Premmereur, Christine 175

Armani, Giorgio 144, 145
Armstrong, Lisa 182
Assoun, Paul-Laurent 172
Atlas, Charles 114
Avrane, Patrick 189
Avril, Jane 21
Azzedine, Alaïa 179, 180, 181

Bak, Robert C. 138, 140
Balenciaga, Cristobal 108, 110
Ballard, J.G. 167
Balmain, Pierre 108, 109, 186
Balsing, Anne-Sophie 160
Bancroft, Alison 152, 154, 155, 156, 158
Barbette 64, 65
Barcan, Ruth 38
Bard, Christine 62, 63
Barthes, Roland 168, 183
Barzini, Benedetta 160
Bataille, Georges 88
Bataille, Sylvia 88, 100
Baudelaire, Charles 138, 150
Baudry, Emilie 88
beard 17
Beaton, Cecil 111
Beaumont, Mademoiselle de (Chevalier D'Éon) 6, 7
Beauvoir, Simone de 7, 97, 119
Beecroft, Vanessa 164
Bell, David 205
Belle Époque 49, 108, 158

Bellmer, Hans 88
Benjamin, Walter 207
Benthien, Claudia 171, 172
Berenson, Marisa 160
Bergler, Edmund 10, 11, 107, 108, 110, 112, 116–17
Bernard, Augusta 78
Bernays, Edward 28
Bernays, Martha 13, 17–18, 19, 20, 23, 27
Bernays, Minna 23
Bernheim, Hippolyte 21
Bernini: statue of Saint Teresa 154
Bettina (model) 110
Bick, Esther 175
Binet, Alfred 25, 26
bisexuality 7, 44, 45, 63, 64, 66
Black Panther Party 119, 120
Blanks, Tim 198
Bliss, Sylvia 59
Blondin, Marie-Louise 100
Blow-Up (film) 130, 132
Blum, Dilys 99
bodily ego 7, 173, 175
body dysmorphia 90, 168, 180, 200
body image 9, 88, 91, 97, 180
body modification 130, 177, 185
Bolas, Christopher 70
Bondage Suit 132, 133
Bonham Carter, Helena 1, 2
Bonner, Grace Wales 201
Bornstein, Kate 198

Bourdain, Guy 130
Bowie, David 144, 200
brassiere 140–2
breast 28, 74, 140, 152
Breton, André 88
Breward, Christopher 79, 109
Brewer, John 3, 4
British Vogue 203
Bronniman, Catherine 46
Bronzino, Agnolo: *Portrait of Guidobaldo II della Rovere, Duke of Urbino*, 82
Brosses, Charles de 26
Brouillet, André: *A Clinical Lesson at the Salpêtrière*, 21, 22
Brown, Patrick Viersen 126, 205, 206
Brubach, Holly 149
Brummel, Beau 18
Bruni, Carla 167
Buffon 88
Business of Fashion 202
bustle 40, 75
Butler, Judith 9, 75, 198, 294

Callot Soeurs 77
Caraman-Chimay, Élisabeth de, Countess Greffulhe 49, 50
Caravaggio
    Medusa 171
    Narcissus 169
Carmichael, Stokely 120
Carpenter, Edward 67
Carrington, Leonora 122
Casas, Ramon: *Decadent Young Woman. After the Dance* 8
castration 54, 55, 80
    fears of 81, 130
Cavallaro, Dani 8
Chalamet, Timothée 137, 145, 146
Chanel, Gabrielle "Coco" 10, 36, 67–71, 72, 85, 110–11, 138, 207
Channer, Alice 177
Chapin, Chloe 79

Charcot, Jean-Martin 20, 21, 22, 25, 26, 27, 88
Charcot, Mademoiselle 23
Chauffeur uniforms 67, 159, 160, 161
cigarettes 28
cisgender gaze 203
civil rights movement 118, 119
Cixous, Hélène 128, 130
Clarke, Alison 29
Clarks, Kenneth 41
Clérambault, Gaëtan Gatian de 55, 56, 89
clothes symbolism 75
clothing ego 189
Cobbs, Price 118
Cocteau, Jean 64
codpiece 40, 81, 137, 143
cognitive behavioral psychology 9
collective unconscious 46
Coltart, Nina 104
Comme des Garçons 94, 177, 178, 188
commodity fetishism 26, 163
"compulsive" buying 28
cone bra 140–2
confrontation dressing 132
Copernicus 15
Copjec, Joan 56
core gender identity 198
corset 3, 21, 27, 40, 79, 99, 108, 140–2, 147, 148, 160
Cox, Laverne 197, 209
cross-dressing 7, 20, 48, 53, 55, 64, 66, 74

Dada 100
Dahl, Sophie 160
Dalí, Gala 86
Dalí, Salvador 70, 85, 86, 87, 88, 90, 93, 97, 104, 112, 114
    Necrophiliac Springtime (owned by Schiaparelli), *The Dream Places its Hand on a Man's Shoulder*, 93
    "Rotten Donkey, The" 88

Three Young Surrealist Women Holding in their Arms the Skins of an Orchestra 93–4
Darwin, Charles 15, 17, 38–40
Davis, Pia 204
Day, E.V. 153, 154
death 2, 45, 93, 156, 208–9
    denial of 206, 207
death drive 206
deconstructionist styles 94
deep surface, fashion as 8–9
defense mechanisms 189
defensive femininity 79
Deleuze, Gilles 209
dell'Orefice, Carmen 160
Deneuve, Catherine 129
d'Éon, Chevalier 6, 7
desire
    associations 104
    same-sex 67, 122
    sexual 32, 44, 48
    sexual difference and 135–65
Diagnostic and Statistical Manual of Mental Disorders (DSM-1) 21, 116, 125
Dichter, Ernest 28
Dietrich, Marlene 109, 129
differentiation 69, 104
Dior, Christian 1, 107, 108, 109, 110, 158, 159, 161, 162, 168
Disney, Walt 95
Dittmar, Helga 28
Dolto, Françoise 103
doppelganger motif 47
double discourse 168
Downing, Ken 200
Dr. H. Anonymous 126
dreams of being naked 36, 40–1, 44
dream theories
    Freudian 31, 32, 34–5, 45–8, 87
    Jungian 45–8
dress 3, 4, 6
Dress Reform 63, 79
drives 7, 9
    death 206
    sex 44, 48, 53

Duberman, Martin 116, 117
Duflos, Huguette 89

École de la Cause freudienne 204
écorches 94
ego 7, 89, 104
    bodily 7, 173, 175, 189
    clothing 189
    skin-ego 10, 173, 174, 175–80, 185, 189, 194
ego psychology 107
Egyptian sphinx 24
Elbaz, Alber 177
Ellis, Havelock 67
Ellison, Ralph 118
embodied subjectivity 7
emotion 7, 8, 175, 188–9, 191
Entwistle, Joanne 4
envy 126, 189, 191
erogenous zone 75, 181, 183
Eros 46, 208, 209
erotic/eroticism 38, 41, 50, 52, 53, 70, 78, 87, 109, 117–18
eugenics movement 79
Evans, Caroline 86, 97, 163
evil eye 35, 172
exhibitionism 20, 44, 48, 49, 78
    female 52–3, 59
    male 78

family 15, 72, 116, 117, 206
family romance 160
Fanon, Frantz 118, 120
fantasy 7, 8, 9, 44–5, 50, 56, 63, 93, 110, 119, 130, 135, 140, 147–8, 175, 205
    sexual 138, 145, 160–3
Farnham, Marynia E. 112
fashion, definition 6
fashion designers 46, 47, 70, 90, 97, 107, 208
    see also under names
Fashion Group, The 119
fashion models 138, 177
    see also under names
Fath, Jacques 108, 110, 111

father 15, 79, 128, 158, 160
Feinberg, Leslie 206
femininity 19, 23, 46, 52, 71, 119, 122, 130, 143, 148, 150, 152, 154, 169
feminism 4, 112, 122, 127
feminist theory 130
Fenichel, Otto 140
Ferreira, Lucy Moyse 93
fetish 53, 55
fetishism 25–7, 48, 53
    clothes 53–6
    commodity 26, 163
    female 56, 59
    sexual 26, 55, 86, 130, 137, 138, 142, 158, 163
fig leaf 38, 40
Fish, Michael 200
Fisher, Will 81
Flaming Youth (film) 62
flapper 61
Fleury, Sylvie 163
Fliess, Wilhelm 14, 41
Flügel, John Carl 10, 75–80, 81, 83, 111, 138, 145
Fogarty, Anne 119, 121
Foucault, Michel 4, 9, 20
fragmentation, body 91–4
French theory 4
Freud, Anna 21, 27–8
Freud, Bella 9, 200, 201
    Fashion Neurosis (podcast) 9, 200
Freud, Jakob 13, 14, 15
Freud, Martin 13, 16, 27, 29
Freud, Sigmund 1, 3, 7, 9, 10, 13, 16, 17, 19, 26, 47, 72, 74, 75, 83, 88, 89, 100, 104, 111, 127, 128, 135, 137, 140, 158–65, 168, 169, 171, 173, 175, 189, 200
    case studies
        Dora 34
        Little Hans 160
    dream analysis 45–8
    French Revolution 88–9
    "libido for looking" 48–52

    lost object 152
    "mystic writing pad" 185
    publications
        Beyond the Pleasure Principle 44, 208
        "Fetishism" 54
        "Hysterical Phantasies and their Relation to Bisexuality" 44–5
        Interpretation of Dreams, The 31, 34, 44, 67, 86
        Introductory Lectures on Psychoanalysis 35
        Jokes and Their Relation to the Unconscious 52
        "Psychogenesis of a Case of Female Homosexuality, The" 122
        Three Essays on the Theory of Sexuality 48, 66
    self-fashioning 16, 23
    "topographical" theory of the mind 8
Freyer, John Ercel 125–6
Friedan, Betty 119, 122
Fryer, Dr. John 126
    see also Henry Anonymous

Galliano, John 1, 10, 152–4, 158, 160, 161, 162, 163
Gallo, Rubén 66, 67
Gamman, Lorraine 56, 165
garçonne style 61, 62, 63, 69, 70, 71, 110
Gardner, Ava 112, 115
Gaultier, Jean Paul 10, 41, 42, 138, 140, 141, 143–5, 146, 147, 148
gay liberation 117
Gay Liberation Front 124
Gay P.A. 124
Gay, Peter 1, 3
gaze 50, 88, 89, 90
    cisgender 203
    exchange of 90
    male 97, 130, 172

of the Medusa 170–3
mother's 90, 168
of Narcissus 168–70
gender-bending fashion 198, 200, 203
gender fluidity 198–204
gender identity 20, 62, 63, 198, 202, 203, 205
Gere, Richard 144, 145
Gherovici, Patricia 11, 198, 206, 209
Gigli, Romeo 176
Girl, Connie 151
Gittings, Barbara 124, 126
Givenchy, Hubert de 108
Gleason, Montserrat Albores 104, 105
Golden, Eve 6, 170
Goldenberg, David 126, 205, 206
Gonzàles, Eva: *A Box at the Théâtre des Italiens* 52
Grandville (Jean-Ignace-Isidore Gerard): *Venus at the Opera* 49
Grant, Hugh 135, 137
Greene, Lucie 200
Greffulhe, Countess 50
Grier, William 118
Grose, Anouchka 9, 22, 97, 104, 143
Guattari, Félix 209
Gucci, Alessandro Michele 47, 198, 199, 200

Hall, Jerry 149
Hamilton, Neil 62
Harper's Bazaar 93, 137, 203
Hartnell, Norman 108, 109
Harvey, John 137
Hauser, Henriette 26, 27
Hays Code 75
Heard, Gerald 80
Hearst, Rachel Alpha Johnson 94
Hegel, G.W.F. 88
Henry Anonymous, M.D. 124
see also Dr. John Fryer
Herbert, Robert 3

hermaphrodite 7
Hermès 148, 152
Herzog, Dagmar 116
heterosexual/heterosexuality 48, 66, 75, 95, 108, 111, 122, 130, 140, 154, 197
Hiler, Hilaire 39
Hingh, Valentijn de 203
Hippocrates 21
Hirschfeld, Magnus 64, 66
history
    of psychoanalysis 7, 9
    of psychology 3
histrionic personality type 21
homophobia 3, 116–17, 118, 126
homosexual/homosexuality 20, 48, 53, 66, 107, 126
Horst 109, 186
Hughes, Athol 72
Hujar, Peter 124, 125
Hunt, Lynn 4
Hurley, Elizabeth 135, 137
hypnosis 20–2, 88
hysteria 20–2, 88

identification 69
Imaginary, the 97
Ingres: *Oedipus and the Sphinx* 24
International Journal of Psychoanalysis 73
International Psychoanalytic Association 100
inverts 63–7
Irigaray, Luce 128

Jack Jacobus, Ltd. 34
Jacobs, Marc 1
Jagger, Mick 144
Jay, Martin 89
Joan of Arc 155
Jones, Ernest 72, 78
Jones, Stephen 160
Jorgensen, Christine 197
Joubert, Catherine 16
jouissance 10, 152–4, 155
Joyce, James 206

Jung, Carl 45, 46, 47, 122, 158
Jungian dream analysis 45–8

Kafka, Franz 204
Kameny, Frank 126
Kaplan, Jonathan 15, 16
Kawakubo, Rei 94, 188
Kertész, André: *Muguet Seller on the Champs-Élysées, 1928* 91
Killers, The (film) 112, 115
Kingsley, Ben 1, 2
Klein, Melanie 28, 72, 73, 74, 90, 111, 140
Klein, William 94, 152
Klimt, Gustav 31, 32
Kohut, Heinz 127–8
Kraus, Karl 53
Kristeva, Julia 128, 130
Kruger, Barbara 51
    Untitled (You are seduced by the sex appeal of the inorganic 50

La Vie Parisienne 63
Lacan, Alfred 88
Lacan, Jacques 8, 9, 10, 75, 86, 88–9, 90, 94–5, 97, 99, 101, 103, 104, 118, 128, 130, 138, 142, 143, 160, 168, 169, 174, 175, 204, 206
    "Aggressiveness in Psychoanalysis" 94
    "Aimée" (Marguerite Paintaine) (case study) 89, 173
    Écrits 88
    mirror stage 89–90
    "Signification of the Phallus, The" 100, 127
Lacan, Judith 100
Lacanian psychoanalysis 4, 48, 88, 127, 138
Lafrance, Marc 189
Lagerfeld, Karl 36, 167, 168
Lahusen, Kay Tobin 124
Lang, Helmut 184
Langdon-Davies, John 80

Langley Moore, Doris 112
Lanvin, Jeanne 41, 42, 71, 140
Lartigue, Jacques Henri 61
Lasègue, Charles 48
Laver, James 4, 75, 111, 112
Le Figaro 167
Le Monde 187
Lemma, Alessandra 90, 97, 168
Lemoine-Luccioni, Eugénie 41, 142
Leopardi, Giacomo 207
Lesage 99
lesbian/ism 20, 61, 63, 122
Lewes, Kenneth 126
libido 48
libido for looking 50, 52
libido for touching 50, 52
Lindbergh, Peter 138, 139, 140
Lingua Franca 4
Llamas, Vernoica G. 203
Loewenstein, Rudolph 100
Logos 46
Loos, Adolf 18
Lopez, Jennifer 181, 182–3
Lozano, Manuel Rodríguez
   El Taxi 67
   Retrato de Salvador Novo 67
Lurie, Alison 4
Lyford, Amy 91

Macan, Ana Carolina 177
Madonna 147–8
Magnan, Valentin 26
Magritte, René: *Les Jours
   gigantesques (The Titanic
   Days)* 45
Mai, Bach 183, 184
Mair, Carolyn 9
Mammen, Jeanne: *She Represents* 65
Man Ray 64, 65, 104
Manet, Edouard: *Nana* 26, 27
Marcus, Neiman 200
Marcuse, Herbert 118
Margiela, Martin 186, 187
Margueritte, Victor: *La Garçonne* 61
Marisol 46
Martin, Charles 39

Martin, Richard 104, 137
Marx, Karl 17, 26
Masaccio: *Expulsion from the Garden
   of Eden, The* 37, 38
masculinity 15, 17, 19, 52, 71, 74,
   81, 143–4, 145, 148
masquerade
   feminine 73, 74, 100, 142
   of womanliness 71–5
Matlock, Jann 55
McAlmon, Robert 63, 64
McCardell, Clare 111
McLaren, Malcolm 130
McQueen, Lee Alexander 10, 47,
   88, 152, 154–8
Medusa 137, 170–3
Memling, Hans: *Triptych of Earthly
   Vanity and Divine
   Salvation* 57, 58
Men's Dress Reform Party
   (MDRP) 79, 80
Menkes, Suzy 7, 8, 160
Meyers, Diana Tietjens 95
Michele, Alessandro 198, 199
military uniforms 19
Miller, Daniel 29
Miller, Jacques-Alain 204
Miller, Lee 104
mind–body dualism 2
mirrors 88, 95–9
Mirror Stage 86, 89–90, 130
misogyny 3, 74, 118, 126, 155, 204
Mitchell, Juliet 127
Modern Woman 61, 67–71, 78
modesty 39–40, 52, 75, 81, 83
Money, John 197, 198
Montaigne, Michel de 81
Montesquiou, Robert de 49
Moore, Colleen 62
Moore, Doris Langley 112
Morand, Paul 70, 111
Moreau, Gustave: *Oedipus and the
   Sphinx* 23, 24
Morel, Geneviève 163–4
Morris, Jan 206
mother 15, 25, 46, 74, 90, 108, 111

Mugler, Thierry 10, 148–50, 151,
   197, 209
Mulvey, Laura 130
Musil, Robert 51
mustache 17

Nadar, Paul 49
naked 36–8, 40–1
nakedness 53, 80–3
Name-of-the-Father 160
narcissism 78
   female 10, 56–9, 170
Narcissus 168–70
Nathansohn, Amalia 13, 15
National Organization of Women
   122
Navarri, Pascale 10, 167, 168
necktie as phallic symbol 35
neuroscience 3, 4, 7, 9, 189
New Health Society 79
New Look 108, 109, 110, 158
New York Easter Parade (1929) 28
New York Times 137, 149, 200
Newton, Helmut 130
Ninomiya, Kei 192, 193, 208
Nixon, Richard 111
No Sesso 204
Nochlin, Linda 149, 150
North, Stella 10, 189
Novo, Salvador 66, 67
nudity/nudism 36, 38, 41, 80, 81,
   172

object of desire 2, 143–5
Objet petit a 152
obsessive–compulsive behavior 28
Oedipus 24, 156
Oedipus complex 3, 14, 23, 158
Orbach, Susie 135
Orlan 154
Ovid 169
Owens, Rick 46–7, 156, 199, 200–1

Pajaczkowska, Claire 38, 44
Pantaine, Marguerite 173
Papin sisters 89

paranoia 88, 89
Paris Vogue 138
Parisian Sphinx 23–5
Parisienne 3, 24
Pasquier, Emile 25
"peacock revolution" 143
Peeping Tom (film) 130
Péghaire Anzieu, Annie 174, 175
Pejić, Andreja 203
Pelletier, Madeleine 70
penis 34, 35, 39, 41, 44, 48, 54, 127–8
penis envy 3, 58–9, 74, 127–8, 170
penis-girls 140
Penn, Irving 71
performative masculinity 81
persona 46
perversion 48, 55, 122, 138, 163
    sexual 20, 26, 63
petit objet a 152
phallic amulets 35
phallic dress 80–3
phallic mother 138
phallic parade 143
phallic symbol 75, 81, 83, 138, 145
phallic woman 10, 138–40
phallocentric bias 7
phallus 34, 44, 81, 88, 100, 127–8, 138, 140, 142–3, 189
phantom limb 91
Phillips, Adam 2
piercing 185
Plato 36
pleasure 41
pleasure principle 41–4
Poe, Edgar Allan 8
Polanski, Roman 2
Posey, Willi 119, 121
post-structuralists 4
post-traumatic stress disorder 44
Prada 1, 2
Preciado, Paul B. 204
prêt-à-porter 128
pride 206
Procrustes 94
protection 38, 172, 177, 192
Prown, Jules 3

pseudo-fetishism 56
psychoanalysis 1, 2
    France 88
    Lacanian 4, 48, 88, 127, 138
    popular culture and 114–16
    United States during the Cold War 10
    see also Freud, Sigmund
Psychoanalysis (comic book) 114, 115
PTRA 104
puberty 16
Punks 130–2

queer leathersex community 137
Qui Êtes-vous, Polly Magoo? (film) 94

Rabaté, Jean-Michel 100–3
Rabelais, François 81
racism 118–19, 126
Rado, Sandor 116
Real, the 154–5, 160, 209
Reich, Wilhelm 117, 118
repression, sexual 41, 51, 80, 100
resentment 205
Ricchetti 22
Ringgold, Faith 119
Riviere, Diana 72
Riviere, Evelyn 72
Riviere, Joan 10, 71–5, 79, 100, 142, 149
Rocamora, Agnès 194
Rose, Gillian 9
Rose, Jacqueline 127
Roseberry, Daniel 103, 104
Rosenberg, Olga 28
Rotten, Johnny 132, 133
Roudinesco, Elisabeth 103
Rousteing, Olivier 185–6
Ruggerone, Lucia 180, 209
Rykiel, Sonia 128, 129

safety pin dress 137
Saint Laurent, Yves 129, 131, 175
Saketopoulou, Avgi 205
Salpêtrière hospital 21

Sánchez-Kane, Bárbara 202
Sanders, Wren 203
sartorial androgyny 7
sartorial phallicism 81
Schiaparelli, Elsa 10, 85–6, 87, 88, 90, 93, 94, 97, 98, 99, 103, 104, 111, 208
Schilder, Paul Ferdinand 91
scopophilia 48, 130
Scott, Jeremy 43, 44
Scottish kilt 144
second skin 180
Segal, Naomi 189
sex 7, 143
Sex Pistols 130, 132
sexology 20, 53
sexual difference 55, 127, 135–65
sexual fetishism 26, 55, 86, 130, 137, 138, 142, 158, 163
sadomasochism 137
sexual identity 20, 63, 67
sexual liberation 61, 130
sexual symbolism 34–6, 53
sexuality 2, 4, 13, 31, 38–40, 48, 55
sexualization 181–4
sexuation 143, 158
Shakespeare, *King Lear* 38
shame 36, 38, 40, 44, 51, 172, 189, 205
Shapiro, Elana 40
shell shock 21
Shocking Pink 87
shoe hat 86–7
Shox, Larry 102, 104
Signs 3
Simmel, Georg 69, 104
sinthome as a framework 206
Siodmak, Robert 115
Situationism 100
skin 7, 38–9, 48, 135, 136
skin surfaces 185–8
skin-ego 10, 173, 174, 175–80, 185, 189, 194
Slimane, Hedi 168
Snow White and the Seven Dwarfs (film) 95

Index

Socarides, Charles 116
social constructivism 4, 198
social psychology 9, 69
Solomon, Gayle 205
Sonia's Clothes 128–30
Sophocles 24
   Oedipus Rex 14
Spellbound (film) 112, 114
Sprouse, Stephen 154
Stern, Sarah 16
Stockman dress form 187
Stoller, Robert 198
Stonewall riots (1969) 122–4, 126
straitjackets 132
Strauss, Renate 180, 209
Styles, Harry 203
surface 2, 7, 8
Surrealism 10, 86, 87, 88, 92, 104, 122
Symbolic, the 209

Takahashi, Jun 47, 209
tattoos 185
Tear-Illusion dress 93, 94
Thanatos 208, 209
Therapy of fashion 119
third sex 63
Thornton, Minna 138
Time magazine 197
Times, The 182
Tiresias 206–9
Tischer (tailor) 19
top hat as phallic symbol 83
touch 50, 52, 128, 175, 189
Toulouse-Lautrec, Henri de 21
trans 7
transgender 7, 11, 64, 150, 197, 198, 203, 204, 206, 209
transphobia 3, 204, 205

transsexuals 124, 150, 204
transvestism 20, 61, 63, 64, 110, 124, 150
trauma 44–5
Turkle, Sherry 103

unconscious 3, 4, 8, 9, 13, 31, 35, 46, 55, 86, 88, 140
Undercover 47, 207, 209
underwear 140
Uzanne, Octave 24

Valetta, Amber 181
Vallotton, Félix: *Intérieur avec femme en rouge de dos* 32, 33
Varo, Remedios: *Woman Leaving the Psychoanalyst's Office* 122, 123
Veidt, Conrad 64
veil 56, 89, 142–3, 154
Vermeil, Lionel 147
Verrall, Joan Hodgson 71
Versace, Donatella 181, 182–3
Versace, Gianni 10, 135, 136–7, 173
Vienna 13, 14, 15, 25, 27
Vienna Psychoanalytic Society 35, 53
Vietnam War protests (1966) 117
Viktor & Rolf 185, 190, 191
Vinken, Barbara 208
Vionnet, Madeleine 71, 96, 99
Vischer, F.T. 24
Vogue 69, 86, 93, 109, 149, 182, 203
Vogue Paris 139
von Krafft-Ebing, Richard 53, 63, 140
voyeurism 48, 130, 172, 194, 206
vulnerability 83, 145, 167, 168

Wallace, Michele 119
Wallon, Henri, mirror test 89
War
   World War One 21, 44, 45, 61, 72, 88, 91
   World War Two 28, 99, 107, 126
Ward, Ivan 38, 44
Warwick, Alexandra 8
Webb, Vernoica 180, 181
West, Katherine 72
West, Vera 112
Westwood, Vivienne 94, 130–2, 140, 141
Why Be Good? (film) 62
Wilde, Oscar 79, 159
Wilhelm, Bernard 188
Wilson, Elizabeth 4, 99
Winnicott, Donald 90, 152, 175
Wipprecht, Anouk 192
Wittman, Blanche 21
woman/women 4, 6–7, 24, 38, 46
women's liberation 130
Women's Wear Daily 203
World War One 21, 44, 45, 61, 72, 88, 91
World War Two 28, 99, 107, 126
Worth, Charles Frederick 49
Wright, Richard 118

Yamamoto, Yohji 177
Yevonde: *Machine Worker in Summer (Joan Richards)* 5

Zaretsky, Eli 72
Zeffirelli, Franco 110
Zhang, Enrique 203
Zucchi, Jacopo: *Cupid and Psyche* 31
Zweig, Alfred 18
Zweig, Stefan 18